SYMBOLISM IN HINDUISM

Compiled by:
Swami Nityanand

CENTRAL CHINMAYA MISSION TRUST
MUMBAI - 400 072.

© Central Chinmaya Mission Trust

First Edition		1983	- 5000	copies
Reprint		1989	- 5000	copies
Reprint		1993	- 3000	copies
Reprint	November	1996	- 3000	copies
Reprint	June	1998	- 2000	copies
Reprint	June	2000	- 1000	copies
Reprint	November	2000	- 1000	copies
Reprint	June	2001	- 2000	copies
Reprint	October	2002	- 1000	copies
Reprint	May	2003	- 2000	copies
Reprint	January	2005	- 2000	copies
Reprint	September	2006	- 2000	copies

Published by:

CENTRAL CHINMAYA MISSION TRUST
Sandeepany Sadhanalaya
Saki Vihar Road,
Mumbai - 400 072, INDIA.
Tel: 91-22-28572367 / 28575806
Fax: 91-22-28573065
Email: ccmt@vsnl.com
Website: www.chinmayamission.com

Distribution Centre in USA:

CHINMAYA MISSION WEST
Publications Division,
560 Bridgetown Pike,
Langhorne, PA 19053, USA.
Tel: (215) 396-0390
Fax: (215) 396-9710
Email: publications@chinmaya.org
Website: www.chinmayapublications.org

Printed by

SAGAR UNLIMITED
28-B, Nand-Deep Industrial Estate,
Kondivita Lane, Andheri Kurla Road,
Mumbai-400 059.
Tel.: 28362777 / 28227699

Price: Rs. 75=00

ISBN 81-7597-149-5

INTRODUCTION

Conceptual thinking is hard to the many. To contemplate upon the formless and therefore the Transcendental Essence is given but to a few. The majority needs some grosser expression of the Pure and the Infinite, for their mind to conceive It and their intellect to contemplate upon It. These "symbols" of the Eternal Ground, the Supreme Truth, are called idols.

Thus, an idol represents an ideal. When we do not know the ideal which a given idol represents, it is something like seeing a portrait in a studio! If it were my beloved's portrait I would have seen in it more than what the black-and-white picture represents. I would experience the warm pulsating menace of my love, the mother of my beloved Children!

In the same way the religious symbols and idols have a deeper depth for us to discover, over and above their mere external shape, the general forms of the symbol and, in each, even the exact arrangements of its various aspects.

To bring out eloquently the voiceless beauty and joy of the Infinite, through unsaid significances of Its finite expressions and symbols, is called Mysticism. All religious idols are mystic-symbols. To learn the art of interpreting them is to experience a harmony in our devoted contemplations heard without ears, seen without eyes!!

I had been indicating some of these depth-significances during my discourses, and a few of them I had written out for publication in our souvenirs and in our monthly journal - Tapovan

Prasad. Some I had dictated and my disciples had written them down, and often they have been published under their own names! All these have been compiled here and after completely editing, we are publishing them in one interesting and instructive volume mainly for the edification of our foreign devotees who have no intimate touch with our deep and sacred Culture.

To the foreigners these have to be alien thoughts having some strange mysticism about them and a quivering charm in them. These expositions can rocket even a modern Indian youth into worlds of fresh discoveries and enchanting poetic visions of the Life Divine.

We congratulate Sri R. S. Nathan (Calcutta-Chinmaya Mission) for bringing his enthusiastic and dedicated interest in compiling, editing these pages, and thus preparing the material for this volume. This is not exhaustive: it can never be; Hinduism is too rich in its mystic-contents.

For each student of contemplation, the mystic depths in our *pauranic* literature open up a rich and unending field to explore and to discover. I hope each reader will learn independently the art of contemplating upon these very same symbols, and come to discover for himself the hidden significances in all other religious symbols.

SWAMI CHINMAYANANDA

CONTENTS

PART I
GENERAL

PART II
MANIFESTATIONS

PART III
THE ITIHASAS OR THE EPICS
AND AUSPICIOUS DAYS

PART IV
SACRED ARTICLES
VAHANAS OR VEHICLES
AND ABSTRACT FORMS

SYMBOLISM
IN
HINDUISM

PART I

GENERAL

THE ART OF GOD-SYMBOLISM

Melody carved in stone is sculpture. Sculpture in melody is music. In colours it becomes painting. Sculptured music, painted in words, is the highest in literature. And this medium of word painting has been chosen by the poet-seer, Vyasa, to describe the Indescribable, in his Puranas.

And there is a definite reason for this choice. The painter in his medium can no doubt, not only express all the details but can, also represent movement; but three dimensions alone can he express in his paintings. On the other hand, a sculptured piece of beauty can express all its rhythm of form overflowing from all its sides. The spectator can move around the sculptured piece and enjoy the beauty of it from all angles. But, at the same time, the expression of a piece of sculpture is an arrested moment in life and there is, therefore, no movement in it. Vyasa felt that he needed a medium which had all the beauty and strength of both painting and sculpture with none of the weaknesses of either, in order that he might express and describe the play of the Infinite among the finite objects of the world. In calling our attention to the Unseen Power that supports and moulds the happenings in life, Vyasa searched for a new art of "sculpture-painting" and it is the weilding of this art that we find in all the Puranas : the art of word-painting.

The theme of the Upanishads is too subtle for the average intellect to comprehend and when one is not able to appreciate an ideal one should necessarily fail to apply one's mind to it. Unless the student is capable of clearly visualising a concept and continuously meditating upon

3

it, he will not be able to experience the highest beatitude that has been promised as the achievable final goal in all the scriptures of the world.

In order to help growing children to understand their country, in all educational systems we use maps, and the teacher points out therein the various cities, rivers, mountains, etc. But the map is not the country – it serves only to help the student understand the relative positions of various places and, thereafter, in his own maturity he will realise the glory of his country in all its details. The map is a physical guide for the student's intellectual growth. In the same way, in order to help the seeker comprehend the Infinite Reality and the philosophical concepts of Vedanta, Vyasa, the mighty teacher, felt the need for supplying some conceivable representations and these are provided in the word-pictures and the stories in the Puranas.

The word-paintings of this master-poet have succeeded in carving for us solid forms out of the Infinite Truth of the Upanishads and they all live and act and move magnificently across the dark despondencies of the world and meet diligently the despairs of man-made situations. These representative symbols of Truth are conceived as 'deities' and the entire Puaranic literature is studded with such blazing pictures of dynamic gods and goddesses.

These representations, we find very often, have normal forms, but it is not unusual for Vyasa to take even impossible anatomical features and structures to describe the All-Pervading Essence of the Self; for, the One Infinite Reality Itself has become the world of endless forms and, naturally, therefore, every form in the universe is, in a sense, but a representation of the Primeval Truth.

Thus, these Puranic stories were written for the benefit of the early students of Spiritual Truth, and, in his pages, the irresistible philosopher and Man of Realization

4

in Vyasa could not remain permanently hidden. Now and then the mask of the teacher falls off and the theme of the Upanishads unconsciously flows out of his pen. As we read the Puranas we find that the drab description, of the man-like deities are enhanced by Vyasa adding effulgent strokes of the Upanishadic concepts to make the gods directly reveal their real essence as the Eternal Soul of the Universe.

This style, called mysticism, is the strain in which the entire Vedas are written. Vyasa being a perfect poet, his pen sings its songs of mysticism and produces for us the palpitating sculptures of comprehensible god-forms. These become the altars at which a devoted seeker, shattered with his own desires and passions, confused with his despairs and disappointments, crushed beneath his duties and responsibilities, could easily find a haven of peace and consolation.

The criticism that, "though God created Man in his own image, man has, in his turn, ultimately created a God in his own mortal form", is apparently true, but on deeper analysis we shall find that there is not much pith in it. The human mind, in its present state of constant preoccupations is so dense that it cannot directly lift itself to the subtler heights of pure contemplation or sheer meditation. Weighed down with its own attachments and desires for the objects of the world outside, the meditative powers in the mind are today lying undiscovered and unexplored. The spiritual master must first of all help the seeker to quieten his mind so that he may discover his own meditative faculties. For this purpose, the method of *Upasana* (worship) has been prescribed even in the earliest *Vedic* literature. The people of that age worshipped the sun, the moon and the stars, the mountains, the rivers, the rain and the ocean as expressions of this mighty unseen Cause of the Universe.

5

In the *Upanishads* we find very many methods-of-meditation *(Upasanas)* which are all techniques to develop the seeker's powers of concentration, which each student has to practise by bringing his entire thoughts channelized into the given line of contemplation. As time passed on , the population increased and, consequently, the competition for existence became more and more severe. In a competitive society, the individual mind gets more and more shattered and, under such continuous tensions, it is difficult for the mind to discover the necessary poise for pursuing the methods of concentration prescribed in the Upanishads. By the time of Vyasa, a psychological situation had arisen wherein it was found necessary that the teacher must provide the students with a fresh kind of technique, if they were to follow with profit the spiritual exercises. In the *Puranas* Vyasa had so successfully inaugurated these new deities and the easier methods of meditating upon them that the Vedic methods fell almost completely into disuse, and in their place the Pauranic gods and goddesses got accepted as the most popular altars of worship amongst the Hindus. Herein I propose to point out the symbolism of a few of the deities most popularly worshipped in the country.

Nothing has so directly helped the Hindus to feel their common religious bond as the worship of these deities, the most important and popular of them being Rama, Krishna, Shiva, Vishnu, Narayana and Devi. In the temples of these gods, Hindus of all classes and persuasions visit, mingle together, worship and feel the exhilaration of the Spirit. For centuries these temples and the common worship of these deities held the Hindu society together, providing a common bond of love and devotion, creating among them a great sense of pride and brotherhood.

The regular study of the Ramayana and the Bhagavata moulded the emotional and intellectual character of our nation, and the millions who were not able to read for themselves the original sacred books "heard" constant discourses upon them given out by the pandits. Besides, many of these inspiring works have been translated into the various local languages both in prose and simple songs, so that these deities have contributed a lot in the formation of the Hindu mind and its thoughts.

No doubt, when the pandits came to merely explain the "Story" without giving the deeper meanings of the text to indicate intelligently the philosophical and scriptural import of these mystic-text and the ideals the personalities stood for, slowly the intelligent and the educated classes stayed away from the study sessions of these Puranas. Once the understanding was not full, the faith in the deities got ruined and, consequently, the temples enshrining them became deserted.

To revive a true interest in the temples, we must gain a clearer understanding of what these "Divine Representations" signify and in what way each one of them suggests some of the aspects of the Infinite Self within. To students of the Upanishads a few indicative pointers are more than sufficient. I leave them deliberately sketchy — these are not exhaustive. But I am sure the well-informed mind can explore these enchanting realms of suggestiveness and discover for themselves much more than what we plan to give here under each god-form. In Self-exploration there is a thrill of discovery and a continuous inspiration to search for more and more meaning in each Pauranic "Story".

SWAMI CHINMAYANANDA

THE MONOTHEISTIC HINDU PANTHEON
or
"EKAM SAT VIPRA BAHUDHA VADANTI"

(Hinduism has been accused of a multiplicity of gods by accusers who have not cared to know that the basic creed of this religion - the most ancient of all the living religions of today, the religion of **SANATANA DHARMA,** *wrongly yet popularly called Hinduism - is* **"Ekam Sat Vipra Bahudha Vadanti" - The Truth Is One, It Is Perceived And Spoken Of In Different Names And Forms.)**

Man's capacity to wonder has been at the root of all his inquisitiveness and search for knowledge. Man, with the emergence of intelligence, observed that everything around him in nature was working for ages with precision and regularlity. He also understood that chance and regularity are two things which can never stand together. Therefore he came to the conclusion that there must be an intelligent cause behind all this. Every religion is a path and a method by which man tried to discover this ultimate cause, or Cosmic Intelligence, and every philosophy is only a humble attempt on the part of man, to express, explain, and identify himself with, this Ultimate Cause.

Man found that everything around him was constantly changing. If you want to see a change, you have to be outside the field of such a change. As man was able to observe these changes, he came to the logical conclusion that there should be something changeless in him and he came to name this changeless factor the Supreme Reality or Infinity after years and generations of search and research

8

leading to the acquisition of knowledge augmented by hundreds of succeeding generations in the grand and continuous march of life.

Now, the thing to be understood was Infinite. And man's equipments with which he could try to understand it, were, and are unfortunately finite. With a finite instrument we cannot measure the Infinite, much less understand it. So man had either to bring down the Infinite to the finite level of understanding, or transcend his finite equipments, evolve, reach, and realise the Infinite. The first method developed into religion, the second into philosophy.

The Infinite, due to the very reason that it is infinite, must be formless because form denotes a limitation, and Infinity cannot have any limitation. And man with his finite equipments, could not conceive of anything without a form. Just as water, which has no shape of its own, assumes the shape of the vessel in which it is contained for the time being, this formless infinity began to be conceived in different forms by different people according to their mind-intellect equipment which was the vessel in which they tried to collect and contain this formless Infinite. *"Saadhakaanam hitarthaaya Brahmano rupakalpana"* - Brahman the formless is assigned forms for the convenience of the aspirant. As no two minds are at the same level of evolution and understanding, there soon came to be a multiplicity of concepts. But the sages declared and emphasised in the Upanishads *"Ekam Sat Vipraha Bahudha Vadanti"* - and *"Akaasat patitam toyam yatha gacchati sagaram, Sarva deva namaskara Kesavam pratigacchati"*. Call Him by whatever name you like, worship Him in any form you like, it all goes to that one Ultimate, Infinite, Supreme Reality. Just as the same person answers different people who call him by different names, each according to his or her specific relationship with him, the Infinite answers, whether you call him Siva or Krishna, Buddha

9

or Arhat, Allah or the Father in Heaven, Tao or Ahura Mazda, provided there is sincerity in the call.

"Hinduism" is a religion (it will be more correct to say that it is a way of life) inadequately understood by the Hindus themselves in general, and either not properly understood or even misunderstood by others. To start with, the words Hindu and Hinduism are not even Indian in origin. In fact there is no religion called Hinduism. "Hinduism" is a wrong yet popular name given to the most ancient of all the living religions of today-and therefore the Mother of all religions-namely, SANATANA DHARMA, which as its very name proclaims is a religion based on the eternal principles and values of life. Again, it is strictly a monotheistic religion misunderstood as a polytheistic religion even by the Hindus themselves. The difficulty comes in mainly because, for the different words *Deva, Ishwara, Brahman,* etc. employed in this religion, there is only one word in English "God". And the greatest tragedy of the modern times is that the Indian of today is trying to understand his own Indian Philosophy through the medium of English, a foreign tongue, the vocabulary of which is grossly inadequate at present to express the highly subtle and suggestive ideas so beautifully and comprehensively expressed in the 'refined' language *"Samskrut",* which is generally considered today by the 'educated and civilised' Indians as a "dead language". But the truth is that it is we who are dead to that great and rich language, the vast treasure-house of real and profound knowledge.

To this intelligent Ultimate Cause, all-pervading Infinite Reality, they gave the name **"BRAHMAN"**, from the word *"Brahat"*, meaning the largest thing ever conceivable by man. And by this very concept, it became attributeless, and therefore, far beyond the understanding by the limited human mind-intellect equipment. And as man began to conceive of that 'inconceivable', it began assuming forms and attributes to suit the tempermental requirements and

10

predilictions of the human mind. Thus came *"Iswara"*, the conceived form of Brahman, with attributes. In the process, the *'Nirguna'* has been reduced to *'Saguna'*. Thus the 'actionless' Brahman, became the 'active' *Iswara,* in whom was vested the creation, sustenance, preservation, and ultimate re-absorption of the visible universe. Gradually the concept of *Iswara* was resolved into *Brahma,* (not to be confused with *Brahman*: the Supreme) *Vishnu,* and *Siva,* depending on the particular aspect in which *Iswara* was conceived of at a given time, to denote the same *Iswara* as the Creator, the Preserver, and the Re-absober respectively. Thus the idea of the personal gods, their personal attributes and requirements to push them into their respective activities had to be provided. Thus came Saraswati, Lakshmi, and Uma, the energy counterparts of these personal conceptions. As correct knowledge of the thing to be created is essential before setting out to create a thing, Brahma's counterpart necessarily became Saraswati, the Goddess of Knowledge. As preservation of the thing already created requires materials for sustenance, the provider was found in Lakshmi conceived of as the Goddess of Wealth and possessions. As re-absorption, or the 'constructive destruction', to be more appropriate, requires tremendous energy, Siva was given Uma the Goddess of Energy. Thus the Supreme Godhead has come down a step to satisfy the mind, the imagination and conception of man. And it has to be remembered that behind all these conceptions of Godhead, man had the fear of God in his mind, and that he was guided and inspired by unalloyed devotion.

And man was not satisfied. He decided that to control the Universe in all its varied activities, God should necessarily have an all-comprehensive, able, unfailing, and supremely efficient administrative set-up. So, minor gods began to spring up in his fertile imagination and they were given the control of the different activities. But it was

11

maintained that the Supreme Godhead was the one single source of power for the entire hierarchy, and in the highest analysis these minor 'gods' were only the different functional manifestations. And in the course of time, the minor gods started acquiring such importance as even to eclipse the Supreme Godhead, which was the source from which they derived their power and sustenance, from the minds of the rank and file.

The learned sages and saints who were responsible for this Hindu Pantheon should have been such pious and well-meaning souls, and their only consideration should have been to instil into the minds of the common people the fear and respect for an all powerful force that controls their destinies, always and in all ways, in all aspects and activities, so that humanity may remain confined to the right conduct in life and thus ensure a happy life herein and a fulfilment hereafter. And if we take a close look at the various concepts and forms we have thus given to the Godhead, we will be amazed to find a richness of conception backed by an eloquent symbology in every case. The Chart attached elsewhere makes a humble attempt (it is not exhaustive, and it cannot be) to present to the readers, a sort of geneological tree of the Hindu gods and goddesses who are generally worshipped by the Hindus of today, from one end of the country to the other. Of course, there are various other forms too in the fold, and they are either not so popular or are not worshipped as such,because the duties assigned to such forms do not attract a worshipful attitude from ordinary men and women.

Now, we will take a close look into the symbology of these various forms as they are presented to us today, subject to the limitations of space, time and knowledge, under which only all are functioning whether we accept the fact or not.

12

1. ISWARA

The immediate personal aspect of the Supreme Impersonal Godhead. It is conceived that the individual soul of man and Iswara are both reflections of the Supreme Godhead (Brahman) in two different media. Just as the Sun gives different reflections in thousands of buckets of water but gives only one reflection in an entire lake, the Supreme Godhead is reflected in thousands of individual minds, which reflections are called Jivas, and the single reflection of the same Godhead in the total Universal mind is called Iswara. Iswara has not yet been given a concrete form for worship just as we get in the case of the other gods and goddesses.

2. BRAHMA

Brahma is the Creative aspect of Brahman, or better still, Brahman is known as Brahma when He is conceived to be engaged in the work of creation. In this he is ably assisted by his spouse Saraswati, the Goddess of Learning and Knowledge. Brahma is depicted as having four heads and four hands. The four heads are said to represent respectively Manas, Buddhi, Chitta and Ahamkara, all of which are essential for the work of creation. He is seated in a lotus arising from the navel of Vishnu. Lotus stands for purity and the *Saatwic* element in man. He himself arises from the navel of the Preserver of the Universe, Vishnu. He is supposed to be doing *tapasya* in that posture on the lotus, and the entire process of creation is a *yagna* in itself.

3. SARASWATI

Saraswati as aforesaid, is the divine spouse of Brahma and is the Goddess of Learning and Wisdom. The name itself means "the essence of one's own self". She can be said to represent the status to which womanhood was raised to and respected in India of the ancient times. She

13

THE HINDU PANTHEON – THE ART OF GOD – SYMBOLISM IN HINDU RELIGION.

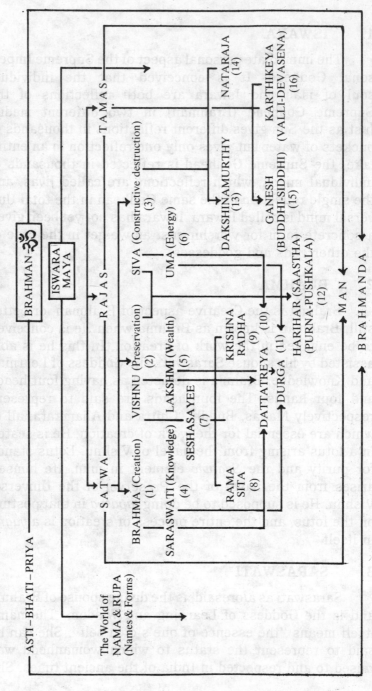

14

too has four hands, and a swan as her vehicle. She has a rosary and a book in her two hands, and the other two hands are engaged in holding a lute on which she is supposed to be constantly playing. The rosary stands for contemplation, the book for knowledge, and the lute for harmony. The vehicle swan is the symbol of purity and stands for discrimination. Mythologically, this bird is said to have the capacity to drink milk alone from a mixture of milk and water and leave the water behind, thus representing the power of discrimination, to absorb the good and reject the evil.

4.   VISHNU

The concept of Vishnu stands for that aspect of Brahman which is engaged in the work of preservation of the creation. He is supposed to be lying in a state of *Yoga Nidra* (a state of Yogic in-activity) on *"Ananta"* the serpent-bed in the ocean of milk. Yoga *Nidra* is the state of deep contemplation and intense internal activity which supplies the force for sustenance. *'Ananta'* as the word implies, stands for eternity, the 'endless time' on which Vishnu rests. Ocean of milk is the symbol of purity and prosperity. The name Vishnu stands for the 'long stride' (Vyapnoti Vishnu – Vyapakatwat Vishnu) that covers within itself the entire Universe. Vishnu has also four hands and he carries in them a fully-blossomed lotus flower, a discus, a conch and a mace respectively. The conch stands for the eternal principle of sound calling man and the entire creation to the higher and nobler values of life. The mace stands for the corrective and punishing power, the discus is the inexorable "wheel of time", and the lotus is the symbol of purity and eternal peace. The complexion of Vishnu is blue, the colour signifying unlimited distance or Infinity in philosophical parlance. He is called *"Purushotama"*, — the ideal in Masculinity (not mere brawn but masculine qualities), the seat of *Kshema*,

15

Sthairya, Veerya and *Vijaya* i.e. prosperity, steadfastness, valour and victory. The concept of Vishnu is widely worshipped as Narayana – the power behind and beyond man.

5.   LAKSHMI

When *Brahman* was reduced in concept to the *"ideal man"*, *"Purushottama"*, the necessity automatically arose to provide a conceptual counterpart in an "ideal woman", and "Lakshmi" was the result. She is said to have risen from the ocean of milk as a result of churning it, and thus stands for absolute purity and all that is *Satwic* represented by the pure whiteness of the milk the *"Uttama Sthree"* for the *"Purushottama"*. She is seated in a fully-blossomed lotus flower, the highest concept of all that is sacred, chaste and pure. She is the Goddess of Wealth and Prosperity and is supposed to provide these in abundance to sustain the creation,which is the portfolio of Vishnu, her devine consort. In fact she represents the *Sakti* (Power) of Vishnu for preservation and sustenance. She has an owl as her vehicle, the mythological bird of wisdom. She too has four hands always engaged in distributing wealth and bestowing prosperity. The Divine Mother in the form of Lakshmi is widely worshipped in India.

6.   SIVA

Siva is the third member of the Hindu Trinity representing Godhead in Its aspect of Annihilator, in charge of the "constructive-destruction" in the continuous process of creation, preservation, destruction and re-creation or transformation. He is the god of austerity. He is clad in a deer-skin (elephant-skin according to some) besmears his body with holy ash, has matted hair, and is adorned with snakes round his neck and arms. He is said to have drunk a cup of poison which has made his neck blue in colour, giving him the appellation *"Neela kanta"*, the blue-necked god. He is said to be seated in deep meditation on the top-most point of the world on Mount Kailas on the Himalayas, facing the south. In this aspect, he is known as Dakshinamurthy "the auspicious god facing the south", the embodiment and dispenser of the supreme Knowledge. He has a third eye in the centre of the forehead, the eye of wisdom as well as annihilation. When the eye of wisdom opens, the universe of names and forms and duality must stand annihilated. Supreme Knowledge cannot but be followed by austerity. The deer-skin, holy ash, matted hair, are all symbols signifying supreme renunciation.

7.   UMA or PARVATI

This divine consort of Siva i.e. Uma or Parvati, the daughter of Himavan, is the "*Sakti*" or power that supplies the energy to Siva. She manifests herself in various forms as Uma, Kartyayani, Kali, Durga, Mrudani Chandika etc.. As Uma she did severe tapasya to obtain Siva as her Lord and husband. As Durga, she killed the demon Mahishasura, who scourged the world in the form of a buffalo, which signifies the conquering and annihilation of tamas or ignorance. As Kartyayani, the Virgin, She blesses the world for all, round prosperity. As Mrudani, she mothers Ganesh, Kartikeya and Saasta, though she never conceived or delivered any of them. It is significant that among the three "*Saktis*", Saraswati, Lakshmi and Uma, it is Uma who is known as '*Jaganmata*', the Mother of the Universe and as such she represents the primal source of everything.

8.   DATTATREYA

Next comes the concept of Dattatreya, a combination of the forces of the Trinity aforesaid on a lower plane, the combination on the higher plane being Iswara as we see in the chart. It seems, in course of time the worshippers of Brahma, Vishnu and Siva, had formed into distinct sects each claiming superiority for their 'god' and a rapprochment was attempted by introducing the concept of Datta-

17

treya, a combination of all the three and their attributes with emphasis on the dissemination of knowledge, as "Dattatreya" is presented as the "Guru" preaching the knowledge of the one and only Supreme Reality. He is presented as a *Yogi* who has renounced everything, with a *Mala* and *Kamandalu* in his hands and ever youthful, as knowledge and the illumined souls are beyond the effect and limitations of time.

9. RAMA and SITA

Here we come to the level of the 'Itihasas'. Rama and Sita are the hero and heroine of the evergreen epic of Ramayana. The time had come to present humanity with an ideal man and woman whom they would understand, adore and emulate. And for thousands of years, Rama and Sita have reigned in the hearts of the Hindu. They represent the culture of India, and are considered the incarnations of Vishnu and Lakshmi. In them the people saw the ideals who lived and moved among them. They were the living embodiments of 'Dharma' who 'lived' in Treta Yuga but continue to live in millions of hearts even today (and their tribe is increasing) and inspire them to the higher and nobler values of life. This was the time when people were not satisfied with mere concepts. They wanted a 'living God', and the divine characters of Rama and Sita satisfied this want. If Rama was the ideal man, son, brother and king, Sita was the ideal daughter, wife, mother and queen, the embodiment of all that is great and noble in Indian womanhood.

10. KRISHNA and RADHA

Here we come to the Purana-Itihasa age. Krishna and Radha, the eternally youthful lovers of Brindavan, have come down to us through the Bhagavata and the Mahabharata, the Purana and the Epic par excellence. We do not get a parallel for the concept of Krishna in any religion or literature anywhere else in the world.

While the concept of Rama, the embodiment of Dharma, in a way lacked universal appeal, Krishna provided that in an abundant measure, and that is the speciality with Krishna, who is accepted in Hinduism as the only 'Poorna Avatara' or the full and complete incarnation of the Godhead. While Rama remains as a hero, Krishna has become a legend. Whether it is the infant or the boy, the youth or the maiden, the middle-aged man or the Gruhasta, the administrator, the politician or the statesman, the soldier or the general, the Yogi or the Paramahamsa, Krishna stands as an ideal for all, and commands respect, devotion, adoration and emulation. This universal appeal, the quality to satisfy any angle of vision in the totality of human life and endeavour, is peculiar to and present in the life and concept of Krishna in Hinduism. The love between Krishna and Radha, the ideal Love with a capital L, absolutely devoid of lust, was the self-effacing love, the love that was the absolute surrender of individuality in the case of Radha, and love that was the absolute divine grace in the case of Krishna. With them it was not 'falling in love', but 'rising in Love'. Five thousand two hundred years after he was 'born' into this sacred soil, we find Him still reigning in the hearts and homes of millions in this country (and now outside too) and He will certainly continue to be so. And thanks to some noble souls, the concept and teachings of Krishna are now beginning to be understood by enlightened people all over the world. And those who begin to understand, stand aghast with wonder and amazement at the ancient learning and culture of this hallowed land that could produce and claim a Rama, and a Krishna as its essence.

11.   SAASTA, GANESH and KARTHIKEYA

Though we take these deities after Rama and Krishna, they are in fact far anterior in concept to Rama and Krishna. While Rama and Krishna are 'Vaishnava' in origin, the three deities in the present heading are all *'Saiva'* in conceptual origin. It can be said that Saasta is a reconciliation between *Saivism* and *Vaishnavism,* while the other two are pure 'Saivites'. It can be seen that all these are anthropomorphic, and the concepts must have all come up according to the requirements of times. He who commands and protects is *'Saasta'-Saasanaat thraananaat Saasta.* His spouses - Sakti or manifesting power in esoteric terms-are two, Poorna and Pushkala, standing for Fullness and Full Glory. Ganesh, the Lord of the *Ganas,* the Commander of the spiritual forces, also called *Vighnaraja* the remover of all obstacles, is represented in a very peculair form with a human trunk and an elephant's head, with a mouse for his vehicle. The uninitiated may laugh at this, but he is only laughing at his own ignorance of the high symbology underlying this representation. Such people are invited to study Swamiji's articles on "God Symbolism". Ganesh also is given two spouses, Buddhi and Siddhi, i.e. Intellect and Achievements which of course, go together. Then comes Karthikeya, the god with six heads, the Supreme Commander of the divine army waging war against the Asuras who represent all evil and undivine forces. The six heads stand for the use of power of discrimination in the six different directions, to keep under control the six qualities that pull down man from his spiritual progress, viz., *Kama, Krodha, Lobha, Moha, Mada* and *Matsarya.* He too has two consorts, Valli and Devasena, representing the pure unalloyed love, devotion and complete surrender which can raise even the 'low-born' to divine heights, and the power to subdue and annihilate all evils and evil-doers.

In conclusion, it could be seen that whatever be the conceptual form of worship adopted, it is not the gross form that is worshipped, but the subtle force behind that form which gives meaning to that form in a particular context. Our forefathers have not given different gods to posterity. They have only given different concepts of the same

Godhead, taking into consideration the limitations of the human mind and intellect, and their emotional demands. That is why at the end of all this, they have come out with the declarations **"EKAM SAT VIPRAHA BAHUDHA VADANTI"**, (Truth is one. Only it is spoken of variously) and **"AAKAASAAT PATITAM TOYAM YATHA GAC-CHATI SAAGARAM, SARVA DEVA NAMASKARA KESAVAM PRATIGACCHATI"**. (Just as rain water, wherever it falls, finally flows down into the Ocean, so also all worship offered to any *'Deva'* ultimately reaches the Godhead , Keshava). If we misunderstand or inadequately understand them, it cannot be their fault.

— HARI OM TAT SAT —

R.S. NATHAN

RELIGION AND THE NEW MAN

*(So long as we are looking at this world from our old levels
of ego and ego-centric ideas of the physical, mental and intellectual personalities alone, we shall fail to see the world
co-operating with us. If only we can lift up to a new amplitude
of consciousness in ourselves, then alone we become mightier
and stronger. When we are mightier and stronger, the present
problems of the world will no more be problems to us).*

The Early Religion

Religion has been with mankind from the very beginning. When man was all alone, there might not have been
any religion. But the moment man started living as a
community, a tribe, as a group, from those days onwards
we find that "a religion" was pursued by man. No doubt
the religion was developing. As man developed the religion
also seems to have developed from time immemorial. And
when we watch the procession of progress of mankind,
we can also observe that, in those societies, or com-
munities, religion has also been evolving. So a time has
come when we can say almost with confidence that the
texture, quality and depth of religion indicated the development of the community, its civilization and its culture.
Thus the crude men in the early historical periods, when
they lived in utter ignorance, their religion was mainly a
fear-complex arising out of sheer fear of nature. In order
to pacify nature, man had to surrender and make offerings to the Lord. During this early stage religion was so
crude because men were also crude.

As man evolved more and more intellectually he
started understanding more and more the nature and the

22

play of life around him. He started to recognise that, in spite of the abominable ugliness of the world around, there was an undercurrent of beauty and melody and a serene composure joyously gurgling. The more he recognised the harmony in the society, the more his religion evolved; and thus, there is a blending between the progress of mankind and the progress of religion.

Religion and philosophy must serve mankind

Those religions that remained without any movement, that could not extend themselves, that had not the elasticity to accomplish, to accomodate the new demands and urges in the community, those religions were smashed and mankind progressively moved forward. The march of man cannot be stopped by anything. Philosophy and religion must come to serve mankind and not mankind forced to serve philosophy and religion. Thus, if there be a religion of Truth and a philosophy explaining the Truth, that philosophy must also be a living philosophy ever growing with the development of the community. The growth of the community cannot be stopped. The new extension of the community will absorb the very laws and overgrow these laws. So, a vital, dynamic philosophy must be elastic – not so elastic that any foolish idea in the community can be allowed to find its way into scriptures but elastic enough to embrace the new urges in the community or society; and that philosophy is alive which can thus embrace its new urges from within.

The great religions of old, such as the Egyptian religion or the Greek religion or even the Roman religion, could not stand this onslaught of the new impulses from within, and therefore they were all stampeded by the march of man. Those religions have now become mee museum specimens or archeological discoveries.

23

The great Banyan tree

Our religion, the Hindu Religion, in this country has got various branches : the Jains, the Buddhists, the Sikhs etc. These are the various branches of the one mighty tree called Hinduism. These branches have got, no doubt, adventitious roots themselves just as a *"Vatavriksha"* or Banyan tree. The banyan tree has got so many branches. In order to support each new branch, new roots have emanated and these adventitious roots strike the earth and thereafterwards serve the mother plant with its own absorption of food. At the same time the branch is well supported by its independent roots. But if the branches were to be cut off, no doubt it is true that the branch can grow on independently but it is not as healthy as the mother plant standing by itself. Similarly the other religions are the various aspects of this one religion – the various branches of one mighty tree based upon the Upanishads, or the Hindu Scriptures.

Unlike other religions, in Hinduism the great philosophy of the Upanishads need not be extended by a vote or by democractic methods because the philosophy itself is declaring the fundamental reality, which is the bulwark on which we are standing and functioning at this moment in the society.

The Amendments and emphasis

Whatever be the extension that you might conceive of and feel within yourself, all those things are already embraced in the thought process of these great scriptures. The Hindu Religion has stood the test of time without amendments from time to time. In fact, to an extent we can say, these amendments and emphases which came, have become different religions. Sidhartha had to become Gautama Buddha to show a certain emphasis of a value as non-violence which was seemingly lost sight of by the society. Therefore he insisted upon it and Buddhism came into exsistence, which is nothing but the ideas that were already in Hinduism. But the society at that time needed this emphasis for the right guidance and thus Buddha came to the forefront and emphasised one aspect of our culture which we seem to have forgotten for the time being. In all other religions we find that it is nothing but an over-emphasis of one or the other aspect which the society in its clamorous forward movement seems to have overlooked and forgotten and become habituated not to recognise these values. To re-establish those values such mighty masters came and emphasised those ideas.

Lord Krishna.......The great revolutionary

Every day we have to meet the various challenges in society and while we are meeting the challenges in the society, the society is ever growing; therefore, the pattern of challenges are also changing from time to time. That religion only is alive which can serve man actually in his every-day life, serve him in his office, or his commercial centres, in his workshop, in his factory or on the roadside, or in his home — wherever he is functioning. The ideas must extend themselves to help him in his inner tranquillity and happiness.

(The Mahabharata age in our country was marked by chaos due to too much of materialism. A time came when the old society in the country was on the threshold of a great civil war. On the eve of the great civil war, a great student of the Vedas started feeling "How am I to kill my own relatives and neighbours? How am I to fight this great battle against those whom I love and revere? This war is a great crime indeed, and what is my duty at this moment?" Thus an individual started thinking.) There we find the great revolutionary of that time, Lord Krishna, who comes and explains what exactly his duty is and how those duties are also implied in the various Upanishads. This extension

25

is only an application of the spirit of dedicated activity in the world outside. How can we act on in the spirit of *Yajna* is being indicated in the Geeta which is an extension of the Upanishads demanded by the necessity of the society at that time.

The culture of a country

The culture of a country has always been serving as a handmaid to man to meet his own challenges in the society. It is only for the last 200 years that religion did not apply itself in our lives and therefore here we are, an ugly caricature of a community which has got the name of a spiritual culture, but we find in our actual life we have not got any flavour of religion. We have started feeling that mere physical religion, physical activity, and material production will bring about prosperity in the country. In spite of all our activities there is nothing but disastrous sorrows and pains, and penury everywhere, only because the inner man is not tuned up at all.

Modern man demands a religion

The old type of religion with ritualisms, the temple, the church, and the mosque seems to be losing its hold on mankind. The religion that suited the man of past centuries is no more suiting him in the present context of things. He is demanding a religion that would equip him to face his vast and fantastic problems.

The cleavage of personality

Science has brought progress and wealth in the society. Science has shrunk the world into a smaller one. Science has made you conquer space and time. You are the children of a Scientific Age. When you are physically the children of an evolved age – the age of science- mentally and intellectually certain readjustments are necessary, without which if you try to live in the world, it will be too dangerous indeed. This pang or the cleavage of personality is because physically in the world outside we are the children of science, but mentally and intellectually we are still living the material ideology of each one wanting his own security only, and not extending himself to come to claim and live as a citizen of the world. To that extent there is this pang, this discordant note thrown into the melodious song of progress.

The felt need of the present generation – the religion of Vedanta

In order to be a real citizen of the modern world, the people must develop or grow into a new stature, altogether a new consciousness or awareness. Politics might give us a political awareness. Economics cannot help because economics can give us only some more wealth and conveniences in the society. Science can give us a little more. Perhaps it may give us a chance to go and habitate in the Moon and Mars but even when we go and live in the Moon and Mars it is self-evident that we carry our own problems there also. What else can there be? So the scientist, the politician, and the economist, themselves cannot help us in this particular way or particular aspect of the growth of man.

True religion perhaps can help mankind

When we say that the modern youth or the modern college student has no faith at all, we are only insulting him, misnaming him because the fact is not that he has no religion, but the religion that is available at this moment is not capable of catering to his demands or his problems at all. His problem is much deeper. His is not a problem of security because he is born in the age where he knows life is nothing, it may go off at any time. So he has not placed any great value on life. All that he wants is only to live dynamically. The threatning condition of a danger,

27

and a feeling of the total annihilation of the world – it is under that cloud that the poor young boy has grown up and as he grows up he finds no consolation, no strength in himself to face this great challenge of this new age. At that time the old religion comes with the ringing of the bell or throwing of the flowers or offering of sweets. He thinks "Why should I offer to these silent Gods?" He has no more understanding of it because it is not bringing him anything. The poor boy is demanding a new religion which would give him the new fire and enthusiasm, make him greater than what he has created for himself out of his own intellect.

The Philosophy

The religion of Vedanta can alone satisfy the modern man. We can teach him that in him alone is the Master of the mighty, the centre-most Reality. That Reality cannot be, that divine God cannot be somewhere yonder there because it is from that Reality the whole universe has emerged.When the effects emerge from a cause, the cause must necessarily be inherent and concurrent in the effects. The great Omnipotent,Omniscient Reality in ourselves is the Atman...the Self...the Pure Spirit. The Spirit in me functioning through the matter vestures, is the expression of the individual that I am bringing out into the society, and our intellectual eminence with which in the modern scientific age we are able to extend our knowledge so much, is the expression of the Truth, or the Infinite functioning through our own well-developed intellect. Man should discover in himself the essential knowledge that "I am nothing but the Spirit and as the Spirit I am the universal entity and not an individualised speck identifying with and limited by my body or mind or my intellect." If he is given the capacity to de-condition himself and experience his nature of pure divinity, then alone can he ever be converted to religion. All the rest is only a political or economic programme. The conversions that are going on, the ringing of the bell and the chanting that are going on, are all, at best, to the modern man only an external expression, an external symbol which does not go deep into him, does not touch him. But if it can be explained to the modern man in terms of his own modern science, the nuclear science of the outer world and the modern well-developed or developing science of psychology, if he is taught that the psychological and emotional entity in him is the expression of something deeper, something vaster, and something higher than all, supra-mental, that beyond the mind there is a mighty source in each one of us, to realise and experience that dimension in ourselves, that path would be the modern religion fit for the modern man. All barriers should then be removed. There should be oneness in our life and endeavour. It can be apprehended and appreciated, and we can contribute to it, only when we rise to a new dignity in ourselves. So long as we are looking at this world from our old levels of ego and ego-centric ideas of the physical, mental and intellectual personality alone, we shall fail to see the world co-operating with us. If only we can lift up to a new amplitude of consciousness in ourselves, then we can become mightier and stronger. When we are mightier and stronger, the problems of the world will no longer be problems to us.

Bharat — the fountain source of culture & true religion

The secret or the source or remedy lies with us only, and it is here, in our country. It has been dead for some centuries because of lack of correct usage, but our religion is even now very much alive.

See the words of the Pope.

"So much of religious and spiritual fervour I have never seen in any part of the world and it seems that everybody in India is a spiritual child." — This is not a mere exaggeration. It is a fact which would have been felt by any mystic who practises spirituality in himself. Had the

29

Pope felt that there was no religion in this country, it would have been only an exhibition of the lack of spirituality in him.

India has always been the *Guru* of the world. The time has come. Our generation has been called upon now to lead and guide the world, not in killing, not in destroying, not in warfare, but in learning and understanding how to face the problems of the outer world. For that, the study of the Scriptures is absolutely necessary and we must also learn to practise it in our every day life.

SWAMI CHINMAYANANDA

UNIVERSAL SYMBOLISM

(Dr. Mees of Holland, known also as "Sadhu Ekarasa", was often here in Bhagavan's lifetime. He made a special study of symbolism, on which he published a weighty volume. He is no longer alive, but the author of the following article, who was then a young pupil of his, is now an authority on symbolism in his own right).

So much has been said and written on symbols that it might prove useful to reflect for a moment on the meaning of the word itself. We then find that the word comes from the Greek, "sum-balloo" denoting : "I throw together", "the throwing together". What is being thrown together in the symbol is, on the one hand, its form, its literal value, and on the other hand, the life which it leads in us, understood or misunderstood, in the conscious or in the unconscious. As such it is different from a sign, although there are instances when signs can become symbols. When the sign becomes inseparably fused with inner life, it stops being merely significant, it gets additioinal value, it becomes symbolic.

The opposite of the symbol is the diabolic. This word finds its origin in "dia–balloo", meaning : "I throw apart" or "to throw apart". If the sign and its life get thrown apart, separated, nothing remains but the empty form, the dead skin, and if an estrangement arises between the sign and what it originally signified, (as is unavoidable in the process of cultivation : slowly the bullock loses its significance in association with agriculture), then the sign ceases even to be merely significant.

31

But it is the first part of the process – or rather degeneration – which concerns us here. The opposite of degeneration is general, and the root of that word we also find in that old scripture, Genesis, containing some illustrative material on the subject. For there the opposing symbolic and diabolic are laid down in the commandment concerning the forbidden fruit, "for in the day that thou eatest, thereof thou shall surely die", as against "And the serpent said unto the woman 'Ye shall not surely die.........".

The fruit is eaten and the culprits do not die literally. Since it seems unlikely that the story wants to draw attention to some mistake on the part of Almighty, we must seek for another explanation. The following becomes evident : the commandment is meant to be understood symbolically and its breach is punished on the same level with a symbolic death. The serpent here represents the voice of literalism and materialism. It is always or nearly always in close contact with the material element, Earth, its uplift plays a great part in all culture. In Genesis it is not uplifted. On the contrary, its voice is listened to and advice taken. Then symbolic death results. The meaning is separated from the commandment and the misdoers die a death, in that they are driven out from paradise, from the peace and Bliss which would have been theirs if they had stuck to the path of Genesis, the path of becoming.

It will not be superfluous to go through the relations between the five lower elements and their corresponding aspect in man. The Element Earth (in the *Panchabhutas, Prithvi*) represents the physical body of man and his material interest in life. The Element Water – the element-in-motion par excellence is used to denote the fleeting, flowing element in man : his emotional life (in the *Panchabhutas, Ap*). The Third Element is that of Fire (*Tejas*) and is symbolically connected with the mental life in man from whence his urges and passions are supposed to spring – and even today we speak about the solar plexus near the digestive organs and the thinking faculty of man. The fourth Element is that of Air (*Vayu*) and as in Latin (*Spiritus* – air, but also spirit) the close relationship between the airy and the spiritual can be clearly perceived. (*Atman*-to breath, but also soul, spirit). The spiritual would include the inspiration (literally : the intake of air and intuition/inner intuition). Presiding over the four elements, we are told, is the quintessential faculty of insight (inner sight). It is interesting to note that the "quinstessence" of a matter, that is its centre and core, really means the "fifth element".

Groups of five, sometimes with the two additional spheres added, we find in all traditions : For Christians the pre-Christian symbol of the Man on the Cross became all important. The four points of the cross symbolise the four Elements, while the quintessence is the Man curcified on it. The initials INRI written above the head have been explained by some to represent the four Elements once more : *I* am (Water), *Nur* (Fire), *Ruach* (Air), and *Labeshah* (Earth). Christ is often designated as a "Ruler of the Elements". The Egyptians had (to take one example) the pyramids in which the same principle was laid down with the four corners as the four Elements and the top of the structure, pointing upwards, as the Quintessence. In Hinduism we have the *Panchabhutas* which underline the *Kosas* (body-sheaths) Yamas and *Niyamas*, the *Panchavati* etc. The "Body-Sheaths" or *Kosas* have reference to the five "Elements" in man as follows : 1) the *Annamayakosa* represents the material and physical in man, 2) the *Pranamayakosa* stands for the fleeting, emotional functions, 3) the *Manomayakosa* is connected with the mental faculty, 4) the *Vijnanamayakosa* is the spiritual aspect of man's 'aspirations' and 5) the *Anandamayakosa* represents the sheath of Bliss, the result of insight.

We find the same connection also in the five *Yamas* 1) *Ahimsa,* non-harming, non-hurting refers purely to the

33

physical sphere, 2) *Brahmacharya*, chastity, finds its true source in the emotional life and is thus connected with the Element Water, 3) *Asteya*, or non-stealing refers to the mental faculty – for is it not the mind which, in guiding the hand, is the thief rather than that hand? 4) *Satya*, truthfulness is at heart a spiritual quality and 5) *Aparigraha*, non-coveting, is the result of insight into the whole.

People are said to benefit from meditation near the Panchavati, the five trees harmoniously grown into one. Once the symbolic implications of the values of each of the trees are understood, the idea makes sense. The connection of the five trees with the several aspects of man's being is said to be as follows : 1) the *Amalaka* or neeli : the Element Earth, 2) the *Udambar* or fig : the emotional (including the erotic, also evident in Roman Tradition) 3) the *Margosa*, the fiery neem, for the fiery mind, 4) the *Vata* (or banyan) is with its air roots, symbolic of the spiritual Element Air, 5) the *Asvatth* or bodhi tree, the faculty of insight that the root "bodhi" is related to "*Buddhi*" as found in Buddha, the "Enlightened".

The additional two spheres referred to above are the Moon-sphere and the Sun-sphere, symbolic of the creative power of Consciousness as a reflection of being or Reality. These symbols have been taken from nature, where the moon is a mirror of the sun reflecting the light of that source of life.

Example of methodical attempts at integration in which groups of seven are found, are perhaps even more numerous and are also found all over the world. Hindu ritual has probably been the least corrupted and the aim of integration is easily discernible, once the importance given to the Elements is understood.

The ritual of Puja is an example. 1) *Naivedya*, the offering of food which afterwards comes back in the form of *Prasad* sustains the body, the Element Earth. 2) *Pushpa*, the flowers, having grown from water, symbolize that Element and, as the procreative part of a plant, they are especially connected with man's procreative and emotional life. 3) *Gandha,* the sandal paste, gives off a nice smell. Smell is (in the group of the five senses) symbolic of the mental faculty. It is, in fact, the 'animal mind' or the mind of the animal, for beasts rely largely on their smell. The sandal paste giving off a nice smell, is believed to cool and soothe the (fiery) animal mind and serves a symbolic purpose. 4) *Dhupa,* the incense, rises up in the spiritual Element, Air, when burning. With the act of offering the incense, expression is given to a desire, namely, that the mental faculty may be raised up into the realm of the spirit. 5) *Deepa,* as light is that which gives the onlooker a clearer view of the image of the Godhead, symbolically representing some sort of inner sight. To complete the group of seven we may add the *"kumkum"* placed on the forehead, on the spot between the brows where the *Yoga* teachings have it that the seat of Consciousness is situated, the creative power of the Moon-sphere. Above it the holy ashes are smeared. Since they are the only matter which cannot be destroyed and are truly *"avinasi",* or *"avikarya"*, they symbolize the indestructible in man, that which remains after everything has been burned up, including himself. The ashes are therefore a reminder of death and the Eternal at the same time, and constitute a true symbol of *Advaita,* the ultimate Oneness.

J. J. DE REEDE

(Courtesy – Mountain Path, October '66)

THE NECESSITY OF TEMPLES

To reject the necessity of temples is to reject the necessity of God, religion and earthly existence.

Temples and images remind us to renew our renunciation and dedication from day to day. They remind us "Do not forget the original of the idol, in whatever you see!" If you believe that God pervades everything, you must believe that you cannot enjoy anything that is not given by Him. A man of prayer regards what are known as calamities as divine chastisement. It is chastisement alike of individuals and nations.

I know of no religion or sect that has done or is doing without its House of God variously described as a temple, a mosque, a church, a synagogue or an agiari.

Nor is it certain that any of the great reformers, including Jesus, destroyed or discarded temples altogehter. All of them sought to banish corruption from temples as well as from society.

Some of them, if not all, appear to have preached from temples.

I have ceased to visit temples for years, but I do not regard myself on that account as a better person than before. My mother never missed going to the temple when she was in a fit state to go there. Probably, her faith was greater than mine, though I do not visit temples.

There are millions, whose faith is sustained through these temples, churches and mosques.

They are not at all blind followers of a superstition, nor are they fanatics. Superstition and fanaticism are not their monopoly. These vices have their root in our hearts and minds.

To reject the necessity of temples is to reject the necessity of God, religion and earthly existence.

We, the human family, are not all philosophers. We are of the earth, very earthly, and we are not satisfied with contemplating the Invisible God.

Somehow or other, we want something which we can touch, something which we can see, something before which we can kneel down.

It does not matter whether it is a book, or an empty stone building, or a stone building inhabited by numerous figures.

A book will satisfy some, an empty building will satisfy some others, and many others will not be satisfied unless they see something inhabiting these empty buildings.

Then I ask you to approach these temples not as if they represented a body of superstitions. If you will approach these temples with the faith in them, you will know each time you visit them you will come away from them purified, and with your faith more and more in the living God.

It depends upon our mental condition, whether we gain something or do not gain anything by going to the temples.

We have to approach these temples in a humble and penitent mood. They are so many houses of God.

There, of course, God resides in every human form, indeed in every particle of His creation, everything that is on this earth. But since we, very fallible mortals, do not appreciate the fact that God is everywhere, we impute special sanctity to temples and think that God resides there.

And so, when we approach these temples, we must cleanse our bodies, our minds and our hearts, and we should enter them in a prayerful mood and ask God to make us purer men and purer women for having entered His portals.

MAHATMA GANDHI

THE GODS OF OUR RELIGION

"Is not God one for all? How is it that for you alone there are 33 crores of Gods!" This way the people of other faiths make fun of us.

It is true that God is only one. It is to Him that we refer when we speak of 'Daivam'. But 'Daivam' really means 'Destiny'. But we use that word in the sense of 'God'. People of other religions ridicule us for our 33 crores of Gods in the belief that 'Daivam' and 'Devas' are one, and some of us join in this ridicule.

But 'Daivam' and 'Devas' are really different. In our religion too 'God' is only one. He alone takes different forms. As Brahma He creates; as Vishnu He protects; as Rudra He destroys. But, in truth, these three, Brahma, Vishnu and Rudra, are not different from one another.

When the Tahsildar goes to his office, he puts on his suit. But when he sits for puja in his house he wears a Panchakacha in the orthodox style. When his wife is not at home and he has to do the cooking, he wears only a towel round his waist. Thus, ordinary mortals that we are, we change the dress according to the work that we do at the moment. Similarly, the omnipotent God changes His form also according to his functions.

But the difference between Him and us is this. At different times we put on different kinds of dress. But God who is omnipotent,is engaged at the same time in various kinds of work, and appears differently at one and the same moment. But in ordinary parlance we refer to them as forms of different gods. The several gods (devas) that we worship are distinct from God (Daivam).

39

I shall tell you who they are. The myriads of creatures, created by God in the countless worlds, require a shelter to live under, food to eat, etc. God provides them with the means to this by appropriately mixing together what are known as the five elements – ether, air, fire, water and earth. This is like our preparing thousands of eatables with the materials which have one or the other of the six tastes. So too mixing in diverse ways the five elements, God provides the means of subsistence for all creatures.

He must protect the creatures by adapting the five elements and their combinations to needs. God has entrusted this duty to the 'devas' who are a class by themselves. Even as the king or the government protects the subjects with the aid of several officers who are appointed by the king or the government, so too has God appointed 'devas' to protect all the worlds. A king or the government has an army, a navy and an airforce to guard what belongs to that king or government on the land, the ocean and the sky. So too does God have the army of the devas to keep guard on the five elements.

In our government, in addition to the military personnel, there are officers in charge of irrigation, public works, transport, and the like. Similarly, in God's Kingdom, to convert the five elements to the welfare of mankind, the devas function in different ways.

Among us, there are officers in charge of water supplies, to make breaches by which flood waters could escape, and to construct dams to store water against drought. But these officers cannot themselves produce water for drinking or irrigation. To apportion the water which He creates, He has nominated the engineer (of engineers) namely, Varuna, (to do that duty). In the same way Agni is in charge of fire and adapts it to the needs of men. Vayu adapts air to human needs. Thus there are many gods. The lord of them all is Indra.

We directly see with our eyes several kinds of living beings who belong to the human species. We also see the species of animals, birds and plants. As we go down the scale of creation, we find an increase in physical prowess. Man does not have the strength of a lion or of an elephant. He does not know how to build nests like a sparrow or a bee. But he has more intellectual capacity than them. The living beings who have infinitely greater physical and intellectual power, than men are called devas. Even as among men there are different races like the Mongols, the Negroes, etc., among devas too there are different kinds called Kinnaras, Kimpurushas, Yakshas, Siddhas, Saranas, Gandharvas, etc. We are not able to see the devas with our physical eyes. On that account we cannot deny their existence. They are invisible like air to our naked eyes. But if we use a fan we experience the presence of air. If we perform the prescribed *karmas* we can surely experience the blessings of the devas.

You may ask : What is the connectiion between our performing karmas and the devas? I shall tell you. The government pays salaries to its servants. But where from does the government get the money with which it pays the salaries? It gets through taxes levied on its subjects. So too does God provide sustenance for gods from the karmas we perform. In return for converting the five elements to our service, we provide food to them through our yagas and yagnas. We can get the help of the devas only if we pay taxes to them in the shape of the prescribed *karmas.*

What a vast difference there is between the worm and man among living beings! Can a worm understand the ways of men? Similarly, we cannot comprehend the ways of gods. Those who belong to the class of gods are not subject to old age and death like us. Yet God has ordained that they should get their oblations from us.

The gods are the highest among living beings and

41

they have three forms. In the *devaloka,* every deva has a resplendent form. It is called *aadidaivika* form. If men acquire superior power by their penance, they can communicate directly with these divine forms. In addition to their celestial forms in *devaloka*, these devas are formlessly present in every part of the five elements. This is called the *aadibhautika* form. In water everywhere Varuna is imperceptibly present in *aadibhautika* form. So, wherever we pollute water, he knows it. This is the great difference between our government officers and the devas. Government officers get to know about the lapses and crimes only if we submit petitions to them,but any sin committed in any place is immediately known to the particular 'devata' invisibly present in the respective elements. If a person pinches me in any part of my body, do I need a petition from another to be aware of the pain? It is like that.

Devas have a third form called *adhyaatmika.* Each one of them is present in some degrees in animals. Not only are they present in the five elements which suffer at man's hands, but are also present in the limbs of the wrongdoer. So, the gods cannot be deceived. They will protect us only so long as we do not transgress Dharma, and perform the prescribed *karmas.* Else, they will certainly punish us.

Even a deva is being endowed with life. As we would suffer if we have no food, devas too will suffer if we do not provide them with food. Hence the *puranas* tell us that they complain to God whenever there is a large scale decline in the observance of *karmas* prescribed by the Vedas, and on those occasions there is an *avtar* of God in the world.

I shall tell you some more strange things about the devas. They do not have to perfrom *karmas* like adhyayana of the Vedas and the performance of yagnas. Do you know why? We address our Vedic prayers to the gods ; we perform sacrifices to propitiate them. But whom will the devas address? As we worship Indra and Surya, Indra and Surya cannot worship themselves. Hence it is that Vedic *karmas* are not prescribed for them.

Though they do not have to learn to recite the Vedas like us, they are proficient in them without going through the process of learning. Hence it is that they are ready to bless us when we intone the Vedic *mantras*. They are endowed with Vedic knowledge as part of their nature, even as a fish knows how to swim in water. Due to that they are called *Swayamprathipathi vedas* those who know the Vedas by themselves.

Sri Adi Sankara says that devas too can inquire about *Atman*, and become one with *Brahman*. Though *karma* and *upasana* (worship) are not prescribed for them, they are qualified for *jnaana maarga* (path of knowledge).

God,who resides in us,also resides in the devas. Even as among us there are people who are not aware of God in them, devas too are unaware of this fact. Are not many of our officers personally unacquainted with the Rashtrapati? So too many among the devas do not know of the supreme God.

If we engage in an inquiry into the *Atman*, at the end of it, it will be clear that God is in us as our very self. When that stage is reached we have no use for the devas. Then all *karmas* will fall away from us. But, until then, we must obligatorily do the *karmas* directing them to the gods.

SANKARACHARYA OF KANCHI
(Courtesy : Bhavan's Journal).

THE HINDU SAMSKARAS

OBJECTS

The nearest English word for *Samskaras* is sacraments. They are rituals and sacrifices, by virtue of whose performance the life of the Hindu receives a higher sanctity. They cover his entire life from the moment he is conceived in the mother's womb till his death – inclusive of his funeral ceremonies and further on, for the smooth passage of his soul to another world.

Just as gold or diamond that is dug out from the ore needs refining in order to shine in all its splendour, man too needs these Samskaras or purificatory ceremonies in order to shine in his best form physically and spiritually.

The objects of Samskaras, as can be seen from the mantras and symbolism used in the ceremonies, are several. First of all is the popular, if superstitious,one,namely, the removal of hostile evil powers that beset human life at various stages; and secondly to invoke beneficial results from kindly gods so that man can prosper.

Samskaras aim in the first instance at material gain to the individual as when, during some ceremonies, prayers are offered to gods for gain of cattle, children, wealth, health, intellect, etc., which contribute to mystic and social felicity. Samskaras mirror self-expression of joys and sorrows, hopes and ambitions, which man exhibits in a dignified way when he celebrates these functions with feasts, presents, decoration, music and also in funeral ceremonies in an appropriate mood.

Samskaras also create an awareness of the attainment of social status and privileges for the individual. The boy who is given the sacred thread acquires the right to study the Vedas; the married man gains the title to perform the dharmas mentioned in the Vedas.

Samskaras bring about cultural gains. The ancient lawgivers underscored the introduction of higher religion and sanctity in the lives of those who undergo Samskaras, for some impurity is inherently attached to the prenatal stage itself and Manu and Yajnavalkya see in the Samskara ceremonies, the removal of those impurities, so that man's body is made fit to become a temple for the pure soul or God to live.

There is a moral purpose too. Sage Gautama opines that Samskaras along with the eight Atmaguns take one to Brahman or Moksha.

In fact, Samskaras were never considered an end in themselves. They constitute but the early means by which the individual is helped to develop moral virtues. In other words, they are ethical attempts for the moral uplift of the individual over material benefits. That is the true function of Samskaras. They are moulders of character.

Sage Angirasa poetically refers to the development of personality which the Samskaras endow on its adherents : "Just as a picture is painted with various colours, so the character of the individual is formed by the proper performance of the Samskaras."

In short, the whole gamut of Samskaras is designed to channel the entire energy of man towards the creation of a perfect secular as much as spiritual lift in himself in a manner that is not only ingenious but essentially practical, dignified and compulsory in the interest of all-round human welfare.

45

To quote Max Muller, the prescription of these ceremonies, by the ancients disclose "the deep-rooted tendency in the heart of man to bring the chief events of human life into contact with a higher power, and to give to our joys and sufferings a deeper significance and a religious sanctification".

HISTORY AND SOURCES

There appear to have been no hard and fast rules of Samskaras during the Vedic period. The earliest suggestion of Samskaras is, however, found in the Rig-Veda. Hymns now used in the rituals of marriage, conception and funeral are to be found there, besides others that are generally recited during all rituals. Beyond this the Rig-Veda does not contain positive or systematic rules of Samskaras.

The Sama Veda hardly has any material on the subject. In Yajurveda we have references to the tonsure ceremony, which, however, is common to the Srauta or Yaga ceremonies too. The Atharva Veda is a rich source of mantras relating to several of the Samskaras like marriage, funeral, initiation for Vedic studies, etc., although there is no systematic treatment.

Coming to the Brahmana period, Gopatha Brahmana contains refrences to Upanayana, or the thread-ceremony. The word Brahmacharya is to be found in Sathapatha Brahmana. Taittiriya Aranyaka contains mantras for cremation, Chandogya Upanishad relates how a Brahmachari is admitted to the guru-kula. Mention of Gayatri-mantra is made in Brhadaranyaka Upanishad. Taittiriya Upanishad contains the famous convocation address. We also find in it mantras used for begetting a learned son and also relating to the funeral ceremonies.

These, in a nutshell, constitute the beginnings of Samskara rituals and ceremonies. Presumably, they were

46

observed nominally or by convention at this period. It is reasonable to conclude that they were developed, amplified and codified and given an institutional bias in later years with the development of civilisation or needs of the time for giving stability to the community.

The rituals constituting the Brahmanas received systematic treatment only in what are called Kalpa-Sutras which are exegetical texts of the Vedas. The need for them arose because short manuals were required by the priests as an aid for their daily performance. Among these texts, those that deal with Vedic sacrifices are called Srauta-Sutras and those that deal with Vedic domestic rituals are called Grhya-Sutras which, though not valuable as pieces of literature, are yet valuable as "Folk-Lore" journals of ancient India. They give an accurate picture of the social life, popular customs and usages of ancient India.

Here are some important Grhya Sutras : (1) Apastamba (2) Aswalayana (3) Baudhayana (4) Bharadwaja (5) Gobhila (6) Hiranyakesia (7) Jaimineeya (8) Khadira (9) Manava (10) Praskara (11) Sankhayana and (12) Varaha Grhya Sutras. They belong to different Vedas and Sakhas and hence slightly differ in their contents.

There is another class of texts called Dharma Sutras which are an extension of the Grhya Sutras. These texts deal mainly with secular and religious laws relating to the Asramas. Since in ancient India there was no clear-cut division between the two spheres, Samskaras, too, figure in the second class of books.

These are, again, supplemented by what are called Parisishtas or addenda; the Commentaries, of which 25 are known : Prayogas, of which 24 are known and a dozen Karikas or specialised treatises on individual Samskaras.

Over and above these are Apta-vakyas, or the words of the Saints and elders following the Sanatana Dharma. They have the sanctity of Smritis in cases of doubt.

47

These, then, are the real sources of information about the Samskaras. It can easily be seen from the number of works on the subject, how important the ancients considered the Samskaras.

The Samsakaras are forty in number. They are (1) Garbhadhana (2) Pumsavana (3) Seemantha (4) Jatakarma (5) Namakarma (6) Annaprasana (7) Chowla (8) Upanayana (9) Prajapatya (10) Saumya (11) Agneya (12) Vaiswadeva (13) Samavartana (14) Vivaha (15) Deva-Yajna (16) Pitr-Yajna (17) Manushya-Yajna (18) Bhuta-Yajna (19) Brahma Yajna (20) Anvashtaka (21) Parvana (22) Stalipaka (23) Agrahayani (24) Sarvani (25) Chaitri (26) Aswayuji (27) Agni-Adhana (28) Agni-Hotra (29) Darsa-Purnamasa (30) Agrayana (31) Chaturmasya (32) Nirooda Pasubandha (33) Shantaramani (34) Agnishtoma (35) Atyagnishtoma (36) Uktya (37) Shodasi (38) Vajapeya (39) Atiratra and (40) Abdoryama. Some writers mention forty-eight of them.

These Samskaras describe the rituals and ceremonies connected, among others, with conception, birth, namegiving, first outing, first feeding, first tonsure, thread-giving ceremony (initiation to Vedic study), completion of studies, etc. etc.

The rituals connected with Samskaras contain both secular and religious ceremonies. There are certain common constituents. Agni or Fire, for instance, is an invariable constituent of the functions. It personifies the living god, the patriarch of the home. He is Grahapati or lord of the house, protecting the members of the household. He is also the Sakshi. Sacrificial fire is another form by which it is worshipped with appropriate rituals for the fructification of different objectives.

Where there is fire, there is always water or God Varuna. Often, water is sanctified by the gods being invoked in it with mantras and the sanctified water is sprinkled or sipped to wash away impurities and sins.

Prayers, of course, are the sine qua non of rituals. By means of them the appropriate gods are appealed to for protection and prosperity, and the removal of affliction. When it is for the gain of virtue, prayers turn into an instrument of morality, to wit, the Gayatri-mantra. Again there are mantras in the form of blessings and are uttered by the priests, as representing the gods invoked.

Symbolism is another major constituent of the Samskaras. Stone, for instance, that is used in marriage symbolises permanance, ever as the Pole Star (Dhruva Nakshatra). Sesame seeds and cereal rice symbolise fertility; panigrahana or clasping each other's hand shows assumption of responsibility, a bond; looking at the sun assumes absorption of tejas, etc.

A conscious effort at inculcating an elementary or suggestive information on hygiene, diet, eugenics and medicene are often noted in the Karmas.

All told, the total effect of the paraphernalia of Samskara is the creation on the different occasions of an atmosphere redolent with spiritual significance and its awareness on the part of all concerned.

I shall now give the meanings and purpose of the principal Samskaras.

GARBHADHANA

We can call it the conception ceremony. There are certain do's and don'ts during the "ritu" period of the woman, which are of great psychological significance. The propitious day and time are fixed astrologically for Garbhadhana and the ritual follows a set pattern. The mantras uttered in this Samskara are essentially prayers offered to God to help the bride conceive a good son. The mantras make use of occasional metaphors of joint action. They can be freely translated thus : "May we produce strong and longlived sons as fire is produced by friction; may he be well-behaved. I am part of God and I shall produce good sons to liberate my ancestors. May we beget shining, wealthy children. May we donate liberally to the needy and attain moksha; May God make you fit for conception. Let the evil spirit flee from you. Let your child be free from defects like lameness, deafness, etc. Be you like the divine Kamadhenu, etc."

Procreation is a compulsory duty enjoined on the Hindu to repay his ancestral debt, except when either or both the partners are functionally unfit.

PUMSAVANA

This ceremony is performed in the second, third or the fourth month of pregnancy. The meaning and object of this ceremony is to **"QUICKEN A MALE CHILD"** in the woman. The Rishis are divided in their opinion as to whether this ceremony must be performed before each child-birth. Mitakshara opts for the first pregnancy alone. There is an option to perform this ceremony along with the Seemantonnayana ceremony. The Pumsavana is performed on a day of male nakshatra. In the ritual, a few drops of the juice of the banyan stem are poured into the right nostril of the pregnant lady with a prayer for the birth of a son or a worthy child. According to Susruta, the great Ayurvedic writer, the juice of the banyan tree has all the properties of relieving trouble during pregnancy; Sanctified thread is tied to the left wrist of the lady by way of protection. The mantras, freely rendered, pray : "May God Isana fulfil our wishes; May Dhata bless the world with children and wealth. May he bless this household too with children. May the immortals live in this house. May Agni bless me with sons. May Indra bless me with children. May I have handsome children".

50

SEEMANTONNAYANA

The third in the series of prenatal Samskaras, this is performed during the period between the fifth and eighth months of pregnancy. The ceremony derives that name because of the fact that the hair of the pregnant lady is parted at the centre of the head, which is also the etymological meaning of the term. The parting of the hair symbolises the removal of undesirable shocks to the would-be mother and for keeping her psychologically cheerful and free of care. The child will be well-proportioned.

The specific materials used in this karma, which is for the lady only, are the quill of the porcupine, an ear of ripe paddy and a bunch of Udumbara leaves. The deity invoked is Raka, presiding deity of the full-moon. Their implications are – that pregnancy should be fruitful; that the child should be fruitful; that the child should be beautiful like the full-moon. The gist of the mantras is as follows : "I beseech the goddess Raka. May she bless this ceremony. May my son be sharp of intellect".

Music, specially on the Veena, is indicated to be played on the occasion. This increases the mother's suckling power besides conferring other psychological benefits. Ladies are asked to sing : **"BE A MOTHER OF HEROIC SONS"** thus creating a heroic atmosphere. The mother fasts and keeps silent after the ceremony till the rise of star and at the close of the ceremony she touches a male calf, symbolising a son.

V.A.K. AIYAR

SYMBOLISM IN HINDU MYTHOLOGY

The term "Symbol" signifies a Mudra, a Seal or a Mark, importing certain implications and ideas. In the term "Mudra" lies concealed, an expression of Truth through a suggestive pose or posture of the body or a limb, capable of depicting a vast source of wisdom underlying the same. For example, Shri Sankaracharya is said to have held the "Bhadra Mudra", a combination of the tip of the forefinger and the thumb. He was silent in the midst of his disciples seated under the shade of a Banyan tree giving them a very eloquent speech in absolute silence while holding up the Bhadra Mudra before them to clear their doubts, reveal the ultimate Truth, and lead them to the aim and destiny of the human soul. "Mounam Sarvartha Sadhakam" was the effective policy adopted by him to induct the truth of Brahman into the minds of the yearning disciples. He was more eloquent in silence than in speech in deference to the general principle "the more we talk, the more the confusion, the lesser we talk, the lesser the confusion, and if we do not talk, there is no possibility of any confusion at all," because everyone is left to himself to have his doubts cleared according to his own light and intellectual development at the given time.

Doubt is the property of the mind, which is in the nature of conflicting beliefs and ideas equally valid and reliable through authority or experience or both. The doubt is for one and not for all, and the doubt of one can be cleared and truth affirmed only by a correct and clear understanding of the problem as well as its solution. Faulty and flimsy issues of life give rise to doubts being overvalued and over-estimated and when their application to life and contribution to the realisation of Absolute Truth is judged from the angle of pragmatism and rationalism, they stand to lose their substantiality. "Heard melody is sweet, and those unheard are sweeter" (Byron) is only too true a statement which stands the test of examination and experience. The Upanishadic statement, "Vacho Vig-napanam hi tat", is proclaiming the same truth. So Shri Sankara employed the golden means by keeping silent and holding up his palm with Bhadra Mudra implying that the total release from the cycle of births and deaths and the enjoyment of Supreme Bliss are possible only when the forefinger is in union with the thumb, (metaphorically) which is the life-giver to all the other four fingers, which in their turn represent the four values of life, namely Dharma, Artha, Kama and Moksha, and until and unless the forefinger, which is the nearest to Brahman (the Thumb as we have seen above), dissociates from the other three representing the three states of our experiences and the three values as aforesaid, it cannot attain the state of Ananda, the Supreme Brahman Itself.

Symbolism is employed to simplify human effort to expose the ultimate Truth and the underlying principles, giving adequate opportunities to the aspirants to interpret it in a way in which they will get their answers from and in themselves. Such and other devices are nothing new to other religions either because the ultimate aim and end of man is expressed only through Symbolism. The Cross of Christianity is symbolic enough to import the idea that the Lord Jesus Christ sacrificed his life at the instance of heretics and truth should always be prepared to face and endure martyrdom at the hands of heretics and non-believers. SYMBOLISM IS THE SAFEST AND SUREST and at the same time the most effective way of propagating the Truth because it can be appreciated and enjoyed by the truly deserving devotees, each according to his or her light and vision.

A mass of ideas are composed into one mark or symbol, and the history of a nation or the legend of a life, can be read through it. The raising of a forefinger in anger against another creates fear in his mind, and he attempts to run away to save his life, unless he is capable of effectively retaliating, in which case the former would have thought twice before raising his finger against him. A man makes himself better understood by signs and symbols and,if language fails to prove his case or cause, he establishes the same through the movements of his limbs or to supplement or emphasise his arguments. This science has developed into Tantra Sastra, and the Tantrics are adepts in this art and achieve their ends through the practice of Mudras. In Kerala there is a highly developed folk-dance called Kathakali, wherein the different characters effectively play their parts and communicate with each other, only through Mudras or Symbols and not through words. The ideas contained in the background songs are expressed through the movements of the body and the limbs, and they are all well understood, highly appreciated, and thoroughly enjoyed by all those in the audience who know the techniques of the art. All sentiments of the human mind are expressed effectively and the audience sit through in rapt attention.

In this connection, let us come to the Hindu Trinity and their spouses. Lord Siva, the first and foremost of the gods, is represented with matted hair, tiger-skin apparel, triple-eyed, adorned with snakes, besmeared with ashes all over, residing at the top-most point on the earth on the Himalayan peak called Kailas, perhaps also the coldest part of the earth in proximity to human habitation. The place is covered with snow and everything is snow-white. He has a trident in His hand, and the other hand is held in "Chinmudra". The matted hair proclaims the length and intensity of his "tapas", and the cobra around his matted hair signifies that even the most poisonous becomes harmless because the one that has identified himself with the Supreme has gone beyond all the effects of matter on his senses or organs and has become immune even to the deadliest of poisons. The third eye in the midst of the forehead represents the concentration of Jnana and therefore the Absolute Power to destroy Tamas and all its manifestations and attributes all around. During meditation, the aspirant is advised to concentrate at the spot between the eyebrows – which spot is known as the Aajna Chakra or the Commanding Wheel – according to Yoga Sastra. The blue colour of the neck, and beyond the neck, symbolises the pervasiveness of Maya or Avidya up to the neck is the seat of Jnana leading to Eternity and Immorality. Blue colour represents distance. This can as well warn us about the vast distance that we'll have to traverse from the realms of the body and the heart to the realms of the intellect and beyond. The ashes that besmear the body recalls to us that this body of which we are proud and obsessed is ultimately bound to end up merely as ashes, which realisation is really the starting point in the march towards the final emancipation. It can also mean the complete dehydration of all the Vasanas at the mental level. The Trident stands for Sama, Dama and Vairagya, which dispel and destroy the six qualities which pull us down, namely Kama, Krodha, Lobha, Moha, Mada and Matsarya. By directing the Trident mercilessly against these weaknsses, one becomes conscious of the worthlessness of this worldly existence as a slave to these degenerating qualities and this awakening helps one to forge ahead to the summum bonum of human birth and existence – Liberation. He revels in the cremation ground, the place of death and the haunting grounds of ghosts and evil spirits. Siva, by his tapas, austerities, and consequent wisdom, has conquered the concept of death and all its hideous retinue, and they are all under his overlordship and command. The tiger-skin apparel stands for Vairagya and absolute unconcern for the body and its supposed needs. The Chinmudra in which he holds his hand teaches us that our ego – which is concentrated on the index finger – must bend and that our individuality must end as represented by the symbol 'Zero' which the index finger produces when it bends and touches the middle of the thumb in the Mudra. So, the form of Siva is depicted in such a way that each and every aspect of his personality has a much deeper significance to convey. The eternal truth is expressed more in dignified silence than in vociferous eloquence.

Siva's spouse is represented as Durga,who is said to be invincible. She is the manifesting power of Siva, both potential and dynamic, functioning through the means and medium of Lord Siva. Siva left to himself is impotent and inactive, and it is only through association with her 'sakti' that He becomes efficient of manifestation. The Devi cult of worship is anterior to the Deva cult because the saints and the sages worshipped Power more than Form. As the electric energy is creative, sustaining and destructive at the same time, so also the primordial power functions through different forms and names in different aspects. Her name differs according to the functional names of her Lord, as when he is Rudra she is Rudrani, and she is Bhavani when he is Bhava,etc. She is pure white when she is Santi Durga, and blesses her Upasakas with Bhakti and Mukti. She becomes multi-headed and multi-armed when she is engaged in fighting with Mahishasura, Chanda, Munda,etc., which only represent the multitude of undivine qualities to conquer which a multi-faced and multi-pronged attack is necessary. She can change her form at will, as conditions and circumstances demand and she is named after her success in the warfare. So she is called 'Mahishasura Mardini', 'Chandika', 'Chamundi', etc.

Lord Vishnu is represented as the lord of protection, with four hands, with four symbols, with a crown, and a spouse who is called Lakshmi,the goddess of prosperity. Her feet are on a fully-blossomed lotus – which stands for the Sahasrara Kamala, the fully-blossomed seat of divine prosperity. She is with four hands representing the four Purusharthas – Dharma, Artha, Kama and Moksha – the four spiritual virtues and values of life which every spiritual aspirant is enjoined to adopt and practise as laid down in our Scriptures. Her personal charm is par excellence, and around her is the aura of divine happiness and prosperity. Her smiling face with a look of compassion is the prize which the devotees seek for mental consolation, mundane contentment, and spiritual satifaction. Her one palm which is spread downwards represents her character of "Daana" (giving offering) and the other palm held up stands for encouragement and spiritual blessings. Born of the Ocean of Milk, she is the essence and personification of Purity, Chastity and Generosity, and represents magnanimity and depth of love and compassion. She is integrated with Lord Vishnu who has become "Narayana" only due to her association – known as Lakshmi-Narayana, the resort and refuge of all for material prosperity and spiritual redemption.

The Conch – the Samkha – in the hand of Lord Vishnu represents the source of the primal sound the "Pranava" – the Nada Brahman – the source of all knowledge, the Vedas, and stands for the call to the devotees to listen to the voice of the divine in them. The "Chakra" – the Discus – is the Wheel of Time, which turns at His will and decision, under the revolution of which everything is changed and transformed according to the requirement of time. The fully-blossomed lotus in one hand stands for the Sahasrara, – the thousand petalled lotus – which, according to the Yoga system, is the point where the divine wisdom dawns in man. The Mace in the fourth hand symbolises the authoritative and punishing capacity and aspect to those who stand in need of the same to turn them Godward and on to the spiritual path and the higher values of life. The palm turned upwards assures protection to the distressed and the dissipated and the "Bhadra Mudra" signifies that spiritual prosperity and divine bliss await the devoted and the virtuous. The devotee feels his oneness with God, in respect of time, place and proximity. All His incarnations assure us that He is present everywhere in all forms and names to protect the virtuous and uphold Dharma according to the requirement of time, conditions and emergency.

Lord Brahma, the Creator (as distinct from Brahman the Supreme), is the seat of Knowledge and hence Creation. He is situated on a fully-blossomed lotus which represents spiritual wisdom, with the power of projection and procreation. He is the physical form of the Invisible Principle. His two eyes represent the Sun and the Moon, and his nose the Cosmic Wind. His four hands stand for the four Purusharthas, and the four faces are the four Vedas or the Sources of Knowledge. The garland of beads in one hand points to his incantation of the holy mantra "**OM**", from which the whole Universe has evolved. His spouse is the goddess Saraswati, the Mother of Learning and Wisdom. She is the seat of all the sixty-four kalas or accomplishments in the various branches of arts and sciences, and holds a book in her hand to show that the study of the sacred scriptures is indispensable to know her depth and extent, as also to show that knowledge is endless, as even the Mother of Wisdom still needs to hold a book. She is depicted as playing on a lute to mean that she sings the melody of life, and invites the devotees to merge into Nada Brahman. All students and seekers after material knowledge and spiritual wisdom, invoke and worship the goddess Saraswati. Even today, great scholars and orators are invoking the power of Saraswati through Japa, Dhyana and Upasana, for their effectiveness, superiority, and invincibility.

Sankaracharya was a great devotee of Parasakti – Rajarajeswari – the Mother of Literature, Fine Arts and Spiritual Wisdom. In his "Soundarya Lahari" he invokes the mother in her various powers and faculties through praises and adulations. The first sixtyfour verses of Soundarya Lahari – which means intoxication by beauty and personal charm – are to be represented by sixty-four "Chakras" starting from "Swastipadma" and the greatest of them is the "Sri Chakra" in the centre of which stands Rajarajeswari,the bestower of spiritual light and wisdom. Lalitha is one of the forms of Durga, wherein we have the intersection of innumerable triangles both upright and inverted, and in the middle of which is the "Bindu" which is her seat of power and propagation. Each "Chakra" is symbolic of the physical forms of gods and goddesses and the centre of each crossing triangle is symbolic of the seat of emanation of light and wisdom. This is "Tantra Sastra", which has to be learnt from the traditional scholars. The Science of Forms and Figures is known as "Yantra Sastra", where the forms and parts are depicted as geometrical figures, each one with its deep and intense implications and meanings capable of deeper interpretations. Kerala, Karnataka and Bengal have made tremendous studies and progress in these branches of science. Physical sciences are with reference to known realities and Mantra, Tantra and Yantra Sastras are dealing with unmanifest realities and the immense potentialities of Nature. The human body is the noumenon of the Cosmos and the various powers of nature can be developed within this body through the help of, and Upasanas based on, the Mantra, Tantra and Yantra Sastras. It is said that the concentration of the mind at a single point is nuclear in its effect and powers can be developed and invoked either for construction or destruction as the case may be. There is definitely an intelligent and invincible power that sustains and regulates the Universe, and the invocation of that power for the benefit of humanity is the aim and end of all symbolic worship. The secret is known only to the adept for he draws the diagram within himself and assigns to it different parts and powers of the Cosmic organism. Every symbol is a Yantra complete in itself and represents the Cosmic circle in one aspect or another. Even today there are living Siddhas in Mantra, Tantra and Yantra Sastras, in Kerala especially, who are able to invoke the powers of unseen forces to ward off the evil effects of undivine forces from places and individuals known to have been adversely affected by them. Yantras drawn on metal plates (Gold, Silver, Copper, etc.) and reinforced with Tantras and Mantras are effectively worn by men and women on their persons, to ward off the evil effects of undivine and undesirable forces, popularly known as "Evil Spirits, Ghosts, Bhutas, Pretas, Pisachas", etc. Whether such forces and spirits exist or not is not within the purview of this article. Suffice it to say that forms and figures are only symbols of powers which are not ordinarily comprehensible to human minds and words. In short, Religion is Symbolism and Symbolism is Religion.

DR. S.R.D. SASTRY

DASAVATARA SYMBOLISM IN SPIRITUAL SADHANA

Puranic literature in Hinduism is well-known to be only an exposition of the highest Advaitic principles in the form of stories which can be understood and appreciated even by the common mass of people in the light of their own life's experiences.

The Dasavataras of Shree Maha Vishnu have been a source of inspiration and solace to millions of Hindus through the centuries, and the ideals embodied therein have kept them in the straight and narrow path of Dharma, even when sorely tempted to stray by alluring forms of Adharma. To the spiritual Sadhak however, they convey quite another secret import. To that soul who is all set to climb the mighty peak of self-realisation, the serious student and practitioner of Vedanta, these symbolic stories show the stages in the spiritual journey to Perfection. This path, one has to traverse all alone to the Alone.

The ten Avataras of Bhagvan Vishnu are :-

1. Matsya or the Fish
2. Kurma or the Tortoise
3. Varaha or the Boar
4. Nrusimha or the Man-Lion
5. Vamana or the Dwarf
6. Parasurama – Rama with the axe
7. Sree Rama – The Ideal
8. Sree Krishna – The Perfect Joy
9. The Buddha – The Enlightened
10. Kalki – The ruthless striker of the evil

MATSYA – the Fish

The ego of the Sadhak, before he becomes one, is wallowing in the mire of sensuality and gross ignorance. It is encompassed by the dark night of Tamas, and almost drowned in the ocean of Samsara with its various trials and tribulations. At this moment comes a very faint light and the Lord in his own bosom manifests, as a desire to do Sadhana in some form. He seeks a Guru, and does spiritual practice, taking the first tottering steps on the path to God. A faint ray of divine light leads him ever onward to save him from the slime and dirt all around.

KURMA – the Tortoise

Having started on the path, the Sadhak is told to do daily introspection and self-analysis to discover his weaknesses. A multitude of evil tendencies are discovered, some even masquerading as divine traits. The good is found to be minimal, almost negligible. A divine desperation urges him not to yield but fight out the battle with all his might. Resolving to do intense Tapas, he fixes the rope of his mind to the churning rod of his own discriminative intellect and begins to churn out the ocean of Vasanas in himslef, to draw out the nectar of Immortal Bliss. And in this Purashartha or self-effort, it is the Lord in him that serves as the solid rock of support to the intellect, to guide and help, even as the Kurma avtar supported the churning rod of the mountain Mandhara during the churning of the ocean by the gods and the demons.

VARAHA – the Boar

Thereafter, the Satwic tendencies, become predominent in the seeker, for by constant abhyas or practice, he has by now learnt to stand apart from his own ego. But even now there are lurking desires, deeply hidden evil traits which have to be literally dug out of the subconscious before they can be eliminated. This calls for intense self-analysis, rigorous inner probing, unpleasant though the process may prove.

This is the symbolism of the Varaha or the Boar diving down into the very bowels of the earth to discover the demon Hiranyaksha and destroy him. So deeply entrenched are some Vasanas that they have to be dug out painfully from deep within and eliminated. Else, further progress is impossible.

NRUSIMHA – the Man-lion

The seeker now stands well-up on the stage of evolutionary growth, half-God half-man, as shown in the Nrusimha avatara. Many God-like qualities, love, compassion, kindness, have developed in the head and heart, he is towering above the common level of mankind. A few Rajasic qualities, however, still continue to plague him – spiritual arrogance, pride of learning, etc., – which have to go before he can forge ahead, so comes the next stage.

VAMANA – the Dwarf

The dwarf boy-saint comes to the great king Bali to beg for three feet of land. The Vamana avatar emphasises the important role of humility in the sadhak. Until and unless he has overcome pride in his own progress and sub-limated the spiritual arrogance, he is bound to be humbled by a great fall, when he least expects it. The seeker must always be humble enough to recognise his weakness and obey the words of wisdom of elders and teachers in the spiritual field. Had Bali obeyed his Guru Shri Sukracharya, who warned him against granting the boon to the dwarf-child Vamana, he could not have been crushed as he was.

PARASURAMA – Rama with the Axe

Truly humble and sincere though he be, in the last phase of his spiritual Odyssey, the seeker has to give battle to a horder of Rajasic traits symbolised by the Kshatriya kings annihilated by Parasurama in a blood-bath. This avtar also highlights the intense detachment which must be available in the inner personality at this stage, for did not Parasurama kill his own mother on the command of his father and Guru? The strongest bond of affection has to be thus overcome, before Perfection is attained.

The Rajasic elements to be conquered are no longer the gross ones like lust and anger that were prominent earlier. Alas! these are subtler enemies, truly kingly in stature. Pride of mastery of the Vedas, complacency in being able to hold large audiences spell-bound by the power of oratory, occult powers etc., come to tempt the Sadhak, and he must resolutely say a NO to them and kill them ruthlessly. Only then can man become the Super-man or the next avatar.

SREE RAMA

Grown perfect now, the God-man emerges as the culminating ideal Rama, the perfect ideal Man, born only to show suffering humanity, how man may truly live as a god on earth. An ideal son, husband, brother, king, the acme of Perfection is thus the Rama avatar.

And when the Sadhak has passed through all the previous stages of sadhana, he emerges as the Prince among seekers, a completely enlightened soul.

SREE KRISHNA

And after Perfection is achieved, it is all joy, for ever after. Supreme, scintillating, permanent ecstasy all around and within himself, for he has become the eternal Self in all selves of the Universe. Who or what can contain Him?

This abounding joy is symbolised by the leelas of Lord Krishna, His enchanting divine pranks, which held the Gopi maidens in thrall. The Krishna avatar is one where not a tear was shed ever. The smiling Lord laughed his way through all His splendid colourful life of intense activity.

Hail to Lord Krishna, the Perfection in action and in love.

BUDDHA

And after this deep unchanging ecstasy has been lived and experienced as a permanent Reality, the now Self-realised Saint is transformed into the deeply compassionate Buddha. He yearns to help others, actually his own reflections, to become or rather *be* what he is. And Lo! The Teacher of the world, the Sadguru emerges, even as the Buddha did, his only reason for his existence being to teach and show others the path leading to unending joy. He may choose to be silent like Ramana or walk the path of lecture tours like Vivekananda, and yet both are there only to teach those who are seeking the path and the goal.

KALKI

Last, and yet to come, is the stage where riding the horse of his own dynamic personality, the Saint becomes a force to be reckoned with battling for the cause of the Right and striking down all evil anywhere and everywhere; the world looks on in wonder and amazement at the Saint-Man, who is   God in his own right; strong and perfect as Sat-Chit-Ananda (Existence-Consciousness-Bliss).

May the eternal principle within all of us grow and manifest through all these stages of Sadhana to produce at length the God-man which is only His Self made manifest.

"From the unreal lead us to the Real
From darkness lead us to Light
From death lead us to Immortality
OM Santi! Santi! Santi!!!

V.A.K. AIYAR

65

THE SYMBOL IN ART AND RELIGION

Art seeks to capture a vision; recollect an experience, and convey its meaning through symbol and suggestion. Religion too, aims at something similar, but, while the accent in religious expression is on authenticity, that of Art is on Beauty. In all forms of Art, Music, Poetry, Painting, Sculpture, we have a vision – an experience – and a symbol – an expression. Similarly religion is rooted in experience, an immediate, ineffeable encounter with Reality, a direct vision of Truth. Rituals serve as channels of religious expression.

Art is predominantly a sharing in the experience. Religion is essentially an awakening in the experience. When the man of vision, the mystic, or the artist has undergone the experience, he does not absorb it all to himself or by himself. He must burst forth into forms of expression. He does so spontaneously in response to an inner necessity. The excellence of Art is mainly in the spontaneity of expression. Beauty itself is a spontaneous overflow, as in the song of the bird, or in the fragrance of the flower, no less than in the achievements of the poet or the painter. Nature is the prototype of Art.

Expression flows from the plenitude of experience, and in turn kindles experience in kindred souls. Then the expression acquires the status of a symbol, and serves as a perennial source of meaning. To the symbol belongs the meaning. The substance is beyond expression. Controversies in religion have only a symbolic relevance.

If the satisfaction which Art could give should be complete and final, it must in a very real sense be religious, not

66

"superficially religious" as a mere creed or a dogma, but "essentially religious" as an inward exprience reaching down to the depths of one's own being. In so far as any Art falls short of this, and serves merely as an expression of material quality or a mental mode,without revealing the spirit that animates and sustains it from within, it fails to satisfy finally and fully. The superior forms of Indian Art, through the ages, were ultimately expressions of spiritual experience.

Art is like the outer precincts, "Prakara", of a shrine. As in a temple, the "Prakara" provides material for the experience and enjoyment of Beauty. But the meaning and purpose of all this flow from an inner source in the Sanctum Sanctorum which symbolises the substance of spirituality. Forms of Art draw their inspiration from the experience of the soul. The ecstasies of beauty are consummated in spiritual experience.

The Symbol, whether in Art or in Religion, is only of initial importance. The symbol suggests but does not establish. It touches off, it gives us a glimpse of that Reality which it hides as it fleets, leaving us to our conjectures and speculations; no symbol is of intrinsic worth and therefore none can satisfy in itself; rather it whets the soul's appetite and seems to play hide and seek with it. It is inadequate, but in a sense indispensable. Its real purpose is to induce an experience similar to that which inspired it. Having lit the spark, it must recede, for, if it persists, 'it would distort. The experience may be induced directly or by stages, according to one's capacity and inner constitution, one's equipment and acquisition from the past, one's "Samskara". What it means to us is conditioned by what we bring to bear on it as our own past. Where the past has been shed, the symbol is altogether irrelevant.

In this limited sense Art has its own "revelations" even as the essence of religious experience is believed to be "revealed". In both, what is revealed is not precisely or expressly stated, but just suggested. The revelation as such is real, but its expression being inadequate and fragmentary, is liable to be distorted. That is why Scripture, as revelation, admits of an endless variety of interpertations, claims and counterclaims. So are also certain forms of Art. Where expression is spontaneous, raw, elliptical, explanations are innumerable and diverse.

Consider images that echo the "revelation" seeking to capture and hold a vision through forms of art or as centres of spiritual power. Neither the artist absorbed in the contemplation of the beauty of the image, nor the man of faith established in the authenticity of its essential significance, needs an interpretation. It is only the vainglorious, little intellectual who seeks an interpretation, and misses its beauty as well as its Truth, for no mere interpretation, however sound logically or etymologically, can transmit the beauty or convey the Truth.

PROF. K. SESHADRI

(from T.P. - January 1971)

HINDU GODS
AND THEIR MANIFESTATIONS

The great exhortation of the Vedanta is that each and every soul, in whatever sphere of the Universe, shall rise above all mortality to the realisation of Brahman, that is to say, that the personal soul shall come to realise that it alone is reality, the process being a gradual expansion of consciousness. All relative ideas and relationships about which consciousness builds itself in the weaving of desire must be transcended. The state of progress and becoming, which is the soul's constant experience, must attain its climax culminating in Pure Being and Absolute Perfection. Then, all ideas of birth and death will have ceased to be, and time will have sunk into eternity. Sensation will have for ever passed into beatitude, all progress will have died out, for That which progress tends will have been realised. Then all the fraud of personality will have vanished with its relative freedom and bondage of will. For, Infinite Freedom has then been attained beyond all struggle, beyond all desire, and beyond all bondage. When the personal soul realises the Supreme, then verily it is Brahman. "Tat Twam Asi" – "Thou Art That" – is the spirit of all Vedanta teachings, That being the "OM TAT SAT" or the state of immeasurable knowledge, eternal experience and unfathomable bliss.

The Hindu conceived of the Truth in the categories of the real and the unreal. Thus something may exist, being however at the same time unreal in the highest understanding of reality. Whatever is relatively real, or possesses aspects of reality, is of the essence of Brahman. Man exists as personality. Higher than man are the Gods and the Devas and other superior beings. The reality of all is Brahman. With this as the background, the mind immediately recognises the synthesis of Hinduism. Polytheism, Theism, Monism, all are one in the vision of the Highest. The Gods are personal forms or aspects of Brahman and because Brahman is real, even so are they real. They are "idea forms" of Brahman. More real are they than man, relatively speaking, because they are more immediate forms and emanations of the Infinite Reality and more conscious of reality than man. The humblest Hindu peasant knows this.

According to the needs of time and place and the surrounding circumstances, and according to the varying necessities of the human mind, these spiritual images of Brahman vary. Sometimes Brahman is conceived of as the Divine Father or the Divine Mother, or as the Eternal One wrapt in meditation, or as the Terrible One, the personification of Infinite Force, or as the Preserver or the Destroyer or the Creator, or as a Divine Incarnation full of sublimity. The incarnation is the God-man who realises and preaches the state or consciousness of Brahman. He is God born as Man. There are in Hinduism innumerable Gods or visualisations of Brahman, which the human mind had made unto itself, but underlying the apparent Monism. In the end, as every Hindu knows, all these seemingly different deities are one, first because they are manifestations of the one and the same reality, and secondly because they represent the consciousness of Brahman in different aspects. So there is ultimately only one Personal God. All the Gods are One Person in that they have the same divine consciousness and because all are Brahman. But there is still a higher purpose. The majority of men recognise the Personal God in their own particular objectification of Brahman. It may be Krishna, Buddha, Rama or even Chaitanya, even as with the Christians it is Jesus the Christ. There is no clash of religion in India, however varied the religious belief or

70

worship and that is the reason why it is a secular state, no distinction being made on the ground of religion. Instinctively every Hindu worships all the Gods, bowing to the great ideal of which each one is a separate embodiment. We therefore see in India a Hindu passing before a Church recognising there the existence of the Supreme Being and inwardly accepting that it is the "dwelling of God". He sees the underlying oneness and unity of the different concepts recognising Brahman in them all. It is a racial characteristic, a racial inheritance. This vision is pecularily Hindu in the understanding of religion. Thus every God in Hinduism represents aspects and symbols of the One Eternal Reality.

Therefore the Indian Polytheism is the highest Monism in the essence. The many forms of henotheism or the deification of any one representation of Brahman as Super-Personal God is also, as a consequence, Monism in the essence.

Monotheism itself becomes a spiritual Monism, for eventually the individual soul finds that its own reality is the same as that of the God worshipped. "Whom then to worship?" asks the Hindu. He says that the worshipper and the worshipped and the ideal of worship and all the Gods and all the souls are One. It is because of this unifying supereme outlook of the Vedanta that devotees can sincerely worship all the Gods or take any one God as his chosen ideal of worship. The Impersonal Brahman within their own soul offers equal assurance that all religions and all religious philosopohies lead only to the same goal. Thus India, seeimgly so divergent in her religious beliefs, traditions and customs, is one in this great thought. In the vision of the Hindu, even a stone has the divine substance in it.

The final conclusion of Vedanta is that all these Gods are visions and personifications of Brahman, created by the soul itself. All stand for various "torch-light ideas" of the human mind. As man develops, his conception of the Gods grows, but the Gods do not change. Brahman is ever the same. It is man who changes, it is man who grows. Finally the soul in its most luminous insight discovers that even as all great ideas are only aspects of one all-including Truth, even so are the personal Gods manifestations of the same divine Nature and Consciousness. All external forms of divinity are superimpositions by the inner Divinity of the Soul upon the special vision it entertains at any given time. Ultimately, when all superimpositions die out and all the Gods merge in their true nature, the One and Indivisible only Brahman, only Reality, remains. The Gods are Brahman, the Soul is Brahman, and the Truth is Brahman. Verily the Universe is Brahman, and all paths, however diversified in the religious ideas and worship, lead to the same goal, Brahman, whether the worshippers are Hindus, Christians, Mohammedans, Buddhists or Zoroastrains, or the followers of any other prophet.

No wonder therefore that the Hindu philosophy teaches the importance of the Soul and Its reality, and that on death the body becomes a useless mass of flesh prone to destruction and disintegration, and therefore the Hindu believes that, after the soul has departed.and mixed itself into the Divine, the body is like a discarded piece of old cloth fit to be rejected and burnt. How foolish therefore is the concept that, the soul will remain waiting till the day of liberation dawns, when all the dead will rise, and till that time the body also will remain to join the soul! After death the soul mixes with the Super Being of which it forms a part and the body which covered the soul is thrown down as waste as soon as the soul has departed.

PRAMILA JAYKAR

72

WHAT IS BEHIND SYMBOLS?

(All religions have their symbols, often more than one. These may be visual like the Cross, or auricular like OM. They may represent God as Power like the Sivalinga, or point out the path to Perfection as in the case of the Dharmachakra, or signify the Saviour and his religious system as in the Cross or the Crucifix).

A reverent study of these symbols of the great world religions is as fascinating as it is spiritually rewarding.

OM OR PRANAVA

 Pranava or OM is the universally accepted symbol of Hinduism. Literally the word Pranava means "That by which God is effectively praised". It also means "That which is ever new".

Pranava has been extolled highly in the Vedas, the Upanishads and the Geeta as also in other Scriptures. The Gopatha Brahmana of the Atharva Veda relates a story according to which god Indra successfully overcame the demons with the help of OM. The story can be interpreted to mean that man can conquer his beastly nature by having repetition of OM.

The Yajurveda exhorts us to try to realise Brahman through repeating and remembering OM. The Kathopanishad declares that OM is Parabrahman Itself. The Mundakopanishad advises the spiritual aspirant to meditate on the unity of the Atman (the self) with Brahman (God) using OM for Japa. Sri Krishna avers in the Geeta

73

that He is OM among words and that all religious rites are started with the repitition of OM. Not only that, if anyone succeeds in chanting OM at the time of his death, simultaneously thinking of God, he will attain the highest Truth. The Yogasutras of Patanjali declare that Pranava is the symbol of God and that one can attain Samadhi by its repitition, and meditation on Him.

Actually OM comprises three independent letters A, U, and M, each of which has its own meaning and significance. The letter 'A' represents the beginning (Adimatwa), 'U' represents progress (Utkarsha) and 'M' represents limit or dissolution (Miti). Hence the word OM represents that Power responsible for creation, development and dissolution of this Universe, namely God Himself.

SIVALINGA

Literally Siva means auspiciousness, and Linga means a sign or symbol. Hence the Sivalinga is just a symbol of the Great God of the Universe who is all-auspiciousness. Siva also means One in whom the whole creation sleeps after dissolution. Linga also means the same thing – a place where created objects get dissolved during disintegration of the created Universe. Since, according to Hinduism, it is the same God that creates, sustains and withdraws the Universe, the Sivalinga represents symbolically God Himself.

Sivalingas may be 'Chala' (movable) or 'Achala' (immovable). The Chala Lingas may be kept in the shrine of one's own home for worship or prepared temporarily with materials like clay or dough or rice for worship and dispensed with after the worship, or worn on the body as Ishtalinga as the Virasaivas do.

The 'Achala Lingas' are those installed in temples. They are usually made of stones and have three parts. The lowest part which is square is called Brahmabhaga and represents Brahma the Creator. The middle part which is octagonal is called Vishnubhaga and represents Vishnu the sustainer. These two parts are embedded inside the pedestal. The Rudrabhaga which is cylindrical and projects outside the pedestal is the one to which worship is offered. Hence it is called the Pujabhaga.

The Pujabhaga also contains certain lines technically called Brahmasutra, without which the Linga becomes unfit for worship.

SRICHAKRA

 The Srichakra is perhaps the most important and the most widely used symbol of the Sakti Cult, the cult of the votaries of the Divine Mother. If God can be conceived of as the Father in Heaven, He can as well be conceived of as the Mother Divine also. Though God is neither masculine nor feminine, human nature being what it is, it is but natural that anthropomorphic nature of worship is resorted to in religion. Once this principle is accepted, what form of the Deity can be more fitting for worship and contemplation than that of the all-loving Divine Mother?

Though the three consorts of the Trinity – Saraswati of Brahma, the Creator; Lakshmi of Vishnu, the protector; and Parvati of Maheswara, the destroyer – are the main Deities in the Mother Cult, it is the various aspects of Parvati that are most widely used in worship, Japa or contemplation. In fact, an entire branch of Hindu religion, the Tantra, has developed around this Deity.

Again, Durga, Kali and Lalitha, are the three forms of Parvati which are most widely used for worship. The Srichakra is the symbol of the Lalitha aspect of the Divine Mother. It is essentially a Yantra, a geometrical diagram representing the form-pattern of the Goddess.

75

The Srichakra consists of a dot – Bindu – at the centre, surrounded by nine triangles – trikonas – of which five have their apexes downward and the other four upward. The mutual intersection of these nine triangles forms forty three triangles in all. This is surrounded by two concentric circles of eight lotus petals and sixteen lotus petals. This again is surrounded by three more concentric circles. Finally on the outskirts, there is a square – Chaturasra – of three lines, the lines one inside the other, opening out in the middle of each side as four portals.

URDHVAPUNDRA

Literally the word means a religious mark (Pundra) which is worn upright (Urdhva). In common parlance it is called Nama. Since it has been ordained by the Vaishnava scriptures that, while marking the various parts of the body with the Urdhvapundra, names of Lord Vishnu (like Kesava) are to be repeated and that the respective mark represents the respective aspect of the Deity indicated by that particular name, the word Nama has become synonymous with the Urdhvapundra itself.
Invariably associated with the Sankha or the conch on its left side, and the Chakra or the Discus on its right side, this forms the chief symbol of the followers of Ramanuja, who are known as Srivaishnavas.

The word Vishnu literally means one who pervades everything, one who has entered into everything. So Vishnu is the Cosmic Spirit, the Absolute, which pervades everythying. For purposes of religious worship and meditation, He is described as endowed with a beautiful form, deep blue in colour. He has four arms wearing Sankha (Conch), Chakra (Discus), Gada (Mace) and Padma (Lotus). He wears the jewel Kaustubha on His chest. Single-minded devotion is the best and easiest means to please Him.

76

The Sankha or Conch has the form of a multiple spiral evolving from one point to ever-increasing spheres. It thus symbolises the origin of the Universe from a single source, viz, God. Being found in water, it symbolises the causal waters from which the universe has evolved and into which it gets dissolved. When blown, it produces a sound, which represents the primeval sound from which creation developed. It is also taken to be the representation of the Cosmic Ego. Its involute curve can represent, on the plane of the microcosm, or the individual, the egoism which involves him in Samsara or transmigratory existence.

The Chakra or the discus represents the Universal Mind, the unlimited power that creates and destroys all the spheres and forms of the Universe, the nature of which is to revolve or to change. It also represents the Lord's will to multiply. Its six spokes represent the six seasons of the year, hence the changing Universe, set on the unchanging axle, the pivot represented by the magic syllable 'Hrim' of the Lord. The circle round the wheel is Maya the divine power of illusion. On the microcosmic plane, it can be taken to be a true representation of the individual's mind, which is ever-changing like the rotating wheel.

THE BULL OR NANDI

Nandi, the happy one – the Bull on which Lord Siva rides – is another common symbol. It represents virility and strength, the animal in man. In Siva temples, there is always a reclining bull placed in front of the chief shrine or just outside it, with the head turned away from the deity but the gaze fixed on it. It is interpreted as the Jivatman, the individual soul, with its animal nature pulling it away from God, but His grace pulling it back to Him.

THE LOTUS

The Lotus bud is born in water and unfolds itself into a beautiful flower. Hence it is taken as the symbol of the Universe coming out of the Sun. It rises from the navel of Vishnu, and is the seat of Brahma the creator. Hence the sacredness associated with it. Psychic centres in the body associated with the rising of the Kundalini power are pictured like lotuses.

SALAGRAMA

The Salagrama, a blackish rounded stone with a hole, is worshipped as an emblem of Vishnu. It is normally found in the bed of the river Gandaki (in North Bihar). Inside the hole are visible spirals which remind one of the Chakra, or the Discus of Vishnu. Though eighty-nine varieties are known to exist, only fourteen are commonly found. They are never installed in temples but are worshipped in one's own home privately. Once a Salagram is kept in a house, its worship,though simple, becomes obligatory. It is supposed to be endowed with mysterious powers. Even possessing and worshipping it will confer certain permanent benefits.

THE SUN

Being the giver of life, light and energy, the Sun has naturally become a symbol of the Creator. The famous  Gayatri Mantra has been addressed to God the Creator, in and through the orb of the Sun. The Sun can also represent the cosmic sacrifice from which the whole creation has proceeded. The Upanishads sometimes describe it as the celestial door leading to Immortality.

THE SWASTIKA

The Swastika is a symbol of auspiciousness (Swasti-auspiciousness). It has
been used as a symbol of the Sun or of
Vishnu. It also represents the
world-wheel, the eternally changing
world, round a fixed and unchanging
centre, God. Swastika marks depicted on doors or walls of
buildings or on animals are belived to protect them from
the wrath of evil spirits or furies of nature.

DHARMACHAKRA

The Dharmachakra or the "Wheel of the Law" is the
most important symbol of Buddhism.

Dharma is the Law which accomplishes the greatest
good of the greatest number. In the individual's life it
becomes manifest as good and noble conduct. 'Chakra'
means the Wheel and 'Pravartana' means setting in
motion. The Wheel of eternal Cosmic Law, though ever in
motion, appears to slow down a little, seems to get bogged
down a little, in certain periods of the history of mankind.
At such critical periods Krishnas, Buddhas or Christs, have
to come down to set it rolling once again. This is exactly
what Gautama Buddha did, when he delivered his first ser-
mon preaching the greatest truth he had himself discovered in his life.

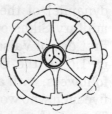

Though the four noble truths, which are
now part and parcel of the religious history of the world, constitute the essence
of dharma according to Buddhism, it is
the last of these truths, the eight-fold path
(Arya Ashtangika Marga), that really
forms the spokes of the Wheel of Dharma as it were. (The
Buddhist Wheel of Dharma has eight spokes) The Wheel
cannot survive without the practice of these eight virtues,

namely right view (**Samyak Drushti**), right resolution (**Samyak Sankalpa**), right speech (**Samyak Vak**), right conduct (**Samyak Kriya**), right means of livelihood (**Samyak Ajiva**), right effort (**Samyak Vyayama**), right mindfulness (**Samyak Smriti**) and right concentration (**Samyak Samadhi**).

It is said that the Buddha himself drew on the ground with grains of rice, the picture of a wheel, an ancient Indian symbol which signifies the round of births and deaths due to Karma, and which man himself keeps in motion through his thirst (tanha) for life. Later the Buddhists developed the Wheel as an explicit symbol. Apart from the eight spokes of the Wheel representing the eight-fold path, at its hub are sometimes shown the three sources of pain – the serpent of ill-will, the pig of ignorance, and the cock of lust.

The Wheel may also symbolise a constantly changing Universe, the Impermanence of everything in the world.

SWORDS, DAGGER AND SHIELD

Sikhism teaches that God is one and that He can be easily pleased by devoted repetition of His name. Obedience and submission to the Guru brings release from transmigratory existence.

Guru Govind Singh, the last (and perhaps the most dynamic) of the Sikh Gurus, established a new order of military Sikhs out of his meek and mild followers. On the first day of Vaisakh (second month of the Hindu Calendar) in 1,699, the Guru declared, to a large meeting of his followers, with a naked sword in his hand, that he wanted five men who would offer their heads to him 'here and now.' Though the whole assembly was stunned by the unusual behaviour of the Guru, five men walked up to him, one after another, ready for the great sacrifice. The Guru called them 'The Khalsa' (the Pure) and 'his very own' and bap-

80

tised them with water stirred by their daggers. And he declared, "Henceforward, the Sikhs (Sisyas or the followers) would all be of one community. The men would wear the five 'Kakas', the Kes (uncut hair), the Kacha (short drawers), Kara (iron bangle), the Kirpan (steel dagger) and the Kangha (Comb). They should always be ready to fight, and if necessary even to sacrifice their all for Dharma."

The swords, the shield, and the dagger represent the martial spirit of the community. They signify that a Sikh must be prepared to fight and even sacrifice his life in defence of his Dharma or faith.

THE CROSS

The Cross is one of the oldest of symbols, found in almost all civilizations of the world. After Jesus the Christ sacrificed his life on the Cross, it has become the perfect symbol of the Christian religion.

During the times when Christ lived, death by crucifixion was commonplace for criminals and was considered to be particularly ignominious. Christ was condemned for treason and was treated like a criminal. He was forced to carry the heavy cross on which he was later crucified. During his last journey he had to undergo a lot of suffering and this is known as the Passion of Christ in Christian theology.

But, by dying on the Cross, Christ raised it from ignominy to glory for all time. It represents the self-sacrifice and redemptive love of Christ for mankind. It has also become identified with the Christian religion and the Christian Church.

There are various forms of the Cross, out of which the Greek Cross, the Latin Cross and the Calvary or the Graded Cross, are more frequently used. In the Greek Cross the vertical and the cross bars are of equal length and it is taken to represent the Church of Christ rather than his Passion. The Latin Cross has a longer upright and the shorter crossbar is fixed in such a way that at the intersection, the upper and the two horizontal arms are all of equal length. The lower arm is conspicuously longer. This cross symbolises the Passion of Christ. Very often a crucified figure of Christ is attached to this Cross when it is called the Crucifix. The Calvary Cross stands on three steps which signify faith, hope and love. This is symbolic of finished redemption, of Christ risen from the dead, and reigning from the throne in heaven.

THE MENORAH

The Menorah is a representation of the creation of the most typical and important of the symbols of Judaism, the religion of the Hebrews or Jews. Judaism has survived to this day because of its monotheistic philosophy and the deep faith of its followers that they are a chosen race destined ultimately to conquer and rule the entire world. The Old Testament is its basic Scripture and the Ten Commandments contain its cardinal ethical principles.

The Menorah is representation of the creation of the world by God. According to Genesis of the Old Testament,

God created the world in six days and rested on the seventh day. The middle light indicates the Sabbath, (the last day of the week, a holy day and a day of rest). The seven branches may also represent the seven heavens created by God.

THE CAULDRON OF FIRE

This is the symbol of Zoroastrianism, popularly known as the Parsi religion.

When Ahura Mazda revealed Himself to Zoroaster and gave him the teachings and the Command, Zoroaster asked

82

Him to give him a symbol. Fire was the symbol given since it burns away all evil and it can never be made impure.

The maintenance of a sacred fire in Fire Temples, called Atar-Beheram without allowing it to be extinguished, is an important feature of Zoroastrianism. It is treated like a King, with a crown hung over it. The cauldron itself may be about three feet in diameter and four feet high. The priests feed it five times a day at prescribed hours. Offering of sandalwood is considered to be specially meritorious for the donors. Ash taken from the sacred fire is used for applying on the forehead by the devout worshippers.

SWAMI HARSHANANDA

(Condensed from Swami Harshananda's book "Principal Symbols of World Religion".)

SYMBOLISM AND LIFE

Today, when man seems to have lost his identity in a wilderness of ideologies, movements and slogans, it is time to pause for a moment to review the past, assess the present, and go forward into the future, with the evaluation, the rejection and the assimilation of experienced norms. To look back is to comtemplate what has been. For this, knowledge of a heritage that is more than five thousand years old has to be acquired. Much of literature and art speaks in terms of symbols, and it is through these symbols that the human mind understands language and communication. Symbols show us the structure of a world gone by, and the values that crested that structure. The depth of the seeking of those poets of the Upanishads,who delved into the profoundest sources of the mysteries of life, enlighten us in the wisdom they gained in all aspects of human existence. They tried, and perhaps succeeded in unveiling and integrating the truths in the great declarations of the Sastras and taught us that we are part of that Supreme Unity which we call "Brahman". "There is a Spirit which is pure and which is beyond old age and death : and beyond hunger, thirst and sorrow. This is Atman, the Spirit in man. All the desires of this Spirit are Truth. It is this Spirit that we must find and know : man must find his own soul. He who has found and knows his soul, has found all the worlds, has achieved all his desires."

But these words are difficult for the common man, so the artists, dancers, painters and writers become the revealers of the meaning of life to the society around them. They studied the symbols that guided the mind towards eternal truths, and through them India's wisdom was wafted through the centuries through stories and fables enacted in dance and drama, depicted in painting and sculptures,that brought into the focus the patterns of life that men should follow for lasting happiness.

First, there was Dharma, the right way of living, of fitting oneself into a proper pattern.

There were duties to be performed, a value-oriented mode of conduct in all conditions of life,and it was in acquitting oneself of these duties that one was sanctified.

Bhishma tells Yudhishtira the story of Tuladhara (a Vaisya to whom Jajali was sent to study) and Dharma Vyadha (a butcher selling meat but well-versed in the duties enjoined in the Vedas); both tales of how a pundit had to go to a merchant and a butcher for enlightenment on Dharma. Dharma, a scholar tells us, is what gives us Hinduism in all its phases, the flavour of a thirst for righteousness in an unrighteous world and a constant yearning for truth wherever it may be found.

As the fisherman said in "Shakuntala", when he was mocked for his lowly status: "However reproachful one's calling us, cherishing each other, let us achieve our common goal of supreme welfare."

These myths direct us how to behave in certain conditions and situations and how to relate to the world around us. Cassirer remarks: "It is the principle of symbolism which gives access to the specifically human world, to the world of human culture. From myths, many of the problems of human beings can be understood and evaluated, and often the wrong values discarded."

A drawn symbol has conscious meaning. It is visual, and immediately creates a response in the viewer. It was originally merely a mark. A mark has no meaning. But, suppose it is used for 2-3, it becomes an action. But, suppose we turn it into a diagonal mark 2 x 3. Again, it is charged with another action. But, then it may become a cross. Now, it represents the heights of martrydom, for it brings into our minds the memory of Jesus Christ who was nailed upon the cross, suffering for all humanity. Another example is a triangle formed of only three lines. Yet how much philosophy has gone into its inner meaning. The Sri-Chakram of good fortune symbolises the cosmic plan, and also represents the three gunas – Satwa, Raja and Tamas. India, it is said, is shaped as a triangle with the Mother Goddess at the top as Gowri-Shankara and the Goddess again at the southern-most tip Kanya Kumari. A triangle also signifies totality in Time-Space-Causation and so becomes vibrant with meaning and action.

The simple wheel of Chakra has also a deeply symbolic meaning. It is the 'Universal law : with its reflection in the moral law of man'; the universal power and the focus of spiritual power in human consciousness; the universal sun and the inner lights of illumination. A 'Chakravartin' is a world ruler. The rim of the Chakra symbolises the world in its entirety, its infinite movement and speaks of the unending cycle of life, death and rebirth. The spokes represent the different paths which lead from the rim to the hub, from movement to peace, from sorrow to nirvana. It also represents the spiritual faculties in man in reference to the seven inner Chakra, of psychic power within the human being, waiting to be explored and invoked.

The wheel of Dharma was also shown as the symbolic axis of the Cosmos, a concept of continuous change. Maya is called the 'Wheel of fire'. Vishnu's weapon is a Chakra, and the Buddhist Wheel of Law is the wheel of existence.

The Bhagvad Geeta says The Lord causes all beings to revolve by His deluding power Maya as if they were mounted upon a wheel.

Siddhanta Siromani, written by the genius, Bhaskara, in A.D. 1150, describes the Quicksilver Wheel, a perpetual motion machine. For Hindus, the Universe itself is a perpetual motion machine. From India, this concept found its way to Arabia and thence to Europe.

Let us now consider a contemporary symbolic structure, a bottle, a bottle of champagne, as described by a western writer, who makes it almost Vedantic in concept. The decision of the shape of a bottle has taken many years, and can be called the 'growing experience' through the centuries. Only the fittest survived, as the form, the thickness of glass and the other details were decided. The corking also, or rather the uncorking, is the ritual in a bottle of champagne, for it shows the true festive spirit of the liquid. The container is the ritual, the content the myth. We observe the bottle, and though we drink the liquid, we also watch the liquid in detached contemplation. So, the drinker becomes the Sakshi, the upadrishta. After the enjoyment, the drinking of the champagne, "the past experience", we are left with the empty bottle. We are told that emptiness is beauty. Empty yourself and let God enter. So the empty bottle is kept as pure art – like the little miniature bottles of Air India that are valued in some houses like exhibits. We may guess the spirit of our times by the "keeping" values, which soon become our "recorded past". But man changes a bottle into a vase or a lampstand, which indicates creativity, the ability to change an already accepted form into something new. But what of the bottles that are thrown away. Are they oversome, forgotten, or are they just garbage? Garbage is our undigested past. If memories are fully assimilated, they become one with nature. Just as an earthen jug dissolves into earth, a wave into water, or a bracelet into gold, even so the universe will dissolve into Me. But are not human beings left with some experiences that cannot be forgotten, like childhood hurts, or psychological mental blocks – 'garbage' that stands in the way of fulfilment?

Through the centuries, creative intellects in India,

turned every manifestation in nature into a symbol; and these symbols were the nucleus of study for understanding the world, both inside and outside. Balanced equilibrium was a constant topic of discussion.India gave to the world the "Yantrarudha", the wheel used in agriculture; the knowledge that Zero was Infinity; and the wisdom that life was a continual change and never ended with 'death'.

India used the logic of symbolic form in aesthetic thought making man alive and alert to the problems of the world he sees around him and also the unknown world, illuminating every detail of life, understanding and aesthetic beauty.

"As a man casts off worn-out garments and dons new ones, so the embodied casts,off worn-out bodies and enter those that are fresh" – Shri Krishna tells Arjuna.

And again in the Katha Upanishad : "The wise one is not born, neither does he die; he came not from anywhere, neither is he anyone, he is unborn, he is ever-lasting".

Indeed, the Sanskrit word for Philosophy is "Anuiksiki" – the survey of all things. There is continually in all Indian art expression, the tremendous feeling of the indestructibility of life, the eternal pilgrimage of the soul to the Ultimate Unity and source from whence it came.

MRINALINI V. SARABHAI

SYMBOLISM
IN
HINDUISM

PART II

MANIFESTATIONS

BRAHMA

Lord Brahma is the first member of the orthodox Brahminical triad; Vishnu being the second and Siva, the third. Brahma is the God of creation. He is traditionally accepted as the Creator of the entire universe.

In Vedanta, the Cosmic-subtle-body called Hiranyagarbha is considered to be the Creator, Lord Brahma. An individual's subtle body is constituted of his mind and intellect, i.e. his entire thoughts. The Cosmic-subtle-body is the aggregate of all the subtle bodies of all the living beings. The subtle body of an individual is responsible for the creation of his gross physical body and the world of objects that he experiences. In other words, it is the mind-intellect equipment that projects the physical body and the world. When this equipment is absent, there can neither be a physical body nor the world. Hence, the sum of all the subtle bodies of all the living beings, the Hiranyagarbha, is said to be the Creator of the entire universe. This Cosmic-subtle-body is personified as Brahma.

The manifested world of plurality has emerged from the unmanifest Reality. To indicate this, Brahma, the Creator, is described as being born from the navel (nabhi) of Vishnu (who represents the Eternal Reality), when He is shown underlying on the great serpent Ananta in the milky ocean.

One of the earliest iconographic descriptions of Brahma is that of a four-faced God seated on a lotus. The Lord has in his four hands a water-pot (kamandalu), a manuscript (Vedas), a sacrifical implement (sruva) and a rosary (mala). He wears the hide of a black antelope and his vehicle is a swan (hamsa).

This description of the Lord, like those of the other deities in Hinduism, bears a mystic symbolism. The Lord sitting on a lotus indicates that He is ever rooted to the Infinite Reality. Lotus represents the Reality, which is the foundation upon which his personality exists.

The four faces of Brahma represent the four Vedas. His four hands, like those of other Gods, stand for the four aspects of man's inner personality (Antahkarna), viz. the mind (manas), intellect (buddhi), ego (ahamkar) and conditioned consciousness (chitta). These four are the ways in which the thoughts function and they are the manifestations of the Pure Consciousness.

The deer skin worn by the Lord indicates that a seeker, who desires to reach the supreme state of Brahma, must first observe austerities like a brahmachari (anchorite). Observing such austerities, the seeker must carefully study and reflect upon the scriptural truths which are suggested by holding the manuscript (Vedas) in one hand of the Lord representing the buddhi (intellect). With such self-control and discipline and having the knowledge of the sastras (scriptures), he must use his physical body in selfless and dedicated service (karma-yoga) for the general prosperity of all. This is indicated by the sacrificial implement held in the second hand (ahamkar/ego). When these three spiritual practices are adopted, the mind of the seeker is withdrawn from its preoccupation with the sense pursuits in the external world. Such a mind, which has become introvert and relatively tranquil, alone is suitable for concentration (dharana) and Japa (chanting with the rosary – mala) provided in the third-hand (manas/mind). Meditation is the last process by which the seeker is transported from his finite limited individuality into the infinite transcendental state of God-Realisation. This is indicated by the holding of the water-pot (kamandalu) – a symbol of sanyas – in the fourth hand (chitta/conditioned consciousness).

Lord Brahma uses the swan (hamsa) as his vehicle. Its significance is that a Man-of-Realization moves about in the world with the unique faculty that a swan possesses. A hamsa (swan), as described in the Hindu mythology, has the faculty to separate pure milk from a sample of milk mixed with water. Similarly, a Man-of-Perfection recognises the one Supreme Truth inherent in the entire pluralistic phenomena.

The Lord of Creation must necessarily possess the knowledge to create. Creation presupposes the possession of a know-how of the process of creation. Hence it is that Brahma is said to be wedded to the Goddess of Knowledge, Mother Saraswati.

Life in this world is a manifestation of the three principles of construction, destruction and sustenance. In fact, these three are inter-connected. The apparent destruction is only an essential forerunner to all construction. Destruction and creation go hand in hand and they are like the two sides of a coin. For example, destruction of the morning is the creation of the evening and the destruction of the evening is the creation of the night. This chain of continuous destruction and construction maintains the day. Similarly, a tree is maintained by the continuous process of births and deaths from the stages of a flower, fruit, seed, plant, to a full grown tree. Hence, the three Gods of the Trinity, viz. Brahma, Vishnu and Maheshwara, representing creation, maintenance and destruction, are essentially the one and the same principle of existence.

The above idea is well portrayed in Lord Dattatreya, in whose form the three Gods are combined. Dattatreya has three faces of Brahma, Vishnu and Maheswara to indicate that the three principles for which they stand are inseparable. Lord Dattatreya is always shown with four dogs following Him. The four dogs represent the four Vedas. A dog is one of the most faithful animals in the world and it follows its master in all environments and

BRAHMA

94

circumstances. So too, the Vedas are said to follow a Man-of-Realisation in the sense that all his actions, thoughts and desires are in perfect accord with the principles enunciated in the Vedic text books.

All creations arise out of Vikshepa (thought disturbances). This vikshepa-sakti is Lord Brahma — the total mind-intellect equipment. Man, being essentially constituted of his mind and intellect, has already invoked this vikshepa-sakti and realized Brahma. Hence worship and invocation of Brahma is not undertaken by anyone.

Yet there are a few shrines dedicated to Brahma. In these He is worshipped and invoked only by scientists and kings (rulers) for generating more creative ideas to serve the world of men and matter. The rulers invoke the Lord in order to surrender their ego and produce plans and schemes to serve the nation. Similarly, the research scholars invoke creative inspiration and flashes of new thoughts revealing the secrets of Nature.

Lord Brahma is not popularly worshipped in India. This is so, because the idea of creation is repugnant to a seeker of Truth. It is the creation of thoughts that has veiled the Infinite Reality. The attempt of all spiritual seekers is to destroy the existing thoughts and maintain this state until the Truth reveals Itself. Hence, Siva (God of destruction) and Vishnu (God of maintenance) are worshipped more than Brahma. In fact, there are very few temples of Brahma — one in Rajasthan and another in Orissa — compared to numerous shrines of Siva and Vishnu existing all over India.

A. PARTHASARTHY

VISHNU – NARAYANA

Analysing the human personality, the Vedanta takes the student to discover the State of Pure Consciousness in the innermost depth of his being, which is the One Source at once for all his perceptions, feelings and thoughts.

This great Self, functioning as the Spark of Existence in each one of us, is the One Eternal Reality. When it expresses through the vehicles of mind and intellect there is the dynamic creature – constantly acquiring and possessing, gaining and achieving good and bad in the world – and this All-Pervading Reality that expresses from behind the mind and the intellect is the theme of all the great scriptures of the world.

Vyasa describes this great Reality in his "Vishnu Purana" as Sri Narayana. Sri Narayana has been shown as resting in yogic-sleep in Vaikuntha. It is described that in an ocean of milk (Ksheerabdhi) Sri Narayana lies in yoga-nidra on a great serpent-bed (Ananta), protected by the hood of the serpent. He is served by Lakshmi, His consort, who is ever at His feet.

Deep in the recesses of our personality (Vaikuntha) lies the Infinite Truth (Vishnu) upon the serpent-Ananta (the mind) who is depicted as thousand-headed. In all religions the serpent represents the vicious mind which, at one and the same time, can think a thousand thoughts and, perhaps, spill its venom through its thousand urges, inclinations, desires and passions. In life it is found that the hooded cobra, to strike its victim, turns its hood away from his body. When the mind is turned towards the world of objects outside, it is capable of spilling its poison on to the world outside.

Here in the description, the hoods are turned upon the body of the serpent and it is lying coiled upon itself, forming a soft bed upon which reclines Lord Vishnu (All Pervading). When the multi-headed human mind turns its attention inward upon itself, and the mind lies coiled upon itself, there is the state of a meditator at the moment the Infinite Vishnu can be recognized as resting upon such a thoughtless mind held in animated suspension in an atmosphere of breathless devotion. The Lord is in "yogic-sleep". It means that, looking from the Pure Consciousness, the world known to us, constituted of the perceptions, emotions and thoughts, is not there at all; just as in our sleep we do not recognize the world-of-plurality. But this is not the ordinary sleep (nidra); it is a moment of positive experience of the All-Pervading Reality, and hence it is called the yoga-nidra.

Such a vision of the Lord can be experienced by the mind when it turns upon itself; and the mind can gain this steady introvertedness only in an atmosphere of supreme purity. Hence it is described that He is resting in the "milky-ocean" in the ocean of the milk of human kindness.

Lakshmi (Wealth, Power and Glory) rests at His feet, serving Him. A Man of Realization, who through meditation has thus experienced the Soul of the Universe in himself, does not thereafter run after the wealth of the world of objects; all glory follows him at his heels, wanting to serve him as his dutiful mistress.

Lord Narayana is the One, among the Trinity, representing the Power-of-Sustenance. He is the one who manifests Himself in the world among mankind at appropriate eras in His various incarnations to rid life of its evil propensities and to make the world ready for greater evolution. When this benign Lord wakes up from His yogic-sleep and comes down to bless those who are His devotees, He assumes the form of Lord Narayana, and the description of Him is given in a dozen places in the "Vishnu Purana",

VIṢṆU - NĀRĀYAṆA

bringing out the entire symbolism in Him clearly. Whether it is in Dhruva's poetic words at the time of his great "vision of Narayana", or in the beautiful song of Prahlada, or in the various songs of Narada, we find the symbolisms described to explain what Vishnu stands for.

Traditionally, He is described as blue in colour clothed in yellow, wearing a crown and standing upon a lotus divine. He has four hands and He holds in them the Conch (Sankha), the Discus (Chakra), the Mace (Gada), and the Lotus (Padma). Every one of these represents a significant symbolism very scientifically employed to indicate that Vishnu is none other than the Divine Mighty Self which is the Changeless Centre of all changes, the Imperishable Essence in the midst of all the perishable finite things.

Blue is the colour of the Infinite and whatever is immeasurable can appear to the mortal eye only as blue; thus a cloudless summer sky is blue to us because the endless distance of space is interpreted by the physical eye as blue in colour. The yellow represents the earth. Anything that is buried in the earth gathers a yellowish hue, and in fire, earth (mud, silica) glows yellowish. Thus, Sri Narayana represents the Immeasurable, All-Pervading Reality (blue colour) clothed in earthy matter (yellow colour), meaning Sri Narayana is the Infinite clothed in matter; He is the Infinite expressed through a form.

When the Self (Atman) thus expresses itself through a form, an individual (Jeeva) is manifested. Every individual acts and accomplishes in the world, not with the mortal two hands alone, but with a subtle set of four hands. These four aspects that function from within the physical equipment are together called the "subtle body"; in Vedanta it is known as the "inner equipment," constituted to the Mind, the Intellect, the Ego and the Consciousness-of-them-all. These four are symbolized in the form-representation of Lord Vishnu having four hands.

The Lord wears a Divine Crown on His head to indicate His Sovereignty and Lordship over all names and forms. He is the sole proprietor of the entire Universe.

This mighty Infinite Lord dwells in the core of our personality as the very Self in us.

His hands are never empty — each is holding a symbol, together indicating how He carries out his Divine duties as the preserver of the Universe. He blows the Conch, calling man to live the nobler values of life so that he may turn away from all his worldly preoccupations and ultimately reach Him and receive from Him the Infinite Bliss of unbroken peace and perfection. This "final goal", indicated in our scriptures, is represented in Hindu tradition as the Lotus.

With a tender anxiety to give the devotee the highest experience of perfect happiness He calls, and man, roaming with his sensuous urges and animal propensities, hears the echoes of the shrill notes of his inner conscience calling him to stop and retire. Generally man has no ears to hear, or even when he hears he has no heart to obey. He still dashes forth in the quest for sense gratifications; it is at such times, out of sheer love, the Lord wields His Mace to knock man down with disappointments, dissatisfactions and a growing sense of restlessness.

Even in spite of these punishments, if the devotee is not turning towards the spiritual path and is not progressively moving towards the final destination, the Lord has the total annihilating power of the Discus, which can destroy the equipment and lift him from his present life of unhealthy circumstances. This is true of an individual, a community, or a nation. Fascinated by the delusory joys of the sense-objects the human mind may dance forth to live a ruinous life of sense gratifications. And if this material and purely sense way of life is continued in spite of the consequent mental tensions and strains, the society dissipates all its higher urges, loses even its common efficiencies and ultimately comes to lose all that it possessed and ends in a pitiful and disastrous fall. This is what history records and commmonsense ever dictates.

We may even consider the 'hand that holds the Conch' as the intellect (buddhi), the 'hand that holds the Discus' as the ego, 'that which holds the Mace' as the mind (manas), and 'that which holds the Lotus' as the consciousness (chitta). The discriminating intellect gives us the call and points out a more rewarding way of life, and in case we ignore this silent whisper of the heart and plunge into a life of extrovertedness, the mind gives endless knocks to that personality. If even then, we are not able to realize our folly and withdraw ourselves from the dissipating ways of living, the arrogant ego fattened by these stupidities of the mind in revolt against the intellect, ultimately drives the individual to his total doom.

On the other hand, in case we are able to listen to the call and surrender our ego and mind in devotion to the Lord, we can surely come to His sacred feet, and receive the Lotus that He is offering to us as an eternal reward for an insignificant renunciation on our part.

When the inner equipments of the mind, intellect and ego are transcended, the Light of Consciousness that illumines them for us is itself discovered as the Pure Infinite Self.

A meditator who meditates thus upon the symbolism represented in the Lord's Divine Form is no more merely gazing at His divine physical form, but the devotee comes to be transported into a realm of Realization of his own inner True Nature. The Lord is ever rooted in this Divine Brahman and, hence, the Deity is represented as standing on a Lotus.

SWAMI CHINMAYANANDA

SESHASAAYEE

Philosophers that we are, even stones and copper are redolent to us of philosophy. If we go on at this rate, all the world, I dare say, will get reduced to five elements just as the idol in the temple is composed of five metals; and you will shortly leave even that idolatry, and proceed to find out the inner meaning of this grand symbol of the world, which is nothing but God, who is, as Sruties declare, subtler than the most subtle, greater than the greatest, firm like a rock and one without a second.

We shall now proceed to discuss the symbol as famous as that of Nataraja, viz., Sri Ranganatha. Curiously enough there is simply a war of words in every land. The Mohammedan plucks out the beard of the Christian, who in his turn shoots him down, his turban and all, only because the former says the true God is Allah, and the latter Jehovah – the Father in Heaven. But those who are impartial will, say however, that Allah and Jehovah mean the same thing, and denote the same Person – if person He be.

Ranganatha and Nataraja mean the very same thing, and refer to very nearly the same conception, only differently expressed. Nataraja is the lord of the stage, so also Ranganatha (Ranga means stage). The stage is the stage of the world, of the cosmos, or better still of the body and the senses. The one dances in Chidambaram, i.e. the sphere of wisdom, the other sleeps on the milky sea.

We cannot sufficiently describe the glory of that conception, the poetry of the ocean of milk, the imagination of the mind that could have originally conveived it; and the grandeur of the idea underlying it cannot be sufficiently done justice to here.

SESHASAAYEE

Our ancient fathers, however poor they might have been in balldresses, arm-chairs and steam-ships, have endowed us with the rich legacy of a silver rock, a gold mountain, a milky ocean, a heavenly river, a generous cow, a liberal tree, a white elephant, a heavenly father and a rich philosophy. We have, fortunately, down below, the Himalayas, the Ganges, etc. In this grand group comes the milky sea.

The real inner meaning of this milky sea can only be ever upon our hearts, lips, and pens. Guru; it is a practical affair, but there is no mystery in it. There is no mystery at organising any esoteric society. To give a glimpse as for as words will permit, the real milky sea is found out when the consciousness of the body is lost; next that of the mind; and next, the idea of vacant space, which is a great hindrance in practical realisation. And the worlds of the sun, moon and colours have all to be left behind, then comes the real milky sea. The sweetness of sugar can only be described as far as words will allow, and not shown, and no reader will get offended with me for saying that the real milky sea is glorious when seen; that it is, to be as exact as words will permit, the sweet undisturbed nectar-like calmness that knows not the distinction of caste and creed, of life and death, of freedom and slavery, of form and no form, devoid of character and name, the calmness divine and perfect that silently pervades all, and plays hide and seek, with the ignorant, the serenity that is light, that is grace that is the ineffable, the effulgent turiya state which is beyond the maddened-monkey-like mind, the highest of the high, which knows not union and separation, or attachment, which knows not coming and going, which is far and near, which is firm like a rock, which fades not, which is beyond the five elements, which is beyond even the consciousness of enjoyment, which is neither one nor two, which is above the prattling tongue and the wandering mind, and which is an ocean of full, undisturbed ecstasy; that is

104

the real sea of milk. It requires the grace of God and the blessings of the real Guru to discover that sea. It is a treasure far beyond the reach of the ambitious, the wicked, the avaricious and the selfish, which is ever a secret refusing to unfold itself to the heart that falters or is false. 'Knock and it shall be opened, seek and ye shall find.'

आदावन्ते च मध्ये च सृज्यासृज्यं यदन्वयात्
पुनस्तत्प्रतिसंक्रामे यच्छिष्येत तदेवसत्
नष्टं लोके द्विपरार्द्धावसाने महाभूतेष्वादिभूतं गतेषु
व्यक्तोव्यक्तं कालवेगेन याते भवानेकाइशेष्यते शेषसंज्ञः

The meaning of the above, roughly translated is –

'From morn to eve and from eve to dewy morn'
That which envelops all the fourteen worlds,
The five elements, and ever shines in all;
During the sleep in which all being lost,
That which remains unlost, that consciousness,
Is called the I or Self, and Sesha forms;
Its inner light is Vishnu great, the Lord,
The Love, the light, the sat, the bliss and strength.

Here is Sesha described, but why the form of the huge serpent? The reason is that the serpent has been selected, not the other snakes, by the common consent of humnanity, as an object of worship in all countries alike. The outspread hood of the serpent, its fine ear for music, which men can never rival, with the fabled gem on its head, its glossy and altogether beautiful appearance, its faculty of hearing with the eyes, its comparative innocence when not disturbed and its real or reputed allegiance to mantras and oaths, which we may call serpent honesty, its intelligence and aptitude, when trained, to besmear human eyes with eye-salve, to mark the human face with sandal, etc., gently and cautiously, and several other fine qualities in it, might

105

have contributed to the universal worship accorded to it. Few countries have been free from the serpent fetichism. Among the Scythians it was God himself; and among the Hindus it has been raised to the rank of an ornament to the Lord Iswara, symbolising the intelligent human consciousness.

Even a higher honour was in store for it; traditions assert that there are five-headed serpents, most beautiful and harmless, and having a beautiful Nagaratna (a precious gem of most wonderful virtues) and wandering in the forests like the Rishis. There is a legend which tells us that Hyder Ali, previous to his Nawabdom, was a poor boy, found sleeping under a shady tree beautifully sheltered by a long five-hooded serpent, which had curled its body round and round, making a seat for itself to a height of about 3 ft. and fully spreading its hoods over the born emperor, with its rich jewel shining brighter than diamonds and rubies, and casting its full lustre upon the beardless face of the orphan boy. Well, if five-hooded serpents are possible here, why not a thousand shining gems in the beautiful sea of milk, especially if it would serve as a grand and true symbol? The serpent, we saw, represents the consciousness, and consciousness is above, below and everywhere-where is it and where is it not? It is in the star above, in the stone below, in the waters that flow, in man, in animal, plant and stone. This consciousness sleeps in the plant, dreams in the animal, and wakes in man. The sun is the same all over the earth : the dead stone like an ignorant man receives that light, but in its dull way; the waters shine in the light, but reflect it not; mirrors, like blessed souls, not merely shine themselves, but also make others shine. This Sesha, then, which is everywhere, manifest or unmanifest, is symbolised by that beautiful serpent. Besides, its infinite coils, all its huge beauty, represent the infinity of that consciousness, its omnipresence and the eternity of that splendour. This consciousness is the Sesha beyond all name and form-beyond time, space and causality. (Sesha means what remains when all else is lost; the undying, the infinite and eternal.) It is on the milky sea necessarily; for until the heavenly calm of the inner soul is realised, the beauty of the universal consciousness cannot be seen.

Vishnu the great God sleeps upon the smooth glossy bed of the serpent-back, it is a wonderful sleep however, for it is sleep without its darkness, it is the sleep, not of ignorance and dullness, but a sleep of light a knowing sleep as it has been called. The idea is that God pervades all the universe 'the atom, the roaring sea, the mountain chains and all', but Himself, like the sun, unstained by the war of the world. The sleeping means "Urdhvapurnam adhahpurnam madhyapurnam" filling the above, the below, the middle, as the Uttara-Gita says, and as the posture is a lying one without North or East or South or West, He fills the world 'from the tip of the nail to the top of the head', as Nakhasikhaparyantam, etc., of the Brih-Upa, means, No clouds can pollute Him, no sin can attach to Him, no grief can enter into Him.

Tasya Kartaramapi Mam Vidhyakartaramavyayam.

Geeta IV, stanza 11.

"Though I am the Lord of creation, as I work without attachment, no action clings to me", said Sri Krishna. So, the great Lord of the universe is in knowing sleep, as the sun, to compare small things with great, though he inspires a multitude of actions, is yet himself free from them. But then, this abstract God, the inner light of consciousness, the Atman, pervades the whole universe, and is everything, even the illusion of phenomena included, and now descending to the phenomenal platform, the Vyavaharika Satta, as it is called, we find creation is real, and the same abstract Brahman is our father in Heaven, our punisher and rewarder. Ranganatha, as we have already seen, means the Lord of the stage, and in the beautiful conception of the milky sea is treasured up in the whole range of philosphy, as "Homer in a nutshell". From the abstract Atman to the personal God, the Father and Creator, the whole range is involved in it, for what are Vishnu's ornaments? – the Kaustubha gem on his broad breast, the Srivatsa mark on his chest, the conch-shell, the bow and the discus in his hands, the Vaijayanti, composed of five precious gems, pearl, ruby, emerald, sapphire and diamond, which adorns his breast. He has a rich store of powerful shafts and a bright sword called Achyuta. For an authoritative explanation of these symbols, we have great pleasure in referring the reader to Vishnu Purana (Book 1, Chapter 22).

The Kaustubha gem beautifully represents the pure and everlasting soul of the world. The pradhana being the chief principle of things, is very well placed as the Srivatsa mark on the chest of the Lord. Intellect is the faculty that shelters us against the arrows in the war of life and is therefore fittingly compared to the mace (Gada). Even our elements,the organs of sense and all their numerous progeny, are very well represented as Isa's conch-shell and bow, the former makes noise, and creation being due to vibration-Sabdanishtam jagat – the conch-shell represents the great function of creation, the bow very well represents the organs of sense, for, like the latter, they go in search of things, and are the faculties of grasping like the bow. But both the conch-shell and the bow (that is, creation and enjoyment – the whole world is described as the Lord 's lila or sport) must have their basis on Ahankara (egoism), the primary delusion of self. As Narada beautifully said to Sanatkumara: "If there be I, then there must be you. There then begins the mischief. If there be I and you, then there must be all the world." The discus (Chakra) symbolises the mind, which shames the speed of the winds and the swiftness of lightning. The universe composed of five elements is a beautiful ornament – the necklace Vaijayanti – to Vishnu the Protector, for nothing better expresses His grandeur and glory, who rules day and night, though sleeping, this vast, infinite and apparently conglomerate household of suns, moons and stars, and clouds and winds and waters.

The sharp faculties of action and perception are very well likened to the shafts which fly from the bow of the senses and intellect. Wisdom is a veritable sword, which fells down the grand tree of Aswatha, which changes every moment (Aswatha, means that which is not next moment), and is at the same time eternal, because Maya or delusion is eternal, which has its roots in that Supreme Lord, Narayana,who is sounding his conch-shell of creation. The Vedas are the leaves of this tree, because they shelter the tree from the sun and other things. The intellect forms the branches from the main trunk, and Ahankara (egoism) the five elements and the deceitful organs of sense are its branches, and the senses are holes in it. Virtue and vice are its flowers; and joy and grief are its fruits. It is the tree on which all souls live. (For a fuller explanation please refer to Gita, XV, 1, 2 and 3 and the elaborate commentaries on the same by Sankara, Ramanuja, Madhva and Sridhara, and Katha-Upa., 11, 61).

As Madhva has beautifully said, this grand tree of Samsara, which has its branches in Heaven, Earth, and everywhere should be bravely felled by the sword of wisdom – Achyuta of Narayana. This sword, however, is most often concealed in the scabbard of ignorance, and we people are therefore going round the tree, instead of felling it but even this ignorance is nothing but Narayana, for the Vedas proclaim that it is merely a sport, a leela of Hrishikesa.

Wilson, referring to this grand symbol in his translation of the Vishnu Purana, Book 1, Chapter 22, which we strongly recommend our readers to see, says: "We have in the text a representation of one mode of Dhyana or contemplation, in which the thoughts are more readily concentrated by being addressed to a sensible emblem instead of an abstract truth. Thus, the Yogin here says to himself: 'I meditate upon the jewel on Vishnu's brow as the soul of the world; and upon the gem on his breast as the first principle of things' and so on, and thus, through a perceptible substance, proceeds to an imperceptible idea." Lakshmi of course represents the pomp, the luxuriance of the world, the Lord's glory or Vibhuti, as it is termed-the Samsara Adambara or Jagajjala Vaibhava, the great neverending festival of illusory existence (Maya as it is called) – She sits near the feet, i.e., the Avidya Pada, i.e., the sphere of ignorance, for ignorance is the mother of creation and the world.

That the Seshasayana symbol is no mere idolatry is further attested by the following extract from Vishnu Purana – Book 1, Chap. XXII: "Thus Supreme Eternal Hari is time, with its divisions of seconds, minutes, days, months, seasons, and years. He is the 'seven worlds,.... First born before all the first-born; the supporter of all being but himself self-sustained; who exists in manifold forms, as gods, man, and animals, and is thence the sovereign Lord of all, eternal; whose shape is all visible things; who is without shape or form; who is celebrated in the Vedanta as the four Vedas, inspired history, and sacred science. The Vedas and their divisions; religious manuals and poems, etc., are the body of the mighty Vishnu... I am Hari, all that I behold is Hari. Cause and effect are from none other than Him. The man who knows these truths shall never again experience the afflictions of worldly existence."

B.R. RAJAM IYER

RAMA

The personality of Lord Rama in the Ramayana stands out unique and the most glorious as compared to any other character described in the scriptural literature. The great sage, Valmiki, has, in his creation of this divine hero, symbolised in Him the ideal of uncompromising goodness. Nowhere else does one find such idealistic perfections in all walks of life combine in a single individual. Thus Rama was, at once, a perfect son, an ideal king, a true husband, a real friend, a devoted brother, a noble enemy and so on.

Different aspects of the human personality, functioning in diverse facets of life, have been separately projected, and in Sree Rama an achievable perfection is indicated in each aspect. While attempting to paint an ideal picture of each aspect of the Lord's personality, the Rishi (sage) would not compromise with the standards of perfection conceived by him. He highlights one aspect of the personality at the expense of the others, so that Rama's conduct and behaviour, in certain instances, appear to be inconsistent with His divine character. Such seeming inconsistencies have created misapprehensions among the students of Ramayana because their deeper inner significance has been lost sight of.

One such instance is the criticism levelled against Rama for leaving his father, King Dasaratha, and going away to the jungle,while Dasaratha was severely protesting and Rama Himself knew that His father would not survive the sorrows of his son's self-exile. This criticism has no bearing when one bears in mind that Rama was only playing the part of an ideal son. In order to emphasize perfection in a son, the sage Valmiki provided an exaggerated

111

environment and situation and yet made Rama take this decision. Consider, it was the eve of Rama's coronation; Rama himself owed a duty to the subjects, who were clamouring for the sacred coronation; the insane demand of his step-mother, Kaikeyi, to coronate his younger brother, Bharatha, and send Rama to the jungle; the inexpressible love that King Dasaratha and Rama bore for each other; in spite of all these, Rama would not compromise in the fulfilment of His duty as a son. His father had promised to fulfil the demand of Kaikeyi and the son's duty was to see that his father's promise was redeemed, notwithstanding the series of obstacles that confronted him.

Another common doubt and dissatisfaction among the critics of Ramayana is with regard to Rama's action in sending away his queen to the forest in response to the irresponsible prattle of a washerman questioning the purity of the queen. Here again, the ideal kingship in Rama is magnified almost to the pitch of an absurdity. A true king, in those days, was one who was accepted by all his subjects, unlike the present system of democracy which is the rule of the majority. Hence, when Rama found even a single dissenting note in the voice of the public, he made the greatest sacrifice in sending his queen away. This action of Rama, though appearing to be absurd by modern standards, portrays the sanctity Rama attached to accepted standards of ideal kinghood in those days.

It is interesting to observe that this kingly action of voluntarily sending Sita away to the jungle was far surpassed by the deep devotion and concern displayed by Rama as the ideal husband, when Sita was carried away by Ravana. From that very moment of her abduction, Rama put forth his superhuman efforts to regain his lost wife. Here Rama provides the proof of an illustrious husband.

Above all, the most criticized portion of the entire Ramayana is the apparent cowardice of the great hero

112

RAMA

113

Rama in having hidden himself behind a tree and shot the monkey-king Vali, while the latter was engaged in a fight with his brother Sugreeva. Here again, Rama was only demonstrating his ideal friendship with Sugreeva. Once a friend, he was always a friend. He would go to the extreme limit and do anything to help a true friend. Besides this the episode has also a deeper mystical significance.

Vali, the immoral and vicious brother, represents lust, the lower nature of man. Sugreeva, the moral and virtuous brother, represents man's higher and nobler nature. The story goes that Vali had earned, through tapas (austerity), a boon by which half the strength of his enemy was transferred to him as soon as any enemy confronted him in a battle. Similarly, the power of lust becomes invulnerable the moment man comes in direct contact with the object of lust. The sense objects overpower man and they leave him a helpless victim of temptation. To avoid this, and to overcome successfully the disastrous influence of the sense objects, man has to stay away physically from the objects in the initial stages, i.e., before he gains an absolute hold and control over them. So long as man remains in the midst of sense objects and tries to exercise his self control over those objects, he can never be successful since the power of the sense objects is almost invincible. To indicate this great truth Rama is described as hiding behind a tree, i.e. physically keeping away from Vali, and shooting him from a distance.

The character of Rama paints the picture of a Man-of-Perfection. He was also an ideal brother, a perfect and chivalrous enemy and so on – thus every aspect of his personality is idealised to absolute perfection.

A peculiarity noticed in the personality of Lord Rama is that he is seen to be carrying his bow and arrows at all times. The wielding of the bow and arrows symbolises his preparedness and strength to maintain peace and justice both within and without. Disturbances may arise within one's bosom or reach him from the external world. Rama is ever prepared to face such challenges with strength. He is the ideal of 'aggressive goodness' as opposed to 'weak and passive goodness'. He would not passively accept anything that is inconsistent with or contrary to morality and righteousness. He stands for righteousness and opposes and destroys all that is unrighteous.

Thus, one finds in the Ramayana a necklace of priceless gems, each gem dazzling with the divine brilliance of the ideal personality of Lord Rama.

A. PARTHASARATHY

KRISHNA

Lord Krishna was a dynamic incarnation of Vishnu. He was an Avatar, in the sense that He was totally attuned to the Supreme Consciousness from his very birth. His incarnation brought to bear upon the Indian thought and life such a profound and powerful influence that it has no parallel in Bharat or elsewhere. There is no aspect of life, of culture and of civilisation which did not receive His revitalising touch — the Indian philosophy and religion, mysticism and poetry, painting and sculpture, music and dancing were all influenced by the Krishna theme and thoughts.

Every aspect of Krishna Avatar and His deeds are pregnant with deep mystical symbolism indicating the highest Truth. Some of them are analysed here to set a direction for deeper study and discovery of the allegoric significance behind subtle suggestions.

The word 'Krishna', in Sanskrit, means 'dark' indicating the Supreme Consciousness. The Consciousness is said to be 'dark' (Shyam), not as opposed to 'light', but in the sense that it is unseen by or unknown to man as long as he remains rooted in the terrestrial experiences. Man's knowledge and experiences are limited only to the three realms, i.e. perceptions, emotions and thoughts, which he gains through the media of his physical body, mind and intellect. The Consciousness is the Pure Self or Atman within, which is the Sentient Principle and which causes man's material equipments to function in their respective realms. The Consciousness is the very Subject of all experiences and cannot therefore be objectively experienced. It is beyond the normal human cognition.

116

The incarnation of Krishna represents the descent of the Infinite Brahman to the material world. The Lord is described as being blue (neela) in colour and donning yellow clothes (peetambara). The colour blue is associated with Infinitude in as much as the infinite expanses in Nature, like the clear mid-day sky or the deep ocean, appear blue to human perception. 'Yellow' is accepted as the colour of earth since earth, when introduced into a colourless flame, emits a yellow hue. Hence the blue form of Krishna clothed in yellow appropriately suggests the Pure, Infinite Consciousness that has come down to earth to play in His finite form.

The infinite, all-pervading Truth donning a finite form of a human being gives the impression that the Truth is fettered and limited. This idea of the illimitable Truth seeming to be limited is well brought out by Krishna being born in a prison. Though the Infinite Being seems to be limited and confined to a human embodiment, It is ever-free and uncontaminated. The Pure Self within is never affected or bound by one's material equipments (upadhis), i.e. the body, mind and intellect. Though the divine child was born in a prison, neither the iron bars nor the prison guards could confine Him. Vasudeva, His father, safely carried Him out of the prison in spite of the severe restrictions imposed upon Him.

Also, Krishna, as the Consciousness or Atman, resides in the core of one's personality. It remains confined, as it were, within the five layers of matter constituting the human personality. However, the Atman, being subtler than the matter vestures, is not bound or limited by them.

Sree Krishna was born in Mathura. His tyrant uncle, Kamsa, imprisoned his father, usurped the throne of Mathura and reigned there along with his cruel minister Chanura. As long as these two men were in charge of the land of Mathura, there was confusion and chaos everywhere. Krishna destroyed the tyrants and restored peace and order in that land.

The word 'madhuram' means 'sweetness'. Man's personality is essentially sweet in the sense that his real nature is the Pure Self, which is infinite peace and bliss. His bosom, like the land of Mathura, is now usurped by two evil forces, viz. his ego and his ego-centric desires, which cause agitations, worries and anxieties within. When these two forces are conquered by the higher nature in man, the original glory and splendour of the Pure Self is restored.

In the rasa-leela (divine sport), the beloved boy of Brindavan is found to be amidst the dancing gopis (milk-maids). Much criticism has been levelled against Krishna's association with these gopis. Little do the critics realize that the Lord is ever an unconcerned and unaffected witness of the gopis' dance even though He may be in their midst. Krishna is like the Consciousness within, the Pure Self which vitalises one's thoughts but remains unperturbed and unaffected by them. The Self is ever immaculate and uncontaminated by the thoughts that run in one's bosom. Thus, if the lives of such God-men are read without an understanding of their mystical symbolism, one comes to wrong and, at times, absurd conclusions.

The gopis performed their obligatory duties throughout the day constantly remembering. Their limbs were ceaselessly engaged in activity while their minds were ever attuned to the Lord. This, in short, is the essence of Karma Yoga, i.e. to dedicate oneself to a higher altar and work without ego and ego-centric desires. Such activities exhaust the existing vasanas (inherent tendencies) in one's bosom and also prevent the formation of any new vasanas. When thus, one strives hard and reduces his vasanas to the minimum, the last traces of them lingering within are liquidated by the Lord Himself without even one's knowledge. Hence it is, that He is branded as a thief,

KRISHNA

119

stealing the butter which the gopis carefully stored in their apartments.

Krishna is described as the infinite, omnipresent, omnipotent and omniscient Reality. Yet, the revered mother Yasoda sees only her child in Him. On one occasion, the little boy Krishna was suspected of having eaten mud. The mother chided him, but the boy denied having eaten mud. Krishna was only telling the truth. The earth is included in His Universal Form. He is the Whole and the world is a part of the Whole. How can the Whole Being eat its own part? The 'Eater' and the 'Eaten' cannot be one and the same. The Lord tried to explain, but the mother could not measure the magnitude and stature of His Infinite Being in her own child. Upon her insistence the boy opened his tiny mouth and revealed, to her utter amazement, the entire universe within, holding staff on one hand and displaying Gnana Mudra (the symbol of wisdom) with the other. The staff is used by the cowherd boy to drive the cattle to their pasture lands. Similarly, man uses the Life-Principle in him merely to drive his sense organs to their fields of enjoyment for mere sense gratification. But a man of discrimination is not satisfied with mere sensual pleasures. He takes the hint from the symbol displayed by the other hand to reach the Abode of Truth — the Goal of human evolution.

In the Gnana Mudra, the Lord holds the little, the ring and the middle fingers erect and bends the index finger to touch the middle of the thumb in such a way as to form a circle. The index finger represents the ego since it is the pointing finger which creates the duality-plurality. When the ego transcends the limitations of the three thought-conditions or gunas (Sattwa, Rajas, Tamas) or the three equipments of the gross, subtle and casual bodies, it becomes one with the Infinite Consciousness. (The thumb stands for the Consciousness). A circle, which has neither a beginning nor an end, represents Infinitude.

120

Thus, the Life-Principle can also be used by man to evolve himself and reach the supreme state of Perfection. The Lord gives man the choice to act as he wishes. He is a mere witness of all that takes place in man and in the world.

Lord Krishna plays the flute and brings out enchanting music. The flute, by itself, cannot give out music. It is an inert, insentient piece of matter. But when the Lord plays it, there emanates divine music which enchants everyone. Similarly, the human body is, by itself, inert and insentient. It contains the sense organs and the mind-and-intellect (the holes in the flute) through which the Consciousness expresses itself and brings out divine harmony and peace both within and without. Thus, by one's identification with one's Divine Self, the melody and music of life can be drawn out of oneself.

A. PARTHASARATHY

DATTATREYA

Salutations to Lord Dattatreya, who is neither short, nor long, neither subtle nor gross, who is without any attributes, and by whom alone all the five elements are illumined.

From Datta Stotram by Narada

For a sadhak, to write or talk on the great undigested, subjective subject is something like trying to gulp a vast thing in a small mouth. But since I was asked to write, I take the name of my Guru and plunge in. But who writes? The finite pen, even though it already contains the ink, cannot write by itself. Somebody has to hold it and then the writing is possible. Similarly, it is the Guru who expresses through the finite equipments (BMI) of the sadhak, the instrument in His hands, and who illumines the seeming activities, i.e. the OET. Yet He is unattached to any of them, like the Sun. Keeping in view this point and being afraid of the false 'I', and 'my-ness', with humble Salutations at the lotus feet of Revered Swamiji, our Gurudev, this effort is being made to state a few words devoted to Lord Dattatreya, who is none other than the Gurudev Himself for the seeker of Datta. Any stupidity or mistake in writing is undoubtedly mine, but the glory or beauty of expression is of the Gurudev.

Datta-Jayanti is to take place in May. It is celebrated in most of the "Datta Temples", especially in Maharashtra, where the Bhaktas are more in number.

In the light of Revered Swamiji's lecture heard on Mahasivarathri, it can be said that Lord Dattatreya is none other than the "Mighty Power", Lord Shiva. Thus it is the

'Datta-Tatwa' or the Shiva-Satwa (The Truth Principle), that functions through the finite things and beings in the manifested world, which constantly undergoes three changes – Creation, Sustenance and Destruction. These three mighty powers are objectively represented as the 'Trinity', Brahma (The Creator-Rajas), Vishnu (The Nourisher-Satwa) and Mahesh (The Destroyer-Tamas) who cannot work without each other... and which qualities are found, more or less, in each one of us.

Thus it is something like three official departments from the One Infinite Office. 'The Datta Tatwa', the Cause-less Cause. The departments are entrusted to the departmental heads, Brahma-Vishnu-Mahesh, and Lord Dattatreya is the main source or the substratum – The First (Sanatana) – Unborn, Eternal, Infinite, All-Pervading Officer of all the world of names and forms as termed in Vedanta. He has opened and formed Branch-Offices in everybody's bosom, which we call the life centre illumining all the seeming activites of the BMI in the individual, like the Sun, which lightens the whole world but which cannot be illumined by any of the 'Searchlights' of this so-called Scientific World.

Dattatreya is called "Sri-Guru-Datta", the Sadguru, who shows us the "Sat-Vastu" through the Guru. The Guru, Teacher; Dev, God; and Datta indicate something 'given' or that which is already within. But we are not in a position now to realise our Real Nature, Sat-Chit-Ananda, because of our ignorance, for which Knowledge alone is the antidote, as the Atma Bodha states. So we see, Guru-Dev--Datta is the unique blending together of Guru and Deity as one. Datta Tatwa is the Atman. And when, with a little devotion, any Bhakta of Lord Dattatreya is led to an established Master like our Swamiji, his joy within becomes spell bound. All of us are really very lucky to get the guidance of our Great Master whose glory can't be expressed

DATTATREYA

in the finite words. Even Mother Sruthi adopts the method of 'not this, not this,' while trying to indicate that Great Truth which is beyond all words.

Saint Tukaram, Gyaneswar and other similar Saints of Maharashtra and at other places also say that there is nothing in the world that can be used as comparison for expressing the glory of Sadguru. In Saint Tukaram's words "लोह परिसाशी न साहे उपमा-सद्गुरू महिमा अगाध तो" even the simile of iron (लौह) and Paris (परिस), by which the iron is said to be converted into gold, is also not sufficient. Thus the glory of Sadguru is unfathomable. This is the point where all the 'Yogis' and 'Bhaktas' meet, though in the beginning of their sadhana they appear as Bhakta, Yogi, Gyani, etc. Samarth Ramdas, one of the great Saints of Maharashtra, has defined Bhakta and Yogi as one who is not separate, or dual, from God. Regarding Yogi, he says one who is not separate in identity or union with God is Yogi. Of course, to reach this state requires efforts and Sadguru Kripa, meaning the one who shows the truth. 'The Kripa' may be called by Bhakta as God's Grace; Gyani may call it the Grace of the 'Self' and for Yogi it may be Kundalini Shakti. But Sadguru is the balancing centre of all, so Dattatreya is said to be the Guru Devata. Therefore, Datta-Jayanti is celebrated not only by the Datta Bhaktas (upasakas) but by others also, who may worship their Deity, who know the non-dual glory of Sadguru.

UPASANA

The difference in the Upasana (worship) of Lord Dattatreya during the preliminary stage may be that Bhaktas worship the Lord in the four-walled temple outside, and the Yogis in the temple of their hearts, by constantly remembering the lotus feet of Gurudev. It need not mean that the sadhaks should not worship the image in the temple. It is up to one to understand the meaning of the temple.

125

The Bhakta, when he worships Lord Dattatreya in the beginning by his gross mind or eyes, objectively perceives the 'Trinity' (i.e. an image having three faces, Brahma, Vishnu, Mahesh, together as a God). He starts feeling at the feet of the Lord that He has the pain and pleasure of Samsar; but it is not so. He is something like a witnessing judge, like the sun, who has nothing to do with the activities of the people, be they good or bad.

Our Gurudev, while explaining the method of Upasana, says, to have a higher vision or to seek something higher in a lower object or idol is the Upasana of the Lord. Datta Bhakta has therefore to bear in mind to seek something higher behind the 'Trinity', that Power which illumines the Trinity and its activities in the world. While contemplating the Truth, as the student of Vedanta, we are concerned with the "eye of the eye", and not the physical structure of the eye. Just as the fountain pen, as we have seen in the beginning, cannot write by itself, similarly there is some power from which the inert eye gets the power of vision to see its object. So also is the case of our other sense organs.

Parivrajakacharya Vasudevananda Saraswati has written a sacred book in Marathi called, "Datta Mahatmya", a unique combination of philosophy and Purana — according to which the word Dattatreya is interpreted as meaning Lord Dattatreya without the three upadhis. Naturally, therefore, in our upasana it must be something beyond the three-faced 'Trimurthi' or Trinity. He is the chief controller of these three departmental heads through which He is functioning in us. This statement is supported by a quotation from Avadhuta Gita, in which Dattatreya states to Himself that Brahma, Vishnu, Mahesh (representing Rajas, Satwa and Tamas) are in the three Mantras of Omkar i.e. AUM, and He is beyond the three. He transcends all the three upadhis. Datta Treya itself means without three. The point is hammered that the sadhak should get himself detached from the false identification of the three upadhis; gross, subtle and causal bodies.

This is to be done through purifying our inner equipment, through hearing, reflection and meditation on Truth, by chanting the glory and name of the Lord, keeping in view our Infinite Abode, Atmapur, for which we have to maintain the 'Sivoham' — 'Aham Brahmasmi' vritti as advised by Swamiji on Mahasivaratri. Thus, by selfless prem, the A-tri or Lord Dattatreya, the OM, may be reached subjectively. Of course, the word-exercise or description cannot be attained in the limited finite words, as it is said to be beyond time, space and causality. It is not obtained by something other than itself, but it is said to be Subjective Becoming. Thus, all the while, this directs us to enter and seek within the cave of the heart the great Truth, with single-pointed devotion and selfless action, surrendered to the All-pervading Narayana-Shiva-The "Gurudevdatta".

Hence, let us put forth every possible effort to study and practise Sadhana at the lotus feet of Gurudev in silence. May He, the Sadguru, bless us and enable us to destroy all the ignorance by constant study of the scriptures. May He destroy all the obstacles in our journey towards Truth. May He bless and enable us all sadhaks to be fit for Guru seva, which is rather impossible without His Grace. And may we invoke the Mighty Power, Lord Dattatreya, on this auspicious occasion of Datta Jayanti.

— **BRAHMACHARI**

MOTHER DURGA

"Mother Durga" is the Power Terrible, which manifested out of the Eternal Truth, which is Paripoorna, and so has in Itself all powers.

Man, the imperfect, the bound, the sorrowful, has a thousand enemies within. He is riddled with negative thoughts, fears, yearnings. These are selfishness, jealousy, meanness, prejudice and hatred – just to mention but a few. The Sadhak must get rid of these lawless villains within. With Mother Kali's Kripa, these destructive masters are to be annihilated. No amount of soft persuasions can avail. The forces of Sri Rudra must be applied. There must be a deep, determined, adamantine resolve, and a fight-royal within, as sanguine as Kali's ferocious sword dripping with blood; and unless the Sadhak is ready to wear about his neck the Skull-mala of these murdered false values there can be no peace or order within.

Invoke the Mother Terrible to help us annihilate within ourselves all negative forces; all weaknesses, – all little-ness. It is these that have removed us from our own selves – the Supreme Parameshwara Swaroopa which we all are.

Now a mere elimination of our weakness in itself is no permanent achievement, for, if the bosom is empty, again they will enter by the 'back-doors'. In short, a mere negative sadhana alone is impotent. We must equally emphasise the positive side in our Right Effort – then only does the Purushartha become complete and whole.

SWAMI CHINMAYANANDA

MOTHER DURGA

SAASTHA (HARIHAR)

On the peak of Sabari Hill at the southern tip of the Sahyadri range stretching southward into Kerala, there is an ancient temple dedicated to Lord Ayyappan,who is popularly known as Sabari Mala Saastha. This temple can be reached only by foot through the jungle which is infested with wild animals.

In Hinduism, the transcendental message of the Vedas has been conveyed to man through the technique of Mysticism. This technique is employed in all religions,but in the Hindu scriptures it has been developed to artistic perfection. Saastha is one of the Hindu deities which has a deep mystic significance.

Lord Ayyappan is the son of Lord Siva and Mohini (Lord Vishnu) in a delusory enchanting form. Ayyappan stands for constructive destruction which is a combination of Vishnu (construction) and Siva (destruction). He is considered the 'Protector' of the weak. He saves mankind from sickness, diseases and miseries of the world and endows them with Gnana (knowledge) leading to spiritual liberation.

The Vishnu Purana describes that in heaven the gods and the demons — the devas and the asuras — decided to sink their differences temporarily, to come to a mutual understanding for a joint endeavour to churn and draw the nectar (amrutam) from the milky ocean, on which Lord Vishnu is described as ever reclining in yoga-nidra (yogic-sleep). The gods and the demons stood on either side, used the Manthara mountain as the churn, and Vasuki, the mighty serpent,served them as the rope. The great churning of the milky ocean started.

130

The churning first produced a deadly poison called Halahala. Seeing this poison spreading in all quarters, the living beings flew for protection to Lord Siva. Siva, in His divine compassion for them, received the poison in His palm and, not knowing what to do with it, decided to drink it Himself. When He swallowed thus the poison to save the universe from disaster, Mother Divine, the consort of the Lord, strangled the neck to prevent the poison from going down the neck. The poison spread over the neck region and hence it is that Siva's neck is blue in colour. He is called Neelkanta (Blue-necked). The churning continued after the removal of the poison and several beautiful and powerful things issued forth from the ocean. They were all given away and the gods and the demons pursued in their churning until the last of the products – the nectar (amruta) – emerged. As soon as the nectar appeared, the demons snatched it from the gods and ran away with it.

The gods prayed to Lord Vishnu to retrieve their loss. The lord answered their prayers and agreed to bring back the nectar (amruta) to them. Meanwhile, the demons quarrelled among themselves as they could not agree upon who should distribute the nectar and how much each should get. In such a state of confusion, Lord Vishnu appeared in the enchanting form of a maiden named Mohini. Fascinated by the seducing beauty of Mohini, the asuras (demons) stopped their quarrel and stood passionately gazing at her divine beauty. Having attracted them thus, Mohini offered to distribute the nectar justly. The demons accepted her suggestion and sat down to receive their share. Before the actual distribution started, however, she objected to their lustful looks, which were offending her modesty, and laid down a condition that they should keep their eyes closed until the distribution was over. Whoever opened his eyes would lose his share. Obediently, they all shut their eyes and waited for their share. While they were thus sitting and waiting with their eyes shut, the maiden ran away with the pot of nectar (amruta-kalasa). The demons learnt it too late that the maiden and the nectar had disappeared.

Upon the request of Lord Siva this episode was narrated by Lord Vishnu. Siva wished to see that enchanting form of Mohini who tricked the demons. He was warned that the Maya-form was too irresistible. Siva insisted, being proud of His continuous tapas (austerity) in Kailas. But lust is the last weakness to leave one's bosom. Vishnu conceded to the request and once again took the maidenly form – the Mohini, one who deludes all. Parameswara was charmed by that divine maiden, and a child was born of the contact of Siva and Vishnu, Saastha was that child.

This simple story has a deep mystic significance. It is an objective representation of a subjective phenomenon. It explains the spiritual path leading to the Goal of perfection; the state of Immortality symbolised by the gaining of amrutam. Amrutam means deathlessness or immortality.

The milky ocean represents the Pure (sattwic) mind. The gods (devas) stand for the higher nature/tendencies and the demons (asuras) for the lower nature/tendencies in man. The serpent is one's own ego. The individual (ego) who desires to spiritually evolve and obtain Immortality (amruta) must first cleanse his mind of its impurities and maintain it in a relatively pure sattwic state (milky ocean). Such a mind is churned by the process of Assertion and Nagation. The seeker asserts that he is the divine Self and negates the perceiver-feeler-thinker and the material equipments as 'not-self'. The whole process of such subtle discrimination and analysis between the good and the bad, the Spirit and the matter, the Real and the unreal is accomplished by the great churn, the subtle-intellect (Manthara).

As a result of such discriminative analysis and contemplation, man evolves spiritually. The evolution is first marked by the purging of low passionate animalistic tendencies (vasanas), which are symbolised by the issuing of the poison from the ocean. These vasanas are detrimental to the well–being of mankind. They pollute the head (discrimination) and the heart (feelings). Hence the consort of Siva, Parvati (representing sattwic mind)– arrested the poison in the throat of the Lord, i.e. kept it in between the head and the heart, not allowing it to poison either the feeling of the heart or the clear thinking of the intellect.

As one evolves further in the spiritual path, one develops higher faculties and powers, siddhis, including the capacity to perform miracles. These are represented by the attractive gifts that arose out of the churning. The gifts were however not meant for self-aggrandisement but for distribution to others. Similarly, if the powers obtained by spiritual sadhana (practice) are not dissipated in selfish and ego-centric pursuits, and the seeker continues in his spiritual path, he gains the final reward of Immortalilty (amrutam) – the state of God-Realisation.

The bad tendencies in man trade even on the spiritual treasure gained by him. In other words, the,y make use of his newly-gained spiritual distinction for self-aggrandisement and low purposes. Such men are easily tempted by the enchanting sense-objects (Mohini). 'Moha' means delusion. Mohini, therefore, is 'delusion personified'. Those who have low animal impulses and passions are deluded by the enchantment of the sensual world and they are blind to their own spiritual beauty. When they are thus led away by the senses, whatever spiritual unfoldment they have gained is lost. This idea is indicated in the demons (asuras) losing the nectar (amrutam).

Lord Ayyappan is the son of Siva and Vishnu. Siva is the God of Destruction while Vishnu is the God of Sustenance. These two powers are combined in Ayyappan since he helps to destroy all low negative tendencies and maintains the pure sattwic nature in the seeker. The

Lord is considered the God of Constructive-Destruction-the 'Protector'. He protects our spiritual wealth and powert by maintaining the thought of godliness and destroys all other thoughts pertaining to the worldly infatuations.

This power of maintaining a single thought of the great Reality is invoked from Lord Harihara Sutha, as He is also known, meaning the son of Hari (Vishnu) and Hara (Siva). Without that great power no meditation is possible. Hence all vedantins invoke His grace for maintaining a consistency in their meditation.

The Ayyappa temple on Sabari Hill, in Kerala, is one of the most popular pilgrim centres in South India. Devotees from all over the country, belonging to all creeds and classes visit this sacred shrine. Unlike other temples, the pilgrims visiting this temple have very strict and rigorous preparations to go through before reaching the divine altar. The usual custom is to observe strict austerities and self-control for forty-one days preceding the visit to the temple. By such tapas (austerities) the mind is made to withdraw from the enchantments of the worldly objects and possessions and it is slowly directed to the thought of the Reality : Ayyappa Swami Saranam. During this period of tapas, the devotee is allowed to wear only black or saffron clothes and a mala and he has strictly to perform the daily rituals. The special clothes indicate that he is dead to the world of perceptions, emotions and thoughts. He remains in constant prayer immersed in the thought of Ayyappan, the Self in him. 'Swami Saranam' is his watchword: "the Lord alone is my protection, my safety".

The way to the temple is through jungle and the pilgrimage is undertaken by foot. The idea is to further develop the concentration of the mind, which has been already prepared by strict austerities. All along the ascent to the shrine, the devotee tries to maintain the one thought of the Lord in his multiple experiences. When such

134

SAASTHA (HARIHAR)

135

single-pointed concentration and meditation is maintained, the Truth reveals itself to the seeker, which is symbolised by the darshan (vision) of the Lord in the temple. The eighteen steps which lead the pilgrim to the plateau where the Lord is 'seen' have their endless mystic meaning in the number eighteen.

A. PARTHASARATHY

SHIVA – NATARAJA

Symbols in Indian civilisation have always been powerful representations of the higher reality. The principle has been understood by the support of its symbolic counterpart on our plane of existence. The link between the worlds, the outer and inner, the higher and the lower, is through the language of symbols. How else can a reality where 'sight cannot go, nor the mind, where we cannot know, we cannot understand' – something 'other than all that is known' – be comprehended?

The dance has been one of the most powerful vehicles for this representation and the dancer is fortunate that, through her entire being, she is an expression of infinity. The images of our deities each manifest, in their visible structures, one particular aspect of the world. But the genius of Indian thought found a marvellous unity of science, art and religious fervour in the sculpture of the Dancing Siva, Nataraja, Lord of the Dance.

Whenever, as dances, we speak in the language of the dance of Natraja, infinite are the possibilities that cross our minds, with the realisation that Natraja imparts wisdom constantly through His famous pose that has been immortalised by the master carvers of Southern India.

The deep significance underlying this image should be clearly understood – not only because this symbol has been alive for six thousand years, but because the message is still significant today.

The upper right hand holds aloft the damaru, representing Nada, the sound, the evolution of the universe. From sound came all language, all music, all knowledge.

The shape of the drum, with its two triangles, tells us of nature and energy which combine together for all creation. The upper left hand in the half moon gesture holds a tongue of flame.

Why does Siva hold the hope of creation in one hand, and the flame, the fire that destroys, in the other? For, creation and destruction are the counterparts of His own Being. They are the two aspects of our life, for as we are surely born, so do we surely die. What then is the answer? The right hand, held in front, in the wondorous gesture of protection and peace, tells us, 'Look, God's grace is ever with you.'

Whether it be Shiva or Krishna, Buddha or Christ, every manifestation of the Supreme, uses this Hasta called Abhaya Hasta in the language of the dance. But let us go on questioning. 'How can we attain that grace, how may we be for ever in Thy care'? The left hand points the way. It lies across the body, directing the gaze to the foot. The hand is in the Gaja Hasta, the sign of the elephant hand. This is the hand movement depicting the trunk of the elephant and herein is a still deeper meaning. The trunk is discriminating. It can pick up and break the heaviest of objects, as well as handle the most delicate. It can choose between the two. So too, should we choose between the higher and the lower, and be discriminating. And to help us, He who owns the trunk, Ganesh, remover of all obstacles, is ever present.

The left foot is raised, telling man that as the Dancer raises His foot, so can man raise himself and attain salvation. While one foot is raised, the right foot upon which balances the whole body of the universe, that which, at this eternal moment of dance, precariously balances the fate of the world, that foot is not on the firm ground, but upon the body of a struggling dwarf, a man who is the embodiment of all that veils truth from falsehood, the Apasmara Purusha, made up of ignorance and forgetfulness. This is the Purusha within us, which prevents us from realising

SHIVA - NATARAJA

139

our own essential divinity. It is for us to firmly crush out the ignorance, if we are to attain the supreme joy which is our true nature, the eternal bliss that man calls God. Around Natraja, is a ring of flames, the Prabha Mandala, the dance of nature, all initiated by the Self in the centre, all emanating from Him, and all dissolving within Him.

While Shiva dances, His matted locks hold the sacred river Ganga, the power and the source of all movement in life, with its waters that purify mankind, and the crescent moon delicate as a new-born babe with its promise of life in all its radiance and glory.

What is perhaps most significant of all in the image is the combination of this God Ascetic, the Solitary One, Master of Meditation, with the frenzied dancer— the Yogi and the Artist. A dancer becomes the being that he impersonates on the stage. In the dance are aroused the entire energy of body, mind, intellect and soul. It is a complete surrender to God. Thus, a dancer is similar to the Yogi, who gives his all to the Lord.

This is a dramatic and vivid comparison. But look at the face of Natraja in the sculpture. It is serene, the epitome of inward absorption. While the body moves in a frenzy like the world with its tumult, Shiva Himself is undisturbed by the activity, depicting most wonderfully the mortal life and the Divine Self. His face, calm and immobile, is a spectator in the external play of His own creative impulse; while He teaches, His eternal Self remains apart, watchful and tender. It is the secret of life open to us all to read, so magnificently portrayed in this masterpiece of sculpture. A seeker of the Truth, need search no further for a symbol of the highest Reality. He only needs to look with eyes that see.

MRINALINI V. SARABHAI

SHRI GANAPATI – VINAYAKA

Lord Shiva's first son is described as the Supreme Leader (Vinayaka) or as the Leader of the "Ganas" (Ganapati), who attends upon and follows at all times Lord Shiva, or as the Lord of all Obstacles (Vighneswara). These names clearly show that He is a Master of all Circumstances and not even the divine forces can ever obstruct His path. Since He is thus the Lord of all obstacles, no Hindu ritual or auspicious act is ever undertaken without invoking Him. With His grace, it is believed that no undertaking can fail due to subjective or objective obstacles.

Ganapati is said to have two spouses, Buddhi (Intellect) and Siddhi (Achievement). Thus He is the Master of Knowledge and Achievement.

In this characterisation Shri Ganapati represents a possessor of Perfect Wisdom, and a Fully-Realised Vedantin. Westerners are shocked to notice that Hindus revere a devine form which is so ridiculous and absurd. But the Elephant-Headed Lord of all difficulties in life indeed represents the highest and the best that have ever been given in our Scriptures. To a Vedantic student, since his "path of knowledge" is essentially intellectual, he must have a great head to conceive and understand the logic of the Vedantic thought and, in fact, the truth of Vedanta can be comprehended only through listening to a teacher and, therefore, Sravana (listening) is the initial stage to be mastered by the new initiate. Therefore, Sri Ganapati has large ears representing continuous and intelligent listening to the teacher.

After "listening" (sravana) to the truths of the Upanishads, the Vedantic student must independently "reflect" (manana) upon what he has heard, for which he needs a sensitive intelligence with ample sympathy to discover in himself sufficient accomodation for all living creatures in the universe.

His intellect must have such depth and width in order to embrace in his vision the entire world-of-plurality. Not only must he, in his visualisation, embrace the whole cosmos, but he must have the subtle discriminative power (viveka) in him to distinguish the changing, perishable, matter-vestures from the Eternal, Immutable, All-Pervading Consciousness, the Spirit. This discrimination is possible only when the intellect of the student has consciously cultivated this power to a large degree of perfection.

The trunk, coming down the forehead of the elephant-face, has got a peculair efficiency and beats all acheivements of man and his ingenuity in the mechanical and scientific world. Here is a "tool" which can at once uproot a tree or pick up a pin from the ground. The elephant can lift and pull heavy weights with his trunk and, at the same time, it is so sensitive at its tip that the same instrument can be employed by the elephant to pluck a blade of grass. The mechanical instruments cannot have this range of adaptability. The spanner that is used for tightening the bolts of a giganitc wheel cannot be used to repair a lady's watch. Like the elephant's trunk, the discriminative faculty of an evolved intellect should be perfect so that it can use its discrimination fully in the outer world for resolving gross problems, and at the same time, efficiently employ its discrimination in the subtle realms of the inner personality layers.

The discriminative power in us can function only where there are two factors to discriminate between; these two factors are represented by the tusks of the elephant as the trunk is between them. Between good and evil, right

GANAPATHY - VINAYAKA

and wrong, and all other dualities must we discriminate and come to our own judgements and conclusions in life. Sri Vinayaka is represented as having lost one of His tusks in a quarrel with Parasurama, a great disciple of Lord Shiva. This broken tusk indicates that a real Vedantic student of subjective experience is one who has gone beyond the pairs-of-opposites (dwandwaatita).

He has the widest mouth and the largest appetite. In Kubera's palace, He cured Kubera's vanity that in his riches he had become the 'Treasurer of the Heavens'. When Kubera offered Him a dinner He ate up all the food prepared for the dinner. Thereafter, He started eating the utensils and then the decorative pandal, and still He was not satisfied. Then His Father, Lord Shiva, approached Him and gave Him a handful of "puffed rice". Eating this up He became satisfied.

The above story narrated in the Puranas, is very significant that a Man of Perfection has an endless appetite for life – he lives in the Consciousness and to him every experience, good or bad, is only a play of the infinite through him. Lord Shiva, the Teacher, alone can satisfy the hungers of such sincere students by giving them a handful of "roasted rice", representing the "baked vasanas", burnt in the Fire of Knowledge. When one's vasanas are burnt up, the inordinate enthusiasm of experiencing life is also whetted.

A Man of Perfection must have a big belly to stomach peacefully, as it were, all the experiences of life, auspicious and inauspicious.

When such a mastermind sits dangling his foot down, it is again significant, in the symbolism of the Puranas. Generally we move about in the world through the corridors of our experiences on our two feet, or the inner subtle body, the mind and the intellect. A Perfect Man of Wisdom has integrated them both to such an extent that they have become One in him – an intellect into which the mind has folded and has become completely subservient.

At such a great Yogi's feet are the endless eatables of life-meaning, the enjoyable glories of physical existence. All powers come to serve Him, the entire world of cosmic forces are, thereafter, His obedient servants, seeking their shelter at His feet; the whole world and its environment is waiting at His feet for His pleasure and command.

In the representation of Sri Vinayaka we always find a mouse sitting in the midst of the beautiful, fragrant ready-made food, but if you observe closely, you will find that the poor mouse is sitting looking up at the Lord, shivering with anticipation, but not daring to touch anything without His command. And now and then He allows the mouse to eat.

A mouse is a small little animal with tiny teeth, and yet, in a barn of grain a solitary mouse can bring disastrous losses by continuously gnawing and nibbling at the grain. Similarly, there is a "mouse" within each personality, which can eat away even a mountain of merit in it, and this mouse is the power of desire. The Man of Perfection is one who has so perfectly mastered this urge to acquire, possess and enjoy this self-annihilating power of desire, that it is completely held in obedience to the will of the Master. And yet, when the Master wants to play His part in blessing the world, He rides upon the mouse – meaning it is a desire to do service to the world that becomes His vehicle to move about and act.

The Puranas tell us how once Sri Vighneswara, while riding His mouse, was thrown down and it looked so ridiculous that the Moon laughed at the comic sight. It is said in the Puranas that the great-bellied Lord Vinayaka looked at the Moon and cursed that nobody would ever look at it on that day – the Vinayaka Chathurthi.

When a Man of Perfection (Vinayaka) moves about in the world, riding on His insignificant-looking vehicle, the "desire" to serve (mouse), the gross intellect of the world (Moon – the Presiding Deity of the Intellect) would be tempted to laugh at such prophets and seers.

The Lord of Obstacles, Sri Vighneswara, has four arms representing the four-inner-equipments (antahkarana). In one hand He has a rope, in another an axe. With the axe, He cuts off the attachments of His devotees to the world-of-plurality and thus ends all the consequent sorrows, and with the rope, pulls them nearer and nearer to the Truth, and ultimately ties them down to the Highest Goal. In his third hand He holds a rice ball (modaka) representing the reward of the joys of sadhana which He gives His devotees. With the other hand He blesses all His devotees and protects them from all obstacles in their Spiritual Path of seeking the Supreme.

On the spiritual pilgrimage, all the obstacles are created by the very subjective and objective worlds in the seeker himself; his attachment to the world of objects, emotions and thoughts, are alone his obstacles. Sri Vighneswara chops them off with the axe and holds the attention of the seeker constantly towards the higher goal with the rope that He has in His left hand. En route He feeds the seeker with the modaka (the joy of satisfaction experienced by the evolving seeker of Reality) and blesses him continuously with greater and greater progress, until at last the Man of Perfection becomes Himself the Lord of obstacles, Sri Vighneswara.

The above three or four examples should clearly bring to your mind the art employed by Vysaya in his mystical word paintings. It must be evidently clear to all sensitive thinkers that the representations given in the various symbolisms are not as many different Deities, but they are vivid pen-portraits of the subjective Truth described in the Upanishadic lore. The student must have the subtle sen-

146

sitivity of a poet, the ruthless intellect of a scientist, and the soft heart of the beloved, in order to enter into the enchanted realm of mysticism created by the poet-seer, Vyasa. To the crude intellect and its gross understanding, these may look ridiculous; but art can be fully appreciated only by hearts that have art in them. When we review the Puranas with at least a cursory knowledge of Vedanta, they cannot but strike us as extremely resonant with the clamouring echoes of the Upanishadic melody.

SWAMI CHINMAYANANDA

SUBRAMANYA – KARTHIKEYA

The second son of Lord Siva and Goddess Uma is known as Subramaniam or Kartikeya or Shanmukha. The picture of Subramaniam, like other Deities in the Hindu mythological literature, has a deep mystic significance, which not only indicates the ultimate Reality but also prescribes the path to be taken by a seeker to reach that Reality.

Shanmukha is represented in the human form with six faces ('shat' means 'six' and 'mukham' means 'face'). He is blue in colour. He holds a trident, a sort of spear or javelin (sakti) in his hand. His vehicle is the peacock. The peacock grips a snake with its claws.

Blue colour is generally attributed to infinity. All infinite expanses in nature appear blue in colour to the human perception; for example, the sky and the ocean. The blue colour of Subramaniam, therefore, indicates the Infinite Reality which exists as the Spiritual Essence in all human beings. In a human being, this Supreme Reality expresses itself through the media of the five sense organs and the mind-intellect equipment. This idea is represented by the Lord having six faces. The Infinite Reality by itself has no expression; however, when it functions through the six equipments there is a manifestation of life, such manifestation being like a multi-faceted jewel reflecting light from its different facets.

Again, the peacock-vehicle of Shanmukha is also blue in colour. Another characteristic of a peacock, which is significant here, is its vanity. The peacock is acclaimed to be the vainest living creature. How evident this is during

SUBRAMANYA - KARTHIKEYA

149

the peacock's lengthy dancing with its colourful feathers propped up in a delightful form!

The suggestion here is that the seeker of Truth must also develop extreme vanity of his Supreme Self, i.e. the seeker must vainfully feel that he is essentially the Pure Self and not the limited perceiver-feeler-thinker (PFT). This idea is figuratively represented by Kartikeya using the peacock as His vehicle. The vehicle on which man moves about at present is his egocentric mind which conceives only the limited individual. Man's attention is constantly focussed upon his body mind and intellect. Identifying with them, he believes himself to be a 'perceiver' at the physical level, a 'feeler' at the mental level and a 'thinker' at the intellectual level. Thus, limiting his personality, he develops the vanity of the 'perceiver-feeler-thinker'. By doing so, man becomes unaware of his infinite potentiality. The Deity of Kartikeya is meant to invoke in man the vanity of his Supreme Self and thereby he will conceive his infinite stature. The one who practises this art of withdrawing his mind from its pre-occupations with the material equipments of the body, mind and intellect and succeeds in maintaining the concept of the Infinite Self, that one becomes the blue-coloured Kartikeya – a God-man on earth.

The Deity also gives the seeker a practical suggestion as to how he can discard the material layers of his personality and reach the abode of the Supreme Reality. This suggestion lies in the peacock clutching serpent with its claws. The peacock is the greatest enemy of the serpent. It can destroy the serpent if it wishes to, but the serpent is held here in captivity without being destroyed. The serpent represents the ego, the fleshy, carnal personality of man which tempts him to use his material equipments for seeking the fleeting pleasures of the pluralistic world. Like the serpent, the ego crawls in darkness created by man's ignorance of the Supreme Light. The serpent carries poison in its fangs but it is interesting to observe that the poison is for its own protection. Similarly, the ego carries with it the poisonous mind, which, when focussed on one's material vestures, assumes the vanity of 'I-ness' and 'mine-ness'. The same mind can be intelligently used for evolving oneself by changing its focus of concentration from body, mind and intellect to the Supreme Self. By this process one unfolds and recognises one's own Real Nature. It is important, therefore to note that the ego is not destroyed. The same ego which lures man to the enchantments of the pluralistic world can be channelised to discover the Supreme Self. This idea is symbolised in the serpent being held firmly by the peacock.

Lord Subramania represents such a Man-of-Perfection who has discovered the Supreme Self. To proclaim his infinite status he carries in his hand the Sakti (a sort of spear). The weilding of this instrument of annihilation symbolises the destruction of all negative tendencies (vasanas) which veil the Divine self.

A. PARTHASARATHY

VISHNU

Vedanta analyses the human being and declares the Pure Consciousness to be the core of his personality, which manifests through his body, mind and intellect as perceiver-feeler thinker, and experiences the world of objects, emotions and thoughts. The Consciousness, functioning as the Spark of Existence in living beings, is the one Eternal Reality which is the substratum of the entire Cosmos as well. This Supreme Reality, which pervades the microcosm and the macrocosm, is described by the sage, Vyasa, in his Vishnu Purana as Lord Vishnu.

Vishnu is shown as in yogic-sleep (yoga-nidra), in an ocean of milk (Ksheerabdhi), on a great serpent (Ananta), which has its body coiled up to form His bed. The serpent has a thousand heads and its hood is turned inward looking at its own coiled body. Lakshmi, the Consort of the Lord, sits at His feet, serving Him.

Vishnu (Narayana) represents the pure Consciousness deep within one's personality, beyond the five layers of matter viz. the Food, Vital Air, Mental, Intellectual and Bliss sheaths. This picture of Narayana lying on the serpent bed in the milky ocean suggests ways and means of recognizing Him as the Consciousness in the innermost recesses of one's own heart.

The ocean of milk, in which Narayana rests, represents the purity of one's bosom. White colour represents nobility and purity. The whiteness of the milk indicates one's sattwic (noble and pure) tendencies or qualities. The serpent is the mind and its thousand heads represent the infinite variety of thoughts that the mind entertains. When a serpent comes into contact with its victim, it injects poison from its fangs into the body of its victim. If, however, the serpent remains coiled up around itself, there is no letting out of the poison. So too, when man's mind is extrovert, i.e. seeking the world of objects, it develops ego and egocentric desires, which veil the Divine Self in him. On the other hand, when a sattwic (pure) mind turns its attention inward, i.e. towards the Self, it develops a tranquility whereby there are no longer any desires or passions arising within him.

The thousand heads of the coiled up serpent are all turned inwards to indicate that the thoughts in a tranquil mind are directed to single pointed meditation upon the Self, the Reality. If such meditation is prolonged in a pure, sattwic attitude (ocean of milk), the meditator locates therein the Infinite Reality Vishnu.

The Lord is shown to be in yogic-sleep. It means that the Realized One, who has reached the state of Pure Consciousness, is no longer aware of the pluralistic phenomena of perceptions, emotions and thoughts. He has awakened to the infinite, all-pervading Reality and He seems to be asleep so far as the terrestrial world is concerned. Hence, it is called yoga-nidra (yogic-sleep). Yoga, derived from the root yuj (to join), indicates that He is attuned to the Infinite Reality; 'Nidra' means sleep and it indicates his transcendence to the Infinite from the finite realm of experiences of the limited man.

As Narayana is thus lying down on the body of the serpent, Ananta, His Consort Lakshmi, sits at His feet and serves Him. Lakshmi symbolises wealth, power and glory. A Man-of-Realization, who through meditation has thus experienced the Highest, is disinterested in the world of objects and achievements. Nevertheless, wealth, power and glory follow him and remain always at his feet. He may use them or reject them without the least thought, because he is ever rooted and revelling in the Supreme Truth.

Vishnu is the eternal Infinite Reality. The manifested world of plurality, which man experiences, has emerged from this Unmanifest Reality. To indicate this, Brahmaji, the Creator, is described as being born from the naval (Nabhi) of Vishnu. The navel portion represents the psychological centre (chakra) from where sound originates in the form of Para Vak (transcendent speech). The inaudible sound passes through two more stages of development, viz. Pashyanti and Madhyama before it becomes audible gross speech called Vaikhari. This audible sound is the quality of his face (akash), which is the first of the five elements that constitute the entire universe. The production of sound, therefore, symbolises creation. This idea is illustrtated by Brahma emerging from the navel of Vishnu.

VISHNU is one of the Gods of the Trinity. He represents the power of sustenance. In order to maintain anything in life, one must have the means to do so. An earning member alone can maintain his family. This idea is indicated by the marriage of Vishnu with Lakshmi, the Goddess of Wealth. Unless Vishnu is associated with wealth, how can there be proper maintenance of the created world? In terms of esoteric philosophy, Lakshmi stands for spiritual wealth and auspiciousness.

Vishnu is shown blue in colour and clothed in yellow. He wears a crown and stands upon a lotus. He has four hands and He holds in them a conch (Sankha), a discus (Chakra), a mace (Gada) and a lotus (Padma). All these are significant symbols which are employed to indicate that Vishnu is none other than the Supreme Self – the Changeless Reality around which all the terrestrial changes take place – the Imperishable Essence in the perishable world.

The blue colour of Vishnu indicates His infinite stature. Blue colour is associated with the infinite since immeasurable entities like the cloudless sky or the deep ocean appear blue in colour. Yellow represents the earth for two reasons viz. (i) earth (silica) glows with a yellow colour when introduced in a colourless flame and (ii) anything that is buried in the earth for a long period of time gathers a yellowish colour. Vishnu, who is blue in colour and clothed in yellow, therefore represents the descent of the Infinite, Immeasurable, Transcendental Truth to the terrestrial realm, i.e. the earth. In other words, Vishnu is the Infinite manifesting Himself in a finite form.

When the Infinite expresses through a finite form, there is a manifestation of an individual (jeeva). The individual comes in contact with and reacts to the world with the help of four subtle equipments in him. They are the four constituents of his Subtle Body, viz. the mind (Manas), the intellect (Buddhi), the ego (Ahankar) and the conditioned-consciousness (Chitta). The four hands of Vishnu represent these four equipments.

The crown on Vishnu's head signifies His supreme Sovereignty and Lordship over the entire world of plurality. He is the One Who maintains and protects all things and beings in the entire universe.

The Deity stands upon a lotus. Lotus represents the Truth. 'Standing upon the lotus', therefore means that the ground or substratum which supports a Man-of-Perfection is the Brahman, i.e. a Man-of-Perfection is ever rooted in the Supreme Truth.

In one of His four hands, Vishnu carries a lotus. The lotus indicates the final goal of human evolution. Vishnu invites mankind to reach this Goal of Perfection, which is the Pure Self within. The Lord blows His conch (Sankha) calling mankind to live the higher and nobler values of life so that they may turn their attention away from their preoccupations with the material world and realise the Self within. This call is the whisperings of the inner conscience, which advises man to give up his sensuous appetites and extrovert living and seek the Eternal Reality. But man does not heed this sacred-voice within. He continues with his passionate living until at last he gets knocked down by disappointment and dissatisfaction with life as such. This 'knocking down' is also done by the kindly hand of the Lord using His mace (Gada). If man, despite the growing sense of restlessness and agitations in his bosom, still persists in his sensual indulgence and does not turn towards the Spiritual path, the Lord uses the annihilating power of His discus (Chakra). The discus is meant to destroy man's present equipment so that he may start afresh, with better equipment and in a more appropriate and conducive environment, for seeking the Truth.

The above is true not only with reference to an individual but to a community or a nation as well. As long as people do not heed the sacred advice of the Scriptures and take to the spiritual values of life, they meet with troubles and tribulations of life. If this warning also is not heeded and the people continue to live extrovertedly, fulfilling merely their sense gratifications, they are bound to meet with utter disaster and death. This is what history has been recording from generation to generation by the rise and fall of cultures, civilisations of nations.

On the other hand, a seeker who listens to the call from within and follows the spiritual path leading to the Truth, does not experience the knocks of the mace or the destruction by the discus. He lives a life of contentment and bliss until he reaches the sacred Abode of Truth and becomes one with Vishnu.

A. PARTHASARATHY

CONSORTS OF THE THREE GODS

(1) SARASWATI – THE GODDESS OF KNOWLEDGE

The Vedic tradition in India from time immemorial has given women the highest place of respect and recognition. Thus, we find our Scriptures referred to as 'Mother Sruti', the Bhagavad Geeta as 'Mother Geeta' and Knowledge itself personified as a feminine deity, Goddess Saraswati.

Saraswati literally means 'the one who gives the essence (Sara) of our own Self (Swa).' Goddess Saraswati is represented as sitting on a lotus, holding the Sacred Scriptures in one hand and a lotus in her second hand. With the other two hands she plays the Indian lute (Veena).

The Goddess of Knowledge and Learning is depicted here as one who has not only the experience of the Supreme Reality but is also the embodiment of the philosophy of the Upanishads. These two are the essential qualities of a Guru, a Spiritual Teacher. The Goddess, therefore, represents the ideal guru who possesses both these qualities. 'Sitting on the lotus' symbolises that the teacher is well established in the subjective experience of the Truth. 'Holding the Scriptures in her hand' indicates that she upholds that the knowledge of the Scriptures alone can take us to the Truth.

The four hands of the Goddess, represent the four aspects of the inner personality of man, viz., Manas (mind), Buddhi (intellect), Chitta (conditioned consciousness) and Ahamkar (ego).

157

The goddess's chitta-hand holds the Scriptures. with the other two hands, representing the mind and the intellect, she plays the lute (Veena). The suggestion is that a truly qualified teacher tunes up the mind and intellect of the seeker and draws out of him the music and melody of life, i.e., the seeker learns to be in perfect harmony with the world. If such tuning is not done, man suffers mental agitations in life and remains ever in disharmony with the world.

Thus, when a seeker lives a life of intelligent self-control (Tapas), deep study (Swadhyaya), continuous reflection (Manana) and steady meditation (Nidhidhyasana), his erstwhile limited ego attains liberation (Moksha). This state of absolute liberation experienced by the individual ego when it rediscovers the Supreme Self within is symbolised by the lotus held by the Goddess in her 'Ahamkar' hand.

Saraswati is wedded to the Creator, Brahma. The Creator needs to be associated with the Goddess of Knowledge, since creation has to be supported by the 'knowledge to create'. All creative endeavours can spring forth from and sustain themselves only by the knowledge of what and who to create.

In the nine-day festival of Devi-Pooja (Durga Pooja), Saraswati is worshipped in the last three days. On the first three days Shri Kali (Durga) is invoked and on the second set of the three days Shri Lakshmi is worshipped. Kali is the mighty power of destruction. She is invoked in order that the seeker may destroy all his negative tendencies within him. Thereafter, Lakshmi the Goddess of Wealth, is worshipped to culitvate and preserve the nobler traits and emotions which are one's inner wealth. One, who has thus cleansed one's inner personality of the negative qualities and substituted them with nobler traits, alone can benefit by the invocation of the Goddess of Learning. The study of Upanishads is futile and it cannot bring about a spiritual awakening unless one's heart is pure. The false values of

SARASWATI

desire, lust and passion must be weeded out and the positive qualities like self-control, love, kindness, etc., must be cultivated before actual learning begins. With the dawn of spiritual wisdom,the little ego in man, his lower nature, is destroyed. The burning of an effigy on the tenth day following the nine-day Durga Puja commemorates the destruction of the ego. This day is also called the Day-of-Enlightenment, Vidyarambha.

(2) LAKSHMI – THE GODDESS OF WEALTH

Lakshmi is the Consort of Lord Vishnu. Vishnu represents the Power of Maintenance. In order to maintain anything in life, one must possess the wealth to do so. An earning member alone can maintain his family. The God of Maintenance has, therefore, necessarily to be associated with the Goddess of Wealth.

Wealth in this context does not mean only money. It also includes the nobler values of life, the power of the mind and the intellect, moral and ethical qualities, etc., which constitute the spiritual wealth. These are the types of wealth to be acquired before one's initiation into actual spiritual learning and knowledge. That explains why Lakshmi is worshipped on the second set of three days in the Devi Pooja.

Lakshmi is expressed as Swarnahasta by virtue of the fact that She pours out wealth to the community. This wealth is gained by invoking the Goddess. Wealth, however, does not come to anyone of its own accord. The capacity to earn wealth remains as an inherent power in man and it has to be drawn out through self-effort (Purushartha). This idea is well brought out in the allegory of 'the churning of the ocean of the milk'.

The story given in the Bhagavata Purana is that of the churning of the ocean of milk by the gods (Devas) and the demons (Asuras) for obtaining the nectar (Amruth). One of the many precious things that came out of the ocean,while

LAKSHMI

it was being churned, was Goddess Lakshmi. The emergence of Lakshmi from the ocean symbolises the creation and development of ethical and cultural values of life in one's bosom when one's pure, sattwic mind is churned by the process of reflection and contemplation upon the Higher Self.

Lakshmi is sometimes represented with four arms, but more often with two. She is described as seated on a lotus. She also holds a lotus in Her hand. The realisation of the Self is the Supreme Goal to be gained by man. This is symbolised by the lotus in the hand of the Goddes.

(3) GODDESS UMA – PRAKRITI

Uma is the Consort of Shiva, the Lord of Constructive Destruction. Uma represents Prakriti (matter). The power of destruction has always to be associated with destructible matter in order that this power could manifest. In other words, destruction ceases to have any meaning without destructible objects. The God of Destruction has, therefore, chosen Uma to be His partner.

The God and the Goddess are the first self-revelation of the Absolute, the male being the personification of the passive aspect and the female, the activating energy (Sakti). Goddess Parvati (Uma) represents this Universal Power (Sakti). Uma and Parvati are Her maiden names; and Mrudani and Ambika are Her post-marriage names.

The Goddess is also referred to as Annapurna meaning 'Bestower of Food' 'Anna', though translated as 'food', has a wider connotation and includes all material objects/ wealth, which are food for the five sense organs. The Goddess is possessed of all types of 'food' to offer Her devotees.

All the three Goddesses together are represented by the fierce-looking Goddess Durga or Kali. She is shown in a fearful form. Kali is worshipped by a seeker to

UMA IN TAPASYAPOSE BEFORE SIVALINGA

invoke his latent power of destruction and thereby annihilate all his negative tendencies and qualities which veil his Higher Self.

A. PARTHASARATHY

RADHA AND KRISHNA

"The love of Radha and Krishna is symbolic of the eternal love affair between the devoted mortal and the Divine.... Radha's yearning for union with her beloved Krishna is the soul's longing for spiritual awakening."

Every aspect of Krishna and His deeds is pregnant with deep mystical symbolism indicating the highest Truth. One must have the subtle-sensitivity of a poet, the ruthless intellect of a scientist, and the soft heart of the beloved in order to enter into the enchanted realm of mysticism. Art can be fully appreciated only by hearts that have art in them.

In Sanskrit, the word Krishna means "dark", indicating the Supreme Consciousness. Pure Consciousness is said to be "dark", not as opposed to "light", but in the sense that it is unseen by or unknown to one as long as one remains rooted in earthly experiences, experiences limited to the realms of perceptions, emotions, and thoughts gained through the physical body and the intellect.

Consciousness is the Pure Self, the sentient Life Principle which enlivens one's material equipments to function in their respective realms. Consciousness is the very subject of all experiences and therefore cannot be objectively experienced.

The incarnation of Krishna represents the descent of the Infinite Brahman to the material world. The ever smiling, lotus-eyed Krishna, with a garland of flowers around His neck, is described as being blue in colour and wearing yellow clothes. Blue is the color of the infinite, and what-

165

ever is immeasurable can appear to the mortal eyes only as blue. Vast expanses in nature, such as the sky at midday or the ocean at its depths, appear blue to human perception. Yellow represents the earth. Anything buried in the earth gathers a yellowish hue; and in fire, earth (mud, silica) emits a yellow hue. Hence the blue form of Krishna clothed in yellow appropriately suggests pure, infinite Consciousness coming down to earth to play in His finite form.

This Infinite Lord dwells in the core of our personality as the very Self in us, for whatever exists in the macrocosm also takes place within the human heart, or the microcosm. The One Infinite Reality has become the world of endless forms. Therefore, every form in the universe is, in a sense, but a representation of the Primeval Truth.

The infinite, all-pervading Truth, donning the finite form of a human being, gives the impression that the Truth is fettered and limited. This idea of the illimitable Truth seeming to be limited is well brought out by the fact that Krishna is said to have been born in prison. His tyrant uncle Kamsa, imprisoned Krishna's father, usurped the throne of Mathura, and reigned along with his own cruel minister, Chanura. As long as these two men were in charge of Mathura, there was confusion and chaos everywhere. Krishna destroyed the tyrants and restored peace and order in the land. Similarly, our bosom is usurped by two evil forces, namely, the ego and the egocentric desires, which cause agitations, worries, and anxieties within. When these two forces are conquered by one's higher nature, the original glory and splendour of the Pure Self is restored.

Krishna, as the Consciousness, or Atman, resides in the core of one's personality. It remains confined, as it were, within the five layers of matter constituting the human personality (food, vital air, mental, intellectual, and bliss sheaths). However, Atman, being subtler than the matter vestures, is not bound or limited by them.

166

RADHA & KRISHNA

167

Though the Infinite Being seems to be limited and confined to a human embodiment, it is ever free and uncontaminated. The Pure Self within is never affected or bound by one's material equipment (upadhis), that is, the body, mind, and intellect. Though the divine child Krishna was born in prison, neither the iron bars nor the prison guards could confine Him. Vasudeva, His father, safely carried Him out of prison inspite of the severe restrictions imposed upon him.

Krishna is described as the infinite, omnipresent, omnipotent and omniscient Reality. Yet, His revered mother Yasoda saw only her child in Him. On one occasion, the little boy Krishna was suspected of having eaten mud. The mother chided him, but the boy denied having eaten mud. Krishna was only telling the truth, for the earth is included in His universal form. He is the Whole.

How can the Whole Being eat its own part? The eater and the eaten cannot be one and the same. The Lord tried to explain, but the mother could not measure the magnitude and stature of His Infinite Being in her own child. Upon her insistence, the boy opened His tiny mouth and revealed to her utter amazement, the entire universe within.

Lord Krishna plays the flute, producing enchanting music. The flute, by itself, cannot create music. It is an inert insentient piece of matter. But when the Lord plays it, divine music emanates from it and enchants everyone. Similarly, the human body is, itself, inert and insentient. It contains the sense organs and the mind-intellect equipment (the holes in the flute) through which the Consciousness expresses Itself.

RADHA'S LOVE FOR KRISHNA

It is said that, long ago, Krishna left His dwelling place in the highest heaven. He came to earth, bringing with Him the things and inhabitants of that idyllic paradise of peace : cow, peacocks, nightingales, and the cowherds and milkmaids (gopis) who loved Him.

Krishna, the beloved boy of Brindavan, is pictured among the dancing gopis. Much criticism has been levelled against Krishna's association with these milkmaids. Little do the critics realize that the Lord is ever an unconcerned and unaffected witness of the milkmaid's dance, even though He may be in their midst. Krishna is like the Consciousness within, which vitalizes one's thoughts (gopis) but remains unperturbed and unaffected by them. The self is ever immaculate, uncontaminated by the thoughts in one's bosom. Thus, if the lives of such God-men are read without an understanding, their mystical symbolism, one comes to wrong, and at times absurd, conclusions.

The gopis performed their obligatory duties throughout the day constantly remembering Krishna. Their limbs were ceaselessly engaged in activity, while their minds were ever attuned to the Lord. This, in short, is the essence of Karma Yoga, that is, the dedication of one's actions to a higher altar, working without ego and egocentric desires. Such activities exhaust one's existing vasanas (inherent tendencies) and also prevent the formation of any new vasanas. When one thus strives hard and reduces his vasanas to the minimum, their last lingering traces are liquidated by the Lord Himself, even without one's knowledge. Hence Krishna is also described as a thief stealing the butter which the gopis had carefully stored in their apartments.

The most beautiful and the most beloved of all gopis was Radha. The love of Radha and Krishna is symbolic of the eternal love affair between the devoted mortal and the Divine. In relation to God, it is said that we are all women. Radha's yearning for union with her beloved Krishna is the soul's longing for spiritual awakening to be united with the One Source of peace and bliss from which it has become separated. This long-forgotten pain of separation is the root cause of all suffering. To rediscover our Oneness is the source of all happiness and fulfilment. In this sense, Krishna is the fulfilment of all desires.

Every human being is constantly seeking a share of peace and happiness, and since one does not know the real source of these, one seeks them in the midst of sense objects. But when, in devotion, one comes to turn one's entire attention towards the higher and the nobler, one experiences the Immortal, the Infinite – as intimately as one experienced the world and its changes before. Bhagavan Himself says in the Bhagavatam: "The mind that constantly contemplates the sense objects irresistibly comes to revel in their finite joys, and the mind that learns to constantly remember Me comes to dissolve into Me and revel in Me." Radha represents this state of devotion and consequent merging with the Lord.

SWAMI CHINMAYANANDA

NATARAJA

Every name and form in which the lord is worshipped has a special symbolic significance of its own. The inner meaning of these symbols is often very grand and poetic, and to enter into and understand it, will certainly be a privilege to those who are striving to realise for themselves the truths of philosophy; for these symbols were devised simply as aids to imagination and many men have employed them with advantage. The meanings of these symbols differ of course according to the standpoint adopted, and the highest,viz., the Vedantic will be the one from which we shall study them.

Nataraja means the Lord of the Stage. The idea is that the world is a stage, a puppet-show which presents the vision of life and activity through the power of the all-pervading Atman or God, the unseen Lord of the Stage. "Who will not dance when thou causest him to dance, and who will not sing when thou causest him to sing," says a poet-philosopher. But for the inner Atman all the world will be mere Jada (inert or dead).

The Atman or Self being the real teacher of the human mind, Nataraja is meant to represent the Teacher or Guru. There are two kinds of Gurus — the apparent and the real, the seen and the unseen. The former is the teacher who instructs the disciple and takes him along the path — this is what we usually mean by the word Guru; but all teaching really comes from inside, not merely in the sense that the outward apparent teacher is but the instrument employed by Atman or God, but also in the sense that all growth is from within. The plant, for example, grows from within; the manure, water, etc., are simply aids to its growth. In the same way, the mind has to grow only from within, Assimilating of course the teachings from outside. Nataraja, then, is the real Guru concretely represented. One of the functions of the Guru, perhaps the most important, is to be what he teaches-to enforce his teachings by example. It is this idea that is the key-note to the Nataraja symbol.

The little drum in one of the right hands is meant to express the idea that God or Guru holds the cause of all the world, i.e., sound,(Sabda Nishtam Jagad – through sound the world stands) in His hand. In other words, all the world is in His hand, to be folded or unfolded at His own will. To the Gnani or wise man the world exists only if he chooses and not otherwise. The deer on one side is the mind, because the latter leaps and jumps from one thing to another as wildly as that animal. The Atman is far beyond the reach of the deer-like mind; and so the deer in the picture is placed near the legs. Nataraja wears the skin of a tiger which He Himself slew. Ahankara or the skin of egoism is that tiger; it is beastly and ferocious and fiercely fights when attacked, but it has to be killed and Nataraja or Guru alone can kill it. On His head He wears the Ganges, i.e., Chit Sakti or wisdom,which is most cool and refreshing, and the moon which represents the ethereal light and blissfulness of the Atman. One foot is planted over and crushes the giant Mayalaka, i.e., Maha Maya, the endless illusion which is the cause of birth and death, while the other foot is raised upward and represents the "Turiya" state, which is beyond and above the three states of waking, dream and dreamless sleep, and leaves behind, the mind, Maya and the world. The second right hand,representing the idea of peace,indicates the blessed calmness,which is the glorious privilege of wisdom. In one of the left hands, is held Agni (fire), i.e., the Guru brings in the Jotis of the Atman itself to attest the truth of His teaching. The idea is that the truth of the Guru's teaching can only be fully understood on practical realisation in experience (Anubhava). The place of the dance, the theatre,is Thillaivanam, i.e., the body (of the individual as well as of the Cosmos) spoken of as vanam or forest on account of the multitude of its components. The platform in that theatre is the cremation ground, i.e., the place where all passions and the names and forms that constitute the vision of the world have been burnt away; pure consciousness devoid of attachment to anything outside and devoid of illusion.

The above are some of the leading features of the Nataraja symbol. The Guru teaches that Maya – illusion – should be crushed down, that the world should become subject to us and not we to the world, that the deer-like mind should be left behind, and Ahankar (egoism) be destroyed, and that man should ascend to the region of pure, unconditioned consciousness free from passion and free from deception, and enjoy the calmness which is his birthright, and bliss, the light and the truth that form the Self. Viewed in the light of this inner meaning,the image of Nataraja is no more a meaningless idol, a piece of stone or copper but a symbol of the highest teaching, an object that can inspire and elevate.

B.R. RAJAM IYER

SHRI GANESH — IN INDIA AND ABROAD

Lord Ganesh is worshipped in different names and forms throughout India and abroad. In Bhereghat (Jabbalpore), the Lord appears in female form (Ganeshini). At Suchindram, in the far southern tip of India, also you can find Ganesh in female form adorning a pillar opposite to the Amman Sannidhi. In Madurai, Vyaghrapada Ganesha gives darshan with a lotus in one hand and the other hand free. At Jalagandeswara temple at the Vellore Fort, the Lord gives darshan as a child creeping on all fours. At Srisailam in Andhra Pradesh, He appears as playing the flute.

He is worshipped as "Mahabini" in Borneo, "Totkar" in Mangolia, "Tchoprak" in Tibet, "Brahganesh" in Cambodia, "Kwanshidiyik" in China and "Vinayaksha" in Japan. Vaishnavites call Him "Vishwak Sena" or Senai Mudaliar. He reveals Himself everywhere, blessing His worshippers. He gives Buddhi to His devotees and Siddhi follows naturally. There is a rock-cut temple in King-Hsein in China for Him. With five faces He is worshipped in Nepal. In the yogic pose of meditation He attracts the imagination of worshippers in Java. In some places in India also He is worshipped in a form with five heads and seated upon a lion. In Tiruvottiyur, He has all the five heads in a row. At Nagapattinam, He has four around and one at the top of the four faces. In Madurai, He is "Mukkuruni Vinayagar". A large measure of rice is shaped into a big ball for neivedya. In Tirunallore, He appears just as Salagrama stone. He appears dynamically poised in Hoysaleswara temple in Halebed, Mysore, in a dancing posture. The credit goes to Vishnu Vardhana for the construction of this

Nrithya Ganesha of golden colour dancing under the Kal-paka Vriksha (tree). In Tirupuvanam and Chidambaram also you can see Ganesha in a dancing posture. At Bhavani near Coimbatore, He appears with a Veena.

We give names to the nameless according to our gunas or temperaments. As we feel and experience our relation-ship with the Lord, we name Him accordingly. As Ekadanta, the Lord has limitless powers. As Heramba, He removes obstacles. As Lambodara, He protects all worlds. As Surpa Karna, He shows compassion by giving the high-est knowledge. Being the elder brother of Lord Muruga, He is Skandapurvaja. All these are various names for Lord Vinayaka, who is the Lord of all and for whom there is no other Lord.

No name or form can completely reveal His true nature (Tattwam). They only indicate His nature. If we can follow different arrows indicated by these names and forms in our deep meditation, perhaps we might land in Him where all these arrows meet.

AJNATANAMA

LORD SHIVA – THE MASTER OF LIFE AND DEATH

For ages past, the Indian people have been celebrating Sivaratri (the sacred night of Lord Siva) as a national Parva. The Hindus associate with it several religious and mythological anecdotes, which give it an aura of pious ceremony. On this occasion, the observance of a fast followed by the worship of Lord Siva during the 'Yaamas' (the four quarters of the night) is enjoined.

The conception is that, on Sivaratri, Siva manifests Himself in the form of a vast Linga (Jyotirlingam). It is interpreted as a Phallic Emblem. There should be no modesty or affected prudery about its meaning. The Linga and Yoni are the symbols of the biological act by which all living creatures are created by nature. There can be no higher and purer symbols of the Universal Parents indispensable for reproducing life. The more one thinks about the divine purpose and the nature of the life principle, the more one is convinced of the purity of the procreative act for perpetuating life or Prana in the Plane of Matter. The true glory of the Phallic Emblem was understood in its purity by the primeval races of mankind.

Another conception of Siva is that of 'Ardhanareeswara' – half male and half female. In fact there is a biological enunciation according to which both male and female hormones are inherent in each individual organism. The latest researches in psychology reveal that every man has a woman in his mind and each woman has a man inherent in her constitution. This is known as the principle of Animus and Anima. Nature has made every individual as

LORD SHIVA

an Ardhanareeswara. To speak in the language of the ancient symbolism each individual is Brahma i.e. Prajapati or the creator unto himself and creates for himself a mind-born daughter who functions as his energy for all creativity. She typifies the principles of intelligence (Buddhi) by which the individual obtains his extension that may be termed as the "Mandala" of his life. This female energy or the principle of intelligence and intellection is the element that makes up the Ardhanareeswara form of each individual.

In the ancient Scriptures, we see an increasing importance attached to Lord Siva. He is invoked as the 'Master of Life and Death and we find that those aspects of his character which inspire terror and strike dread are exalted in preference to that beneficence of nature which distinguishes Him most in the Hymns of the Vedas. He is more frequently identified with Agni, Fire, conceived as an element of destruction. By his side appear 'Bhava' – the Prosperous; and 'Sarva' – the Archer, both of whom are destined to merge in the person of the God; and 'Kaala' or Time which produces and devours all things and which shall also become one of the elements or 'forms' of Siva is invoked as the first principle of all that exists. In the Vedas, Lord Siva is called 'Isaana', 'Iswara', the Lord, and 'Mahadeva' or the 'Great God'. We also meet with the legends that relate to His birth, His triumphs over the Asuras, whose Tripura He destroys, 'The Triple City', namely Earth, Air and Heaven, as well as others which exhibit Him as breaking into the midst of the gods and taking violent possession of the offerings made in sacrifice to them.

Siva is the God with three eyes: 'Triambaka Deva' – the Sun, the Moon and Fire are said to be the three eyes of the Deity, typifying the triple constitution of the life principle or consciousness, and corresponding to the three-fold fires of the Sacrifice. The principles of Matter, Vital

Powers (Prana) and Consciousness (Manas) are combined in the conception of Siva. The perfect integration of the physical man, the vital man and the mental man, constitute the ideal of a perfect Yogi; and Siva is the embodiment of that ideal.

Siva appears with all the criteria of a Deity of purely popular origin, in vital relationship with all the aspects of the rough and tumble of life, which has from time immemorial distinguished India. He and His Gunas, the troops under His command, are invoked as protectors of the house, the fields, the herds, and the roads. He is the patron of craftsmen, cartwrights, carpenters, smiths, potters, hunters, and is himself a crafty merchant; but he is also the head of the army, the God of the brave, of foot soldiers, and of those who fight in chariots, of all those who live by the bow, the sword and the spear. It is his cry that echoes in the thick of the battle, and his voice which resounds in the war-drum. He is the patron of thieves and of all those who go by night in troops and live on plunder. He is also the God of the beggars and the faquirs, of those who wear long and matted hair, as well as those who shave the head. By himself or by the numberless spirits at his back, he is omnipresent, in the houses and the fields, in the rivers and the fountains, in the wind and the passing clouds, in the grass as it springs up, in the tree as it grows green, and in the leaf as it falls. But his dwelling is especially in forests and solitary places, and he reigns over the mountains. He sits enthroned on Kailas, the fabulous mountain of the North, beyond Himavat, surrounded and waited on by the Yakshas and a large number of spirits of different forms. By His side sits enthroned Uma, His spouse, the daughter of Himavat. Like Her husband of whom She is the exact counterpart, She has many names and assumes many forms. She is worshipped as Devi, Goddess Parvati, the daughter of the Mountain, Durga the bright one, Sati the devoted wife, Bhairavi the terror-inspiring, Kali the black one,

179

Karala the horrible one, and countless other designations, which express Her two-fold nature as Goddess of Life and Goddess of Death.

Lord Siva is said to have the Bull for his vehicle. What is the meaning of this and what is the symbolism contained in it? Every individual is an expression of the principle of Ananda. As the holy books reveal, all creatures are processed to the mysterious chemistry of Ananda. The most subtle and refined form of Ananda is Kama. Siva typifies the divine principle of Kama, not as its slave but as its Master; and the Bull, as its name Nandi implies, represents the same principle of Ananda incarnating in matter, and this is the vehicle of Siva. It is said that the Bull, the Life Principle, inheres in Mahadeva, the Great God, the Immortal Divine amongst all mortal beings. Each individual is the Nandi Bull, the vehicle and agent of Lord Siva, the instrument of His creative powers.

Siva is a development of the Vedic Wind or the Storm-God, Rudra. He inspires love and reverential fear and wins the affections of human hearts and is worshipped emotionally. He is not only dreaded but also revered, as the destroyer of evil and evil-doers, hatred, diseases, and is a nourisher who bestows long life.

> Rudra! thou smiter of workers of evil,
> The doers of good, all love and adore thee!
> Preserve me from injury and every affliction,
> Rudra! the Nourisher!!

(Rik Veda)

ANJANI KR. SRIVASTAVA

DAKSHINAMOORTHY

Personification of Eloquent Silence

The Upanishads, the original source of Vedanta, tells us that Brahman, the absolute, is beyond the reach of mind and words (see Taithiraya Up. II - 9 - 1, Kena Up. I - 3). Yet the Rishis have tried to indicate that reality through various methods. In his Brahma Sutra Bhashya, Sankara narrates the story of a Guru being approached by a disciple who wanted to know the Atman; the disciple asks the master three times to teach him the Atman. The Master keeps silent for the first and second requests, but the third time he replies – 'I have been teaching you – you don't follow; the Atman is total silence. The Truth can be discovered only when we observe the total silence of the mind'.

How do we represent this teaching in Sculpture through mystic symbolism ? In the form of Dakshinamoorthy, Lord Shiva in the Guru's role, surrounded by the four Manasa Putras of Brahmaji, viz. Sanaka, Sanatana, Sanandana and Sanat Kumara, we have the representation of this teaching through silence. Dakshinamoorthy – the southfaced Lord – the youthful Guru sitting under the banyan tree in total silence with His hand held in 'Chin-mudra' or 'Jnana-mudra' (sign of knowledge), is surrounded by the old Rishis who were the disciples listening to Silence. He dispelled all their doubts by His 'eloquent silence'. Under His right foot, crushed by it, is Apasmara – a demon.

The ever-smiling youthful Guru symbolises the fact that a man of Realisation has transcended time and has drunk the nectar of immortality which makes him eternally youthful and joyous. The old disciples indicate that the

DAKSHINAMURTHI

seekers of the Ultimate Truth must be mature in mind having tested all the lower Purusharthas (goals in life) like Artha, Kama and Dharma before they are fit for the highest goal of Moksha (Pareekshya lokan karma chitan etc. Mundaka Up.). They are best among (Adhikaris) spiritual seekers.

Silence is the language of Realisation. Unless the seekers make their minds absolutely silent, devoid of all mental agitations (Amanee Bhava – of Mndukya Karika) the Atman is not discovered. This Prashaanti can come only when the three bodies – Gross, Subtle and Causal – have been transcended, when in the fourth state of consciousness the seeker discovers the Atman-Brahman identity. This is indicated by the 'Chin-mudra', wherein the first three fingers are held together representing the three bodies and the index finger standing apart shows its transcendence when the Atman is realised as one with Brahman, the index finger touching the thumb forming a circle. The crushed Apasmara represents the destruction of the ego.

Thus the Truth of Védanta is taught through absolute silence and the sign of knowledge, to the mature students of meditation by a competent Guru. Dakshinamoorthy, the form of Lord Shiva facing the south is indicative of the fact that the grace of the Guru, as His inner realisation, is ever being showered on the disciples, sitting in the south, who are caught up in the net of Yama the Lord of Death (South is the special domain of Yama), representing mortality. The Guru leads the disciple from mortality to Immortality. Thus the highest type of Vedantic teaching is symbolised in the form of 'Dakshinamurthy' the teaching through silence when there is perfect communication between the Guru and the disciple at the highest spiritual level.

SWAMI HARINAMANANDA

ARDHANAREESWARA

Siva – Sakti

Atma – Anaatma

Purusha – Prakriti

Male – Female

To know and to act are the two essential pre-occupations in life. Where there is no knowledge, there no action will be : actions spring from knowledge. And if there be no actions, then there is no life. Ofcourse, knowledge is the expression of our Mind-Intellect equipment, while actions are the expressions of Prana – the Vital Air. Prana does not mean mere breathing. That essential vitalilty which expresses in all our inner dynamic activities is called Prana. In short, Prana is the sum-total of all the gross expressions in life in every living creature : that factor because of which the body moves and acts.

Because of its functional differences, it has five different names. **PRANA**– receives everything into the body; **APAANA** – excretes what is not required; **SAMANA** – receives all that is brought in by Prana and digests and assimilates it; **VYANA** – the circulatory system that carries the assimilated food to all parts of the body; and **UDANA** – protects and serves as bodyguards to the individuality, ego in us, helping it to lift its thoughts to new heights of larger understanding.

Now, the one mighty Essence in whose presence all these act and function so efficiently, that Essence is really meant by the term Prana. This Prana is behind all the transactions of a living being who lives with a world around him. Therefore it is power – Sakti. It is this power that becomes the sense-organs, the mind and the intellect, and controls all the activities, both within and without, in all living creatures.

184

Yet, this Sakti is inert, it has neither knowledge nor consciousness in it. When the instrument of vision (eyes) comes in contact with form (roopa) under the grace of the Sun (light) there happens the action called 'seeing'. The sunlight must fully illumine the object; the eyes and the object must contact each other; then only can we say that the 'seeing' is accomplished. But if one must experience 'I saw', then there must be knowledge to illuminate the mental ripple caused by the 'seeing'. This knowledge or consciousness is not something that comes from the eyes, or rises in the object, or belongs to the sunlight. It is clear to everyone that conscious-ness is something different from them all; and we know that this consciousness functioning through man's equip-ments of Body-Mind-Intellect, is that which makes it possible for him to experience all his perceptions, feel-ings and thoughts.

If this Consciousness (Knowledge) were not there, no equipment would function; all activities would cease. Actions belong to the equipments (BMI) and to the ego (PFT) that identifies with the equipments; not to the Self, the Consciousness.

Thus, we find clearly two categories, one consisting of the Body-Mind-Intellect, Perceiver-Feeler-Thinker, and Objects-Emotions-Thoughts; and time and space; and another the Self, which is the Pure Consciousness that illumines and lends existence and sentiency to all the forms of matter. These two, the not-Self and the Self together in their constant interplay mantain the game of this pluralistic Cosmos.

Of these two, the Self, the Consciousness, is termed as Spirit, Siva and the non-Self, the group of inert equip-ments, etc. is termed as Matter, Sakti. This is the Purusha and the Prakriti pair mentioned so often in our philosophi-cal text-books. The Spirit (Siva) is Knowledge (Jnana) and Light of Consciousness (Chaitanya); while Matter, Sakti is ignorance (Agnana) and darkness (Tamas). When the Light of Consciousness plays through the different sets of equipments, we have the three States-of-Consciousness and the endless varieties of all our experiences as waker, dreamer and deep-sleeper. Just as night and day are for us, who experience the presence and the absence of sunlight, never for the Sun, so too the different states of Consciousness can be only for the individuals and these can never be in the Self, Siva. Thus in Siva, the Purusha (Self), there can never be the pluralistic ever-changing world of sorrow and imperfections, the Jagat. So, in Purusha, the Spirit, there cannot be ignorance, perceptions of plurality, birth and death, change or sorrow. In Prakriti (matter), one shares the qualities of it, and when one identifies totally with Purusha (Spirit) one must be away from all sorrows, revelling in pure Bliss and Knowledge.

When the Consciousness, Purusha, expresses itself through matter, Prakriti, the inert insentient matter gets its knowledge-light, (Gnana-Prakasa) and acts as though dynamic. The primordial matter,Moola-Prakriti, tickled by Consciousness in the Spirit, later on expresses itself as the gross and the subtle, the objective and the subjective world of things and beings, feelings and thoughts. Siva-Sakti, Purusha-Prakriti, Spirit-Matter combination, we call the 'Source of All. '

When this Siva-Purusha comes to play through Sakti-Prakriti, He gets more and more involved with matter, when, He expresses His divinity at different levels, in different intensities, and each of these is defined in our sacred Books by a distinct name of Siva. When He plays through the Space-time principle Siva becomes ESWARA. When expressing through Air, which has both the properties of sound and touch, He is called SADASIVA. Fire has sound, touch, and form, and, when the Spirit, Siva, plays, therein He is known as RUDRA. In Water, which has the properties of sound, touch, form and taste, He is called VISHNU. When

186

ARDHANAREESWARA

the Pure Spirit functions in Earth, which has all the five qualities of sound, touch, form, taste and smell, the same Spirit, Siva, is recognised as BRAHMA, the Creator.

Thus, in each we must recognise that there are its own three distinct aspects:-

ELEMENT (Adhibootam)	PROPERTY (Adhyatmam)	DEITY (Adhidaivam)	FUNCTION (Presiding over)
Space	Sound	Eswara	Sleep
Air	Sound & Touch	Sadasiva	Breathing
Fire	Sound, Touch & Form	Rudra	Distinction
Water	Sound, Touch, Form & Taste	Vishnu	Sustenance
Earth	Sound, Touch, Form, Taste & Smell	Brahmaji	Creation

These three aspects are called in Vedanta as Adhibhootam (Elemental), Adhyatmam (Subjective), and Adhidaivam (Presiding Deity). Where there is a preponderance of Matter (Prakriti) that is Adhibhootam.

The aspect where there is a preponderance of the Spirit (Purusha) is Adhidaivam. And the aspect in which Spirit and Matter (Purusha and Prakriti) are more or less balanced, is Adhyatmam. These three factors we recognise and call the individual (Jiva), the Universe (Jagat), and God (Iswara). Herein the Adytatmam is Jiva, the Adhibhootam is Jagat, and the Adhidaivam is Iswara. All these are but the expressions of Siva, the Purusha. These three expressions together make up the play of life.

When the Adhibhootam predominates in a given personality, he becomes a mere sensualist, a spiritually blind and ignorant person. When in a person the Adhidaivam predominates, he becomes a spiritually evolved person, pure and noble – a Master. One in whom both these are equal is an ignorant one striving to seek a true Sadhak. He is noticed as a person with a spiritual thirst, and he feels in himself inexplicably an urgency to liberate his personality from all its mental hand-ups.

Moola-Prakriti (not-Self) itself comes to manifest as 'Wisdom' (Vidya) when the Self is more in expression, and as 'Ignorance' (Avidya) when the non-Self preponderates in the personality of the individual. This Vidya-state is the Sattwa-nature, and the Avidya state is when the bosom experiences the play of more Rajas and Tamas. The One Self, Pure Consciousness, reflected in Vidya is 'Iswara' (God). The same One Self expressing through Avidya is Jiva (the individual ego); and the delusory misapprehension of all egos put together is 'Jagat' (the Universe).

It is well-known that Brahmaji is the Creator, Vishnu the Sustainer, and Rudra the Annihilator : Sadasiva the presiding Deity of the inhalation-exhalation process of breathing, and Eswara is the Deity in charge of Sleep. These functions and the deities in charge of them are all the same both for the Macrocosm and the Microcosm, and the deities and the fields of their functions are expressions of the Prime Prakariti (Moola Prakriti) indicated earlier. In this primordial 'Ignorance' when all other perceptions, feelings and thoughts, are merged, that quiet state of 'nothing-ness' is deep sleep in the microcosm, described in all the scriptures of the world. In sleep there are Moola-Prakriti (non-apprehension) and the Spirit (Purusha) illumining the 'Nothingness'.

189

Thus, one who is in the Avidya-state, naturally feels that this world is the only real fact, and to him life means a pursuit of the material pleasures, acquisition of wealth, gaining power over other beings and things, etc. For, in his inner personality composition there is a preponderance of Rajas and Tamas, and, naturally, the non-Self alone is valid to him. His efforts are only to maintain his life and to improve and develop the world around him. He comes to live all through his life in his ego-centric state of awareness, suffers the dreadful sense of insecurity in the threatning world of many experiences, their bewildering enchantments and meaningless persecutions, their irresistable might, and impossible cruelities. Fighting against them all alone such a man always feels exhausted, unrewarded, neglected, unfulfilled, and dies in fatigue, with a sad sense of having been cheated of everything all around – even in spite of all his acquired wealth, fame, might, and glory. How sad!!

It has already been pointed out that Pure-Knowlege-Consciousness is Purusha (male) Siva, the Self, and the equipments of the individual and the confusing universe of endless plurality constitute Prakriti, (female) Sakti, the non-Self. The non-Self (Sakti) cannot function without the Self (Siva) playing through her. The combination of Siva-Sakti (Male-Female) is creation. This glorious concept, and all its sacred implications have been entirely accepted by the Hindu culture, and based upon it is the entire way of life designed, and the social values structured among the Hindus. The man-woman form of Siva – ARDHANAREESWARA – represents in art-form the depth-significance in realising the macrocosm and the microcosm as the mere play of the ONE SELF in and through the non-Self.

SWAMI CHINMAYANANDA

SYMBOLISM
IN
HINDUISM

PART III
THE ITIHASAS OR
THE EPICS
AND
AUSPICIOUS DAYS

THE ESSENCE OF THE RAMAYANA

Where a true miracle happens – alas! the average man has no eyes to see it. Only gross magical acts he recognises as miracles. Jesus commanding a lame man to get up and walk, is a miracle. But a fragrant beautiful flower blossoming out of a mere heap of dung, is just an accident! When summer clouds gather and dance in the skies, it is only a routine happening! The very Ramayana started as a miracle......

One day when Valmiki was going to the Ganges to take a bath, he saw a Krauncha couple (a pair of curlews) sitting on the branch of a tree. A hunter shot at one bird which fluttered and fell down dead. The tragic sight evolved in Valmiki the composition of a poem, which in turn caused the gods to request him to write an Epic Poem. Thus came forth the Ramayana – a miracle in itself.

It came out in spite of man, through man. The poem was written by a man well-established in the Ultimate Reality, who was expressing through his work, the pure Advaita Philosophy, the contents of the Upanishads. The glory of the poem is that the ideal states of living are expressed – the ideal brother, son, king, enemy, friend and the ideal man living in society. But all this is mere paraphernalia. The core of this poem is utterly divine – which explains why the glorious story of Rama is so popular even today.

'RAMA' itself means "SARVESHU RAMANTE ITI RAMAH" – that which revels in everyone of us, the pure light of Consciousness, the Atman, the Self, the

Atma-Rama. This spiritual essence in us, can come out only as a son of Dasaratha, one who has conquered all the ten indriyas – five Gnanedriyas and the five Karmendriyas. It will be born in you and reborn only in Ayodhya (Yuddha means conflict, Ayodhya means where there is no conflict, meaning, where all conflict has ended). In that Ayodhya which is ruled only by the self-controlled man (the one given to self-indulgence and pleasures can have no peace and tranquility) Dasaratha's son Rama is born. This Rama, the pure Self, cannot enter into any active participation in life unless wedded to the mind. Seeta (the mind) is ready. She is not born to Janaka by wedlock. While ploughing the land, he finds Seeta. If a girl is got every time the land is ploughed, agriculture would have ceased long ago.

The mind appeared from the most inappropriate place ever. It is absurd to enquire deep into this. Later you find that the same Seeta disappears into Mother Earth. From Mother Earth she came, to Mother Earth she went back. From where the mind comes, and where it disappears during Samadhi, nobody can tell. This is Maya.

Wedded to the mind when Rama returns, he finds that he cannot live in Ayodhya. For, once the mind has come, you start expressing through it. You have to enter the forest of life, self-exiled as it were. Some cause or other must emerge as one enters the forest of existence. So long as Seeta was looking up to Rama, living in Rama, for Rama, by Rama, she never found any difference between Ayodhya and a jungle. But how long can the mind remain constantly centred in the higher divine potential in us? It has to become extrovert. And this is just what happened the moment Seeta looked away from Rama. The golden deer was noticed. The finite, ephemeral, ever-changing objects, start pulling you towards them. The mind demands them. Rama may argue, and all the Scriptures might also argue, that it is all Maya, that it is not real, that it is only a Rakshasa. Yet even Seeta, Rama's own consort, will not accpet it, and she will exile Rama in search of the sense-object. Once desire-polluted, you fall. When Rama goes, he winks at Lakshmana, and they both understand that the poor deluded girl is suffering. Seeta is left in Lakshmana's charge.

Lakshman represents Tapas (austerity). He had no reason to go to the jungle. But he left of his own accord, and he lives in perfect brahmacharya, even without sleep. It is perfect Tapas. But then, one cannot live in tapas. The delusion of the other world will force you to give it up. The moment Seeta hears the sound of Rama's voice, she forgets Rama's glory and might and becomes anxious about his safety. She even urges Lakshmana to go to her husband's aid. And when Lakshmana assures her that the great Rama will never come to any harm, for there is none to match him in skill and valour, Seeta severly rebuffs him. In the original Ramayana, Seeta's words leave much to be desired. Even an ordinary cheap woman would not employ such language. Valmiki was an honest poet. His idea was not merely to bring out the ideal character of a woman, but to portray a spiritual ideal. He painted her in coal tar. The beautiful image of Seeta has been deliberately tarnished by the poet. And why? Once you get intoxicated with a desire, the leprous ulcer of the mind will ooze out puss and blood. When the beautiful ideal woman Seeta utters such malignant words, Lakshmana is shocked into silence. He goes away, drawing a line of demarcation round the hut, urging her not to go beyond it.

Once desire enters your bosom, as an ordinary individual you cannot constantly live in tapas. But you can at least draw a line – thus far and no further. But once tapas has been given up, such lines are of no use.

You readily step over them. And when you do this instead of Dasaratha, you are confronted by Dasamukha, the opposite character. The latter is an extrovert as the former is self-controlled. The sensuous materialistic power persuades Seeta to cross over the line because, as long as you are within the moral boundary, secularism cannot affect you. You go beyond it, and permissiveness starts, and Dasamukha ensnares you.

Dasamukha does not mean having five heads on the right and another five on the left, with one neck in between. If it were so, think of the traffic jam and think what a calamity it would be if Ravana were to catch a cold — he would have to sneeze ten times in every round. Even to clear one nose is a terrible thing. What is meant here is that the five Gnanedriyas and the five Karmendriyas together constitute the Dasamukha. A totally extrovert man lives in the flesh, for the flesh, and by the flesh — it is the rule of the flesh. Such a man is a sensualist and a total extrovert. Materially he can become great as did Ravana who ruled over a prosperous land, Lanka. Compared to this land, Ayodhya was under-developed and village-like with perhaps bullock-carts plying on the roads, while in Lanka the country boasted of the Pushpaka Viman — the herald of the age of space travel. In fact Lanka was so advanced that even at 8 o'clock in the mornings the women folk were found drunk! What a situation!! Even the present day Delhi or New York has not developed to that extent. Drunks are rampant only in the evenings. In Lanka, nobody worked, everybody was supported by the socialist government, and people from all over the world came to pay homage to Ravana, who was supremely powerful.

But does materialism provide anything more than mere physical comfort? It is not a solution to the problem of life. Spiritual and cultural values alone can save the world. This idea is brought out in the Ramayana.

We all know that Seeta was abducted and taken away, but look at the beauty of it. Valmiki decides that she should no more be a citizen of Aryavarta. She may be the consort of Rama, yet she does not deserve to continue to be a citizen of this hallowed and cultured land any longer. She will be given a place in Lanka, another island, no doubt very near, but altogether another land. Even there she was exiled. We are all at this moment "Seetas" in exile. Should we give in to sensuality? To gain back our original Ayodhya, what should we do? We should do exactly what Seeta did. A modern girl in Seeta's place would have said : "Rama was a nice man, no doubt! I can well remember him. But what can I do? Ravana, is constantly asking me. Let me co-operate with him......"

But not Seeta. She realised she had fallen down and to prevent a further fall, she firmly said 'No' to Ravana and remained in the garden under an Asoka tree. Soka means Dukha, i.e. sorrow, Asoka therefore means 'not dhuka' (devoid of sorrow). You and I will have sorrow but we do not recognise it. This is the 'Asoka' state. Under the tree of non-recognition of sorrows, when we want to remain steadfast in character, we will doubtless be tempted and put to a lot of strain. But in that Asoka attitude, we should remain steadfast, constantly remembering Rama.

Seeta was constantly and vigourously thinking of Rama. And we cannot say that Rama did not respond. In the Ramayana, we will find that the scene is alternately changing — once Lanka is shown, the next moment Rama is shown in the jungle. This shows that there is a secret communication between them. The more intense Seeta's cry, the more frenzied does Rama's search for her become. He weeps like an ordinary mortal, not because he is attached to her, but because of his longing to help a devotee.

197

The spiritual essence in man can kill and destroy Ravana, the ten-headed monstrocity of extrovertedness. It can do it with the army of monkeys. An educated man reading this should know what the monkeys refer to. The monkey has two qualities – asthiratwa and chanchalatwa – instability and restlessness. The thoughts in the human mind have these two qualities. They cannot remain sthira – stable. The monkey cannot remain on one branch, it jumps from one branch to another and from tree to tree. If it gets tired and sits on a tree, it will still be restless, and scratch all over. Thus, it cannot keep quiet even for a minute. So too, our thoughts. They can never remain quiet, but keep jumping from topic to topic. The army of thoughts is to be controlled. But, at this moment, Vali - who stands for lust – controls them. This has to be destroyed. And how? It can be only done from behind, and not from the front. It is like a person wanting to curb his desire for alcohol. He cannot do it by sitting before the bottle; for, the moment he does this, not only is half his strength gone, but the pull of the bottle is three times as strong. Hence every time it is your lust that wins, and not you. So, if ever you want to conquer this lust, you have to shoot it from behind the tree. Vali had such great power, that any time an enemy approached him, half the strength of the enemy would drain away and Vali himself would become three times stronger. So, Rama had to kill him from behind. To whom should he then give the kingship of the monkey-clan – the thoughts? To whom better than Sugreeva? 'Greeva' means reins, 'Sugreeva' means well-reined, i.e. well-controlled. When the thoughts are under one's control, the army is then available to cross the frontiers and reach Lanka to kill the ten-headed monster and bring back Seeta.

When Rama regains Seeta after having destroyed extrovertedness, the mind that is no longer extrovert is no mind at all. It (Seeta) has to disappear. Without Seeta, Rama cannot bring about 'Rama-Rajya'. He cannot rule without a wife. Therefore Kapila comes and offers him a Mithya Seeta or Maya Seeta. And with Maya Seeta, Rama returns to rule Ayodhya, with a tranquil and poised mind in a state of perfection, having regained his spiritual status. Though he returns with a mind, it is not really there. It is like the sky which allows everything to remain in space without getting contaminated. So too, Rama, the man of perfection, allows the mind to remain in him, but is not affected by it

Since Rama functioned in the world outside with a perfectly controlled mind, the result had to be a 'Rama-Rajya-, as he created beauty around him as did Jesus, Buddha, Mohammed and all the Rishis of yore. People might laugh at them in their ignorance, and, to please them, the great ones let go their minds. Seeta was banished. But Rama having functioned with her for sometime, something must emerge. It did in the form of Lava and Kusa. From great Masters, Wisdom emerges, generally in the form of books which sing the glory of the Lord. When Lava and Kusa sang the glory of Rama, they were merely singing the glory of the Reality. It is the spread of such literature that has sustained the culture of our country.

SWAMI CHINMAYANANDA

THE GREAT REVELLING
THE MAHABHARATA

"Will you be my charming wife?" whispered the handsome youth in the ears of a lovely maid. The maid smiled and nodded, "Yes, if you promise not to interfere with my freedom."

It was dusk time. The long shadows of the evening were creeping in to clothe the world in a mystery of vagueness. The youth and the maid were standing on the banks of a river.

Thus begins the greatest of the epics, the Maha Bharata. The reply of the maid was not the reply of a sophisticated girl in the International Year for women but was given six thousand years ago in the old-fashioned India.

What followed was a masterpiece of suspense and thrill.

They married and lived a dream of happiness. Then came a jerk and a halt.

Soon a son was born. Before the father could do anything about it, the mother threw the baby into the river to be washed away. Another followed, and yet another, and four more. The horrified, grief-stricken father could no longer contain himself. While the eighth son was being thrown into the water, he stood in the way and stretched out his hands.

"That's enough. Give him to me, the baby is mine." The mother handed over the baby and left without one word or look. All was over between them.

The daring and outrageous manner in which the Epic develops is so dramatic that it can do credit to a modern thriller. though Vyasa Maharshi was not an author of sensational literature. He was a Master Philosopher with a vision and mission for posterity..... Then what is all this about?

The Maha Bharata is called the Panchama Veda — where the esoteric message of the four vedas was dressed and cooked for the ready consumption of an average spiritual seeker. The Vedas, the revelations by God Himself, are so profound that it is difficult for anyone to understand what they mean. They declare how the Supreme alone is, how It becomes apparently the world, and how the individual can reach back his own pristine glory. This profundity of the Vedas is pictured and provided for the ordinary man on the huge canvas of the Epic Story which is called the Maha Bharata or the "Great Revelling". Veda Vyasa himself declared that what is found in Maha Bharata might be found elsewhere, but what is not found therein could not be found anywhere.

How did the Supreme become the poor individual with limitations? The Epic begins at the very beginning.

When the Lord alone was, before the creation, He was the Very Auspicious One — The Sam+tanu. He, the Omnipotent and Omniscient Lord thought "Let me Create." To think is to create.

It is the ordinary man's experience that no creation can be made without knowledge in that particular field; and one who creates something must be united with that knowledge at the time of creation — the musician with his music, the painter with his art, and so on.

So too, the Lord had to be wedded to His Omnipotent Knowledge before He could commence His creation of the world. Thus wedded to the flowing Divine Knowledge, Ganga, He creates.

The raw materials have to be created one by one. Thus the five elements composing the objective world emanate one by one. Next the subjective instruments of experience come out – the mind, the intellect and the egoism.

The Lord does not forget Himself when the five elements are born, nor even when the mind, the sixth, or the intellect, the seventh, is born. His Divine Wisdom consigns them to the flow of the world of changes, but when the eighth one – Ahamakara – is born, the Lord is caught. He forgets Himself and becomes the ego, and the 'I' is followed by 'Mine'. Thus Santanu claims the eighth boy and that is the end of the Divine Knowledge, Ganga Devi, which takes leave.

Now, further fall is not far off. The king falls in love with a fisher-woman, which in turn creates greed in the mind of her father, who demands that his grandsons might be made heirs to the throne.

Thus the ego, attachment, lust and greed together convert the Deva Vratha into an impotent being – Bhishma – who takes the terrible vow not to sit upon the throne, nor even to wed.

What follows next is a series of tragedies – which is the story of the Kuru dynasty, that is the story of action. All men are children of action. They are born because of what t hey did in the past, and in the present life they sow the seeds of their future lives through their current actions. It is a story of dole, disease and despair, which Maha Bharata vividly paints.

Santanu was dead and gone. The two sons born to Satyawathi were also dead. The mighty empire of Hastinapura remained with no one to sit on the throne, with Bhishma who would not occupy it, and three widows.

Somehow the old dowager lady tries to get a heir to the throne by Niyoga and the result becomes fatal – a blind boy Dhritarashtra and an accursed one Pandu Raja were the only result.

Is there a way out from this mess? – enquires a desperate sadhak. For him, is the background given – it is only to show the way out.

The main story depicts the state of a rajasic man, for whom alone the philosophy is intended. A tamasic man is not yet ready, and a sattwic man has gone beyond. It is the rajasic man who has the higher vision but the lower temptations that needs the guidance and help.

Thus the main story starts with the struggle between the children of Dhritarashtra and Panduraja.

A rajasic man has a fine vision but, it is often covered up and veiled by his own selfish low cravings. At that time his intellect is like the blind Dhritarashtra. The mind that is guided by the intellect also consequently becomes blind, like Gandhari. Born to these two blind ones are the hundred and one evil qualities, the Kauravas.

On the other hand, when selfishness does not veil wisdom the intellect is pure sattwic like Panduraj, and the mind guided by such discriminating intellect will be full of devotion like Kunti capable of propitiating and getting boons from the gods. To such a couple are born five wonderful qualities, Dharmaraja the righteousness, Bhima the strength, Arjuna the soft-heartedness, Nakula the beauty of the personality and Sahadeva the knowledge of scriptures. These are all wedded to one Draupadi. Draupadi means pertaining to

Dru pada — quick progress in reaching the Goal (Dru+Pada).

Among these two offsprings is the constant clash whether it be within the bosom or in the outer world of a rajasic man. The evil ones outnumber the good ones and often overpower them. At this stage there is only one way to begin — shed the load of vasanas within, gain efficiency and ultimately supremacy.

From here the story takes a new turn — a huge picture of the Rajasuya sacrifice of the vedic Karma Kanda Rajasuya is the sacrifice prescribed by the Satapatha Brahmana of the Sukla Yajurveda. This is a yaga performed by a Raja, in which some juice is pressed. After the yaga is over, the sacrificer waits for thirteen months. Exactly at the end of the thirteen months, he performs a mock raid over the cows of his kinsmen. Then he sits down and plays a mock game of dice with his kinsmen wherein, by arrangement, he wins. After this the holy bath is taken and the sacrifice is concluded.

The ritual sounds silly and meaningless outwardly. The Maha Bharata explains the inner significance through the story. Raja, Soma and Chandra are the terms used in vedas to indicate the Vasanas within. Rajasuya means pressing out the Vasanas. The Vasanas cannot get automatically pressed out, but only by deliberate, elaborate effort.

First of all there should be an intention to improve and a recognition of the Dharma. Thus in the city of Hastinapura where the Kauravas have the supremacy, the kingdom has to be partitioned and Dharmaraja has to be made the king of Indraprastha or the realm of the mind. In this Indraprastha, the drama of the Maya Sabha, the hall of illusions, starts. The irresponsible and irrepressible Duryodhana wanders about in the Maya Sabha, getting knocks on the head, because he mistakes one thing for another. Draupadi – the spiritual aspect – mocks and laughs at him.

Despite this, when the Supreme Lord Krishna is given the Agrapooja, the Vasana-shedding begins. But it is a long hard struggle. In the day-to-day gamble of life, pitted against his own uncontrollable inferior tendencies, the sadhak remains ineffiecient and gets defeated at the hands of Sakuni (From Sal = able). Inefficiency in the material world hampers the spiritul progress. Thus Draupadi gets insulted in the open court.

Such a sadak has to make a retreat for better control over himself. Thirteen months or 'Trayodasa Masa' is the period fixed by the Satapatha, Brahmana for the completion of the sacrifice. 'Masa', is from the root 'to limit'. The ten sense, mind, intellect and the vasanas are the thirteen limiting forces that are hostile to the spiritual progress.

So the Pandavas go into Aranya for 'Dwadasa Varsha'. Varsha means a rain. The senses, mind and intellect rain down the awareness eagerly into the world, to fight and kick for supremacy. This fighting has to be temporarily stopped and Aranya Vasa – non-fighting – should be started to get better wisdom and divine strength. Thus Dharmaraja spends the twelve years listening to the masters and Bhima and Arjuna spend the time getting divine weapons.

Here too, the spiritual progress Drapaudi, is in danger. It is a withdrawl into the mind, but the mind is a continuous flow of thoughts. So Saindhava (Sindhu meaning flow) tries to kidnap Draupadi.

Last, but not the least, is the entry into the Ajnata Vasa. The vasanas are unmanifest tendencies about which we know nothing. The sadhak has to immerse within himself to sort out the shallow tendencies,

Keechaka (the hollow noises of a bamboo) who is a great danger to Draupadi. She has to be protected by killing him.

When this is successfully accomplished, the rescue of cattle from the Kauravas comes. The Kauravas attack the cattle "Uttara" and "Daskshina" — Gograhna it is called. 'Go' in sanskrit means knowledge. The material knowledge is Dakshina Go (Dakshina from Daksh = to increase). The spiritual knowledge is Uttara Go (Uttara = to transcend).

Then when the knowledge is rescued from the clutches of the Kauravas, the real effort starts - Udyoga Parva. Compromise talks begin.

But there can be no compromise with evil in spiritual sadhana. Thus the fight is a must and the two armies meet on the battlefield of Kurukshetra, which is converted to Dharmakshetra. The heart winces in pain and fear — "Can I undertake this?" doubts the sadhak. If only there is a spirit of surrender in him, the guidance comes from the Lord Himself as the song celestial, and the fight will be over in no time. Dharma is established on the throne with no more opposition. Now the game of life is won, but the sadhak has to go further.

He has yet to sacrifice his ego before he can find his oneness with the self. The ego which is the voracious eater of all experiences is called Aswa. Its sacrifice is called Aswamedha.

As per the ritual the horse is allowed to roam about for a year under the watchful eyes of an army to protect it from being caught. When the horse returns, it is sacrificed.

So too the ego. It has to wander uncaught in the outer world under the watchful eyes of the sadhak. When the wanderings are successfully completed and it

206

is no more caught in the snares of the attractive world, it is ready to be sacrificed.

The death of the ego notifies the birth of Parikshit, the tested one who is dead and revived by the grace of the Lord.

At this stage the Lord gives the Uttara Geeta — the song Transcendental. It is no longer a fight with the evil but a shedding off of the Jeeva Bhava.

Thus the Great Revelling concludes with the ascent to the Svarga. This Svarga is not the heaven of the Indra with his gardens and damsels, but it is a going towards one's self — Svah + ga merging in his own real nature.

In the last phase, it is not an effort, nor even a sadhana. Draupadi drops-out — no haste any more. The twins and Bhima and Arjuna also drop out. The lingering traces of the dying ego, Dharmaraja, accompanied by his Dharma alone, ascends. It is a peeling off, of the last traces of the vasanas, a bud blossoming into a flower.

Even here, he has to pass through good and bad experiences, a vision of the loved ones suffering in hell and the enemies enjoying heaven. This is only a passing illusion. With the final bath in the river of wisdom, the last covering is dropped. The ascent is over.

SWAMINI SARADAPRIYANANDAA

THE CONCEPT OF HANUMAN

Three Sanskrit verses, recited daily by devotees reading the Ramayana, summarise the concept of Hanuman. The verses rendered into English read : "I salute the Lord of the Vanaras, the dear son of Anjana, the great hero, the destroyer of Aksha, the terror to the city of Lanka, and the one who removed the sufferings of Seeta."

I salute the Ambassador of Rama who is swift like the moving wind, who has conquered his senses, foremost among the intellectuals, the son of Vayu and the most understanding among the Vanaras. Wherever the name of Rama is uttered, there, folding his hands above his head, and with tears of joy and Bhakti filling his eyes, stands Hanuman. Him I salute. In the great garland, of Ramayana, Hanuman is the Jewel — Maha-maalaratnam.

It appears that the Indian mind visualised 'The Perfect Man', not in the image of a man, but in the image of Hanuman, the monkey. Ever since Sage Valmiki introduced Hanuman in the Ramayana, his image has grown through the centuries and is reflected predominantly in our sculptural representations. No wonder the Indian people yielded their hearts so thoroughly to him. He was great in every sense of the word. He performed great deeds of valour, of physical strength, which no other living creature of the time could have performed. Deeds which required the greatest strength, the greatest will power, fell to his lot and he performed them with admirable thoroughness of execution.

It is proposed to study the concept of Hanuman in three stages : first as introduced by Sage Valmiki almost 2,000 years ago, second as protrayed by Kamban, the greatest of Tamil Poets, about 1,000 years later and third as visualised by the people of Vijayanagar 500 years later still in about the 14th Century A.D.

Hanuman is first introduced by Sage Valmiki as appearing in human form before Rama and Lakshmana, as an outstanding scholar and a master of the Vedas. After listening to Hanuman's speech, Rama himself says : "One who has not learned the RIK Veda, one who has not mastered the Yajurveda, and one who has not studied the Sama Veda, cannot speak in such a chaste language. Although he has spoken much and spoken long, he has not made a single error. He seems to be a great master of elocution. His speech wins my heart completely and delights my very soul."

Sage Valmiki reveals the greatness of Hanuman through the mouths of every great character in the Ramayana – Rama, Seeta, Lakshmana, Vali, Vibhishana, Indrajit, Ravana and Bharata. He received the admiration of one and all, of men and women, of friends and foes alike.

Hanuman is portrayed as the supporter of Dharma – the vehicle carrying the very Lord Rama and Lakshmana on his shoulders. Though he performed great feats, he never thought that the achievements were his own. He is a character of complete self-efface-ment, a total surrender to the cause of his actions.

Hanuman is depicted as a mighty hero in the Epic. When Vali was about to die, he told Rama : "O Rama, you never gave me a chance to catch the Rakshasas, including Ravana, with my tail and roll them in front of you. Now I am dying. It does not matter. If you want to achieve even greater things, here is Hanuman who can do it for you." Among the Rakshasas, Indrajit was a mighty fighter, greater than even his father Ravana. When he saw the destructions caused to the Chaitya Prasaada, and his brother Akshakumara and the five commanders killed by Hanuman, he exclaimed "All these devastations by a single monkey! What will happen if Rama lands in Lanka with a battalion of monkeys like this?" Indrajit saw Hanuman as an unparalleled hero. So did Ravana.

As a devotee, Hanuman is foremost. He asked Rama for only one thing in life. "Please give me this blessing that my affection for you should never diminish. Do not allow me to think of anything else. I want to live so long as your great name is preserved amongst the sons of men. Let me be for ever and for ever your devotee." As a great warrior, a great scholar, a sincere friend, minister, ambassador, as one wedded to truth and righteousness, a servant and an outstanding devotee, Hanuman reveals the traits that no other Indian creature or character does. Valmiki's power of visualisation had made Hanuman the monkey to be adored and worshipped by the Indian people on a par with even Lord Rama. Yet in Valmiki's Ramayana, Hanuman remains within the human level. He is not raised to the level of a god.

Almost 1,000 years later appeared Kamban, the greatest Tamil Poet, who rendered the Ramayana in excellent Tamil poerty. Kamban, according to competent authorities, lived in the 9th Century A.D. in the reign of the Cholas who ushered in an era of prosperity and peace. A poet of eminence, Kamban elevates the image of Hanuman to greater heights than Valmiki himself. One or two instances could be cited here. According to Valmiki, when Seeta first sees Hanuman in the Ashoka Vana, she suspects him to be Ravana, and states : "You are the very same Ravana, who appeared before me in the guise of a sanyasin at Janasthana. Why do you

210

appear before me now as a monkey and torment me?" Kamban cannot conceive of Hanuman being suspected by anyone and least of all by Seeta herself. He creates a different picture. Seeta, beholding Hanuman at the outset, categorically states that the person standing before her is certainly not a Rakshasa. He is one who has conquered his senses and might even be a god. He is indeed a person of noble feeling. What if he be a Rakshasa, a god, or even merely a monkey! Reaching this place, he brings her the name of her Lord and ignites the hope of survival. Addressing Hanuman, Seeta says : "You have given me solace not only in this world but also in the other world. To me you are the primordial mother and father and an incarnation of grace. What can I give you in return? Even if I had all the three worlds to present to you, that would not be equal to the help rendered by you. I only pray that you live for ever in this world" No nobler expression can be conceived than this, that too coming from Seeta, imprisoned in Asoka Vana, tortured mentally and physically by the Rakshasas and staying a picture of suffering. Hanuman is thus pictured as a symbol of hope, through Seeta, to the suffering humanity.

At the end, after the coronation, Rama distributed presents to all who helped him in the battle. Finally, he turned towards Hanuman and said : "What present can I give you? I can only do one thing. I give unto thee, my own self" On hearing this, Hanuman the great hero, with modesty and bashfulness, head slightly bent, with hands in front of his mouth in a pose of service, stood by the side of his master in all humility. That is the reason why, in all the forms of Hanuman the Chola artists of the 9th century A.D. portrayed, Hanumanis standing in this pose. Almost all the bronzes of Hanuman so far known. depict him in this manner. This, in all probability, is the result of Kamban's imagery. It also reflects the

HANUMAN

taste of the society of those times. The peaceful and prosperous age of the Cholas allowed and encouraged the people to adore this particular image of Hanuman as the visual presentation of all that the noble hero-devotee, Hanuman, stood for. In the superlative bronzes of Rama, Lakshmana and Seeta, belonging to the 10th century A.D., Hanuman is invariably figured as a humble devotee. No image of Hanuman in the Chola age as a dashing hero has come down to us.

From about the 14th Century A.D., a tremendous change is perceived in the concept of Hanuman. The Vijayanagar days witnessed the great challenge to the Hindu faith, Islam posing the threat. While in the North the Hindu traditions were badly shattered, the South accepted the challenge and the Vijayanagar rulers resisted the onslaught, though there was panic and fear witnessed even in the remote villages throughout the country. The one image, to which the age could turn for instilling courage, bravery and at the same time sobriety, was Hanuman. Hanuman, an actor in the Rama Katha, crossed the frontiers of the Rama Story and became an independent god, or deity. His images were carved in impressive proportions and installed in independent temples. Of all the aspects of his character, it was his war-like trait that received adoration. Hanuman as Vira Anjaneya was portrayed extensively, in sculpture, on coins and on flags. The common people believed in the efficacy of Anjaneya worship, in Mantra, Yantra and all forms of Upasanas dedicated to Anjaneya. The profound faith in Anjaneya grew enthusiastically. In the 16th and 17th centuries, monolithic images of Hanuman, reaching over 20 feet in height, were carved, as seen in Suchindram in the extreme south, and Namakkal in Salem district, to cite only a couple of examples. Even a formless stone or a pebble was sufficient to be invoked as Anjaneya.

Other forms of Hanuman also began to appear. Hanuman appears seated below at the feet of Rama holding a palm-leaf and reading the Scripture, and Rama, interpreting the reading as "Para-Brahma-Tatwa", symbolising the fact that the Supreme Reality could be realised with the help and through the image of Hanuman. The portrayal occurs in the 17th Century sculptures, bronzes and paintings. Hanuman as an exponent of music, particularly the Veena, also assumes significance in the 17th century. He is portrayed carrying a Veena on his shoulder. But these forms appealed to and attracted, only the sophisticated thinkers. For the common people, Vira Anjaneya was the real Hanuman. Temples dedicated to him are found everywhere, perhaps in every village.

The Indian people, throughout the ages, have laid great emphasis on the control of the senses – Indriya Nigraha – and the observance of celibacy – Brahmacharya. They adored learning and mastery of language and literature, dexterity and civilised diplomacy in all dealings with men and matters, heroism and valour to fight for the cause of Dharma, devotion and service, and, above all, humility. All the qualities that could be conceived as great virtues were found in Hanuman. There seems to be no other creation in the whole field of Indian thought which combined all the lofty ideals that the country stood for. In the Indian tradition, Hanuman is designated as "Chiranjeevi" – the ever-living. Indeed, his is the one name that lives in every Indian heart.

Born as the son of one of the elements, Vayu, introduced by Valmiki in the form of a monkey, nay as a super-animal, appearing as a man perfect in all fields of activities, Hanuman is raised to the status of godhood, a benevolent god of hope, intellect, courage and devotion. It is not his form but the concept that commands adoration and admiration.

DR. R. NAGASWAMY

RAMA AND KRISHNA

A COMPARISON IN SYMBOLOGY

"Dwividhohi Vedokto Dharma :
Pravruthilakshano Nivruthilakshanacha :

"Vedas deal with Dharma in two categories, one for
the path of Pravruti (action in mundane life) and the
other for the path of Nivruti (redemption from the thral-
dom of Samsara). These are respectively symbolised by
the lives of the two Avatars, Rama and Krishna. The paths
of their lives appear to be diametrically opposite to each
other, and there is an eloquent lesson in that. A comparative study of the main incidents in the lives of the
two great incarnations is very revealing and extremely
rewarding and interesting. There are so many incidents
in their lives which are in striking contrast. A few of
them are enumerated hereunder : these are not exhaustive, but only illustrative. Those who search may find
many more. It is said, "Live as Rama lived, and learn
what Krishna taught."

  1.   Rama was born of parents who had no issues for
long, were pining for that, and who had undergone a lot
of penance to beget children; while Krishna was the
eighth child of his parents who, for that reason and due
to the circumstances in which they were placed, were
not at all eager to get issues.

  2.   Rama was born in broad daylight, in a palace,
as the eldest. Krishna was born in the middle of the
night, in a prison, and was the youngest.

3.   Rama was very fair in complexion, while Krishna was dark.

4.   Rama enjoyed life in the palace as a prince till his twelfth year, while the life of Krishna till his twelfth year was full of dangers and fights for his survival, as Kamsa had employed so many emissaries and strategems to do away with this child.

5.   The first victim of Rama was a woman (Tataka) while the first victim of Krishna in regular combat was a man (Kamsa).

6.   Rama's life was Dharma-oriented (Ramo vigrahavan Dharma); while that of Krishna was Karma-oriented. Krishna even said "Sarva Dharman Parityajaya."

7.   Rama was a man of "Eka Patni Vrata" (devoted only to one woman all his life) while Krishna had "Bahu Bharyatwa", a population of wives, so to say, as the story goes.

8.   Lakshmana, the incarnation of Ananta, was a younger brother of Rama. The same Ananta in his subsequent incarnation as Bala Rama was the elder brother of Krishna.

9.   Rama protected the son of Surya (Sugriva) and killed the son of Indra (Vali) while Krishna did just the opposite. He protected the son of Indra (Arjuna) and killed (caused to be killed) the son of Surya (Karna).

10.   Rama killed Tataka with a poisoned arrow, that is, he emitted poison. Krishna absorbed poison and killed Putana.

11.   Rama was deluded for a time (fainted) in his war with Ravana. Krishna brought back the deluded man, Arjuna, to his full faculties and made him fight to victory.

12.   Rama's wife was forcibly taken by Ravana. Krishna forcibly took away Rukmini and married her.

13.   Rama was the cause for mutilating and deforming a woman, Soorpanakha. Krishna made the deformed woman, Kubja, straight and beautiful.

14.   Rama was a king in his own right. Krishna was never a king himself, but was a King-maker.

15.   Rama never claimed that he was an incarnation. In fact he had to be reminded of that at the last stage in his life. Krishna annoucned that he was the Lord Himself as soon as He was born.

16.   Rama belonged to the Solar dynasty. Krishna belogned to the Lunar dynasty – the Yadava Branch.

17.   Rama represented the perfected Jivatman – (Ramante asmin Yoginaha iti Rama :) while Krishna was the Paramatman - the God (Karshnaat Krishna).

18.   "Ramayana" means the "goings of Rama". He was leading to the goal. It can also mean "going to Rama", just as "Samudrayan" in the case of the river. Whereas in the case of Krishna, he was the goal. He was always calling unto Himself : "Mamekam saranam vraja."

19.   Rama fought the great battle himself : (Jivatman fighting the battle of samsara). Krishna was the "Sakshi" in the great battle, while others fought.

20.   Rama left behind a prosperous Ayodhya, while Krishna had his city (Dwarka) and his entire Yadava race destroyed before he left.

21.   Even the names of the cities in which they lived held out opposite meanings. "Ayodhya" means a city which is not vulnerable to any kind of wars, which should mean the mental state of the "sthithaprajna", while "Dwarka", Krishna's city meant the "Door that

opens into the Perfect State", one being the Means and the other the End.

22. While Rama had to weep many a time in his life, Krishna lived throughout as a personification of cheerfulness. Krishna's eyes became moist only once in his whole life; that was when his childhood friend Sudama called on him.

23. Krishna is accepted as the Poorna-avtara. Rama has not been accepted as such.

24. Even with only one wife, Rama could not lead a happy and harmonious life with her, while Krishna, with an army of wives, could lead the happiest of lives with no complaint from any of those women that she had been neglected even for one evening.

25. While in the forest, Rama goes in search of the golden deer to satisfy his wife, meaning that he went in search of Kanchan to satisfy his Kamini. In the attempt he lost both the Kamini and the Kanchan. Krishna went into the forest in search of the jewel "Syamamantaka" and gets also two Kaminis in the bargain – namely Satyabhama and Jambavati, that is Krishna gains both Kamini and Kanchan at one shot.

26. With the bow and the quiver always hanging on his shoulders, Rama led a warrior's life throughout, upholding and protecting Dharma. Krishna went with a flute in his hands enchanting the world around with his divine music. He too was protecting the righteous and upholding Dharma. While the former did it with his prowess, the latter did it with love.

27. Rama was ready to take up arms whenever required. Krishna refused to take up arms even when everybody expected him to do so.

28. Sita was lost. Rama wandered in search of her, weeping and enquiring of even inanimate objects

whether they had seen her. On the other hand, it was Krishna who had been lost, and the Gopis in Brindavan did exactly the same thing as Rama did in Ramayana.

29. Rama had to go to the forest to fulfil the purpose of his incarnation, whereas for Krishna his mission took him to palaces frequently.

30. Rama was insulted by his enemy insofar as his wife was kidnapped by his enemy, while we see that Krishna was respected by his enemies (the Kauravas) when he entered their Durbar.

31. Rama's sons lived independently of him and were finally crowned by Rama himself before his departure. Krishna's sons and grandsons lived under his shadow throughout, but were annihilated by the grandsire himself before his departure.

32. Rama got a bad name on account of Sita, for which he sent her to the forest when she was in an advanced state of pregnancy. Krishna got a bad name, not on account of a woman but a jewel called Syamantaka. He went to the forest in search of the jewel to vindicate himself, and ultimately got the jewel and two women in the bargain.

33. Rama's name is chanted as "Sitaram" prefixed with that of Sita, his legally wedded wife, whereas, in the case of Krishna, we chant his name as "Radha - Krishna" prefixing his name not with any one of his legally wedded wives, but with that of another man's wife, simply on the basis of devotion.

To crown all these, we find a very interesting fact when we compare the Ramayana and the Bhagavad Geeta – which is the essence of the Mahabharata. They appear to approach the subject from exactly opposite directions. In Ramayana, Valmiki narrates to Sage Narda all the qualities of a "Sthithaprajna" and asks him whether there is any person living who satisfies that description, for which Narada answers that Rama, the Scion of the Ikshwaku dynasty, is a standing example for that. But, when we come to the Bhagavad Geeta, Arjuna does just the opposite. He asks the Lord as to what qualities distinguish a "Sthithaprajna", and the Lord recounts those qualities. The purpose is the same, but the approaches are from diametrically opposite directions.

HARE RAMA HARE RAMA
RAMA RAMA HARE HARE

HARE KRISHNA HARE KRISHNA
KRISHNA KRISHNA HARE HARE

HARI OM TAT SAT

R.S. NATHAN

THE SIGNIFICANCE OF SHIVARATRI

God is Omnipresent and All-pervasive. By the very nature of these qualities, He cannot have any form. He is, therefore, formless. But, in order to bless us, He assumes innumerable forms.

The Linga form in which we worship Iswara is symbolic of both his formlessness and form. It is symbolic of form because it has a particular shape; it is symbolic of formlessness because it has neither head nor limbs, like other images. The very conceptioon of a Linga denotes something which has neither beginning nor end. The literal meaning of Linga is symbol.

The Panchaayatana Pooja generally forms an essential part of worship. For that purpose, we use Baana Linga, representing Iswara, obtained from the Narmada; the Saaligraama, representing Vishnu, obtained from the Gandaki in Nepal; a red stone representing Vinayaka, obtained from the Sonabhadra; the crystal, representing the Sun, obtained from the Vajrateertham at Vallam in Thanjavur District; and a kind of stone with a golden tint, representing Ambika, obtained from Svarnamukhi, near Kalahasti.

It is significant that both Saaligraama, symbolic of Vishnu, and Rudraksha, symbolic of Siva, are obtained from Nepal. Saaligraama has a tiny hole, and if we hold it to the light we can see the mark of a discus (chakra) inside the hole. As in the case of conches and other shells, a kind of worm uses Saaligraama as its abode. The word, Saaligraama, is derived from Saaligraava; *Sali* meaning worm and *graava* meaning stone. In Nepal, the

221

Gandaki river becomes expansive like a lake at one place between four hills and it is from this place that Saaligraama is obtained. A crystal is an undeveloped diamond and according to tradition diamond used to be obtained from Vallam. A crystal (Sphatikam) scintillates in sunlight. Sun's rays pass through a crystal and the wearer of a crystal necklace will feel the scorching heat of the sun when moving about in the open.

A Baana Linga, which is egg shaped, serves to remind us that Isvara has neither beginning nor end. The shape of the sky is another example to denote the state of having neither beginning nor end. If we go into the significance of the symbol of Linga, we will realise that it is intended to bring the Unknown within our mental comprehension.

Isvara assumes various forms in pursuance of His Divine Sport. The prime manifestation with a form of the formless Isvara is known as the Lingodbhavamoorthi and He made His appearance in that form exactly at midnight on Sivaraatri. That is why all devotees keep vigil during the night of Sivaraatri and worship Isvara at midnight.

If we go to any important Siva temple we will find a niche in the outer wall of the sanctum sanctorum, exactly behind the spot where the deity is installed. In that niche we can find a representation of the Lingodbhavamoorthi, a form emerging out of a Linga. We can see neither the top half of the head nor the bottom half of the legs of that form. All the other attributes of Siva, like the axe and the deer will be found sculptured. We will also find depicted a swan in flight at the top of the Linga and a boar burrowing the earth at the bottom. According to the tradition, Brahma took the form of a swan to find out the crown of Siva's head and failed. Similarly, Vishnu took the form of a boar and burrowed deep into the bowels of the earth to locate the feet of

Siva and failed. Thus, in Lingodbhavamoorthi we have the unique combination of Brahma, Vishnu and Siva, impressing in our minds the *advaitic tatva* that God is One, Full and All pervasive. Both the aspects of Isvara with from and without form are thus depicted.

A crystal Linga is believed to be superior to other Lingas in all respects. This is because of the quality of the crystal itself which has no colour of its own. A crystal reflects the colour of the object with which it comes into contact. The significance of this is that Isvara becomes what an ardent devotee desires Him to be. He is the source of all colours and ultimately all colours merge in Him. He is the source of all life and ultimately all life merges in Him. Can there be any Truth loftier than this?

God in his manifestation as Vishnu made His appearance as Krishna at Gokulam at midnight. Exactly 180 days after Gokulashtami, Sivaraatri occurs. Siva, as Lingodbhavamoorthi,also makes His appearance at midnight. Thus the circle of one year is divided into two by these two auspicious days, thereby affording one more example which brings home to us the truth of the Oneness of Siva and Vishnu and teaches us that in one form or the other Isvara protects us all through the year.

The glorious form of the Lingodbhavamoorthi stands out in all majesty to tell us that out of His formlessness Isvara emerged in a form to guide the functioning of the Universe. When the static Isvara decides to assume form, He becomes dynamic and manifests Himself in innumerable forms to fulfil His innumerable functions. One such form is Natraja, Siva in cosmic dance.

There is a verse in Sivaananda Lahari describing this dance of bliss. In that verse, the appellation Neelkanta is used for Siva. Neelkanta in Sanskrit also means a peacock. Peacock, as we know, is a dancing bird. This allegory is employed both in Sahitya Ratnakara and in Sivaananda Lahari. In the former, the dance of the peacock is described with a reference to Siva, and in the latter, the dance of Siva is described with a reference to the peacock!

The verse in Sahitya Ratnaakara is :

Chala Chandraka neelkanta visphuri-
tam naatya vidhou bhuvasthale,
Avalokya bakaasthimalikaa divi bibh-
raama rusheva kaalikaa.

When the summer season ends and the rainy season is about to begin, the sky is overcast with dark clouds with occasional flashes of lightining and peels of thunder. There will also be light drizzling. Inspired by these natural phenomena, and in the presence of its consort, the peacock fans out its tail and dances on one leg.

There is a tradition that while Siva dances in ecstatic bliss, Parvati as Kaalikaa, dances separately a dance of wrath wearing a garland of skulls around Her neck and roaring with anger. This tradition is alluded to in the above verse. The poet uses the term Kaalikaa to denote clouds and describes storks returning to their roost as the garland of skulls round the neck of Kaalikaa. The mate (mayoori) is watching the dance. As the peacock dances, what are known as the eyes (Chandraka) in the tail feathers swing to and fro, even as the crescent moon on the head of Natraja swings as He dances.

Sri Sankara Bhagavadpaada, describing the Ananda Taandava of Siva says in Sivaananda Lahiri :

Sandhyaa gharma dinaatayo hari
karaaghaata prabhootaanka
Svaano vaaridagarjitam divishadaam
drishtischata chanchala;

Bhaktaanam paritosha-baashpa vi-
tati-vrishtir mayooree Sivaa,
Yasminnujvala taandavam vijayate
tam Neelakantam bhaje.

The end of the summer and the beginning of the rainy season are indicated in this verse by pointing out that the time of the dance of Siva is sandhya, the junction of the day and the night. The sound of the big drum (prabhootaanka) played by the hands of Hari constitutes the peels of thunder. The flashes from the eyes of the watching Devas provide the lightining, and the tears of joy flowing from the eyes of devotees are compared to the drizzling. Ambika is the mayoori (pea-hen) for this dancing Neelakanta.

The Lord, who performs the illuminating dance, appears in the form of Lingodbhavamoorthi on Sivaraatri to shower His grace on us. It is our duty on that day to fast, keep vigil and worship Him at midnight at least with one leaf of the Bilva tree. There is a saying that no intelligent dog will touch its food on Sivaraatri day.

There is also a story of how a hunter received the grace of Isvara by even unintentionally worshipping Siva with Bilva leaves on this night. The story goes that a hunter who was pursued by a tiger climbed up the nearest tree. The tiger stationed itself under the tree to catch the hunter as soon as he came down. Lest he should fall asleep and tumble down the tree, the hunter engaged himself in plucking the leaves of the tree one by one and throwing them down. It so happened that the tree on which the hunter found safety from the tiger was a Bilva tree, and the Bilva leaves which he plucked and dropped down fell one by one on the top of a Siva Linga installed under the tree. Even for this act of unintentional worship, the hunter was blessed by Isvara.

225

Let us also spend Sivaraarti in fasting and vigil and in worshipping Siva, particularly at the time He assumed the form of Lingodbhavamoorthi, and earn His divine grace.

SAMKARACHARYA OF KANCHI

(Of Kanchi Kamakoti Peetham)

THE PUJAS I & II

THE PUJAS I

The Pujas are just over. The Durga Puja, Lakshmi Puja, and Kali Puja came in quick succession. We worshipped the Supreme Godhead in three different aspects. We collected money, raised pandals, brought the images, decorated them, installed them, burned incense, offered flowers, ate and distributed prasad, went jubilant and even danced to the accompaniment of drums and cymbals, in some cases sang a few devotional songs too, organised impressive and illuminated processions, and finally consigned the images into the bowels of Mother Ganges in the Visarjan ceremony.

We purchased clothes, footwear and other choicest finery for ourselves and our near and dear ones, and turned out in our best, to see and to be seen. On Vijaya Dasami Day, we celebrated Vijaya or Victory, and liberally sent 'Vijaya greetings' to our relatives and friends. Later we called on them, embraced them, paid respects to them, and renewed our relationship with all of them with all apparent sincerity and affection.

But how many of us had applied our minds to the deep significance of each one of all these actions, the motives with which they have been introduced into society from time immemorial, the purpose for which they have been woven into the fabric of the life of the Hindu, and the effect these periodic rituals should have on our lives both individually and collectively?

Let us look back into the meta-physical side of what we did physically (only briefly, as space does not permit

227

elaborate dealing with the subject here).

Nothing, not even a blade of grass, ever moves in this world unless willed by Him or Her, depending on one's concept of Godhead as Father or Mother at a given time (Please refer to Kenopanishad), though man in his ignorance and ego prides himself as the doer, the dispenser, and achiever of everything, until some incident sometime, somewhere, makes him realise that there is an inexorable and unalterable law governing the working of the Universe with a Supreme Intelligence that is immanent, and transcendent. Whether we realise it or not, whether we accept it or not, we are definitely influenced by the concept of God. There is no atheist in the world. Time and circumstances will bring out the theist in every man. Only the concept may differ on the basis of one's knowledge and evolution at a given time.

DURGA – the meaning of this two letter word in Sanskrit is "that which is difficult to reach or attain" – is worshipped as "Mahishasuramardini" – meaning the conqueror of the buffalo-demon. There is a buffalo in each one of us, the proverbially slow beast symbolising ignorance (Tamas) which is a demon i.e. undivine. It is the vehicle of the god of death meaning, the concept (and fear) of death rides on ignorance. There is no death for the wise. The worship of Durga thus symbolises the conquering of ignorance and all undivine qualities in us, by our own higher Self. Surely that state is difficult to reach or attain. Hence 'DURGA'.

When this is achieved, Goddess Lakshmi is sure to bless us with all prosperity. Once the undivine qualities have been conquered and eliminated, the 'concept of want' undergoes a change and even drops off. That is the highest prosperity. The whole world belongs to such a man – Vasudhaiva Kutumbakam. What more does he want? Prosperity does not depend on your Bank balance.

Your mental contentment is the measure of your prosperity.

Purified of all traces of undivine qualities and consequently enjoying unlimited prosperity based on contentment, we worship Kali at the next stage — Kali, the divine concept that stands for constructive destruction — the destruction of everything changing, for rising to the Changeless.

When we in our hearts begin to aspire for this condition, should we not naturally become jubilant? Will we not dance with a joy that knows no bounds? Will it not be the real victory of the higher Self over the lower self, the real "Vijaya Dasami" in each one's life? And why should it be a 'Dasami'? It is 'Vijaya Dasami' signifying man's victory over the ten — the five senses of perception and the five organs of action.

That is why the ritual is called "Puja", consisting of two letters Pa and Ja. According to the Hindu Scriptures :

'Pa'-kara Papanasana.

'Ja'-karo Janmaviccheda:

Pa — stands for the purification and redemption from all sins and sinful propensities, and

Ja — stands for the consequent cessation of the cycle of births and deaths.

i.e, the Pujas are to be performed as ordained, with the correct mental attitude. Alas it is lacking in most of our actions, including the Pujas.

Now comes the 'Visarjan Ceremony', which is the culmination of the Puja, and is of the greatest significance. God is the Infinite, and man's equipments to understand God are only finite. With a finite instrument, we cannot measure the Infinite, much less understand it. So we try to bring down the Infinite Formless God within the compass of our finite equipments by giving Him a form and a name. "Sadhakaanam hithartham Brahmani rupa kalpate" – Brahman, the formless, is assigned forms and names for the facility and convenience of the devotee. Durga, Lakshmi, and Kali, and a host of other Hindu Gods and Goddesses, are only the Infinite Formless answering and satisfying the aspirants, each according to his or her finite concept. We go from the known to the Unknown, from the forms to the Formless. Through the development aforesaid, we realise that names and forms are changing and transitory, and that we are ourselves the changeless. And we immerse the concept of changing forms and names in the Ganga, which in Sanskrit literally means 'the flow of knowledge'.

Thus we immerse all our dual concepts of names and forms in the river of Knowledge welling within us. Now images are no longer necessary. They have served their purpose. We have identified ourselves with the Nameless and Formless. Visarajan means 'giving up' – giving up the concepts of forms and names, giving up the idol for the Ideal.

And then we went out and embraced everybody. Ignorance overcome, undivine qualities eschewed, contentment cultivalted and spiritual prosperity attained, unreality of this changing world realised, we go out into the world and embrace everything in unlimited love. Our concept of God embraces everything. One sees nothing other than oneself. The whole world for us is one homogenous family – Vasudhaiva Kutumbakam. So far we had 'fallen in love'. Now we have 'risen in love'.

That is the progress of man – the piligrim's progress. Pujas and all other rituals, if performed with the requisite faith and devotion, are intended to purify the mind of man, and prepare him for his final destiny of Wisdom and Perfection.

That was what our forefathers saw and experienced. They introduced these into society so that posterity may evolve mentally, intellectually, and spiritually. But we have not imbibed what they experienced. Ours, at best, is only a superficial imitation and not an emulation as it ought to be. There we stand and stagnate. Let the All-merciful Mother forgive us, for we know not what we do, nor what we ought to do.

— HARI OM —

R.S. NATHAN

THE PUJAS II

The Pujas have once again come and gone. We had our usual revelry once again.

This is the time to reflect : What is a Puja - What is its purpose – and what is it supposed to be?

It is said in the Scriptures of our religion SANATANADHARMA, wrongly yet popularly known as Hinduism, today that :

The letter PA stands for PAPANASANA – the exhaustion of the result of undivine actions, commonly known as PAPA.

The letter JA stands for JANMAVICHHEDA – the cessation of the cycle of births and deaths which state is generally known as MOKSHA.

It is significant that the same two letters constitute PUJA and JAPA, in Sanskrit, in reverse order. It can be seen that the numerical value of these two letters is EIGHTEEN, which number has a special significance in Hindu Scriptures, as it stands for JAYA or Victory – Victory of the higher Self, over the lower self. Puja and Japa properly combined should lead to this Victory.

So a Puja is that action which helps us to spiritually evolve, culminating in the exhaustion of sins and in the stopping of Punarjanma : i.e. any action that purifies us and enables us to merge our individuality and Universality i.e. to realise the Divine within us.

It is worthwhile asking the question ourselves whether our actions have served that supreme purpose even slightly.

232

The details of the external action are immaterial. It is the attitude of the mind that is paramount. The object remaining the same, the impression created in different minds are different. The impressions created in the same mind at different times are also different. The evolutionary level at which the individual stands at a given time decides the quality of the impressions created in him.

It is not what we do that matters, but how we do it – the motive, the method, the attitude.

God is Universal-Omnipresent. The ultimate purpose of a Puja should be to see, accept and realise His presence everywhere, at all times.

What can we give Him? Nothing belongs to us. We came with nothing, return with nothing. We toil and earn for what? To leave behind when we ultimately go back. Everything belongs to Him already. He must be laughing at our vanity and foolishness when we offer Him something which is already His. Is it not robbing Peter to pay Peter himself?

He has everything and therefore He has no need for anything. But there is one thing which He does not have. That is our LOVE. If there is anything which we can give as our own, it is only our LOVE and nothing else. But are we prepared to give that? And if we cannot give that, what is the use of giving anything or everything else?

It is significant that the Pujas commence with "MAHALAYA" and conclude with "MAHISHASURA MARDANA". What do they signify to the reflecting man?

"MAHALAYA" means "THE GREAT DISSOLUTION". It stands for the dissolution of the ignorance within us (absence of Nitya-Anitya Vastu Viveka is called Avidya or ignorance in philosophical parlance) which is symbolised by the killing of the BUFFALO demon on Mahanavami Day. It is a nine days' Tapasya starting on

233

Mahalaya Day, invoking the Goddess of "Constructive-Destruction" and Knowledge. If the Tapsaya is proper, the ignorance within us should be wiped out in nine days. The buffalo is the symbol of Tamas and Inertia. It is the vehicle of Yamaraj, the Lord of Kala – the Great Leveller of Time. Kala slowly yet surely moves forward on the buffalo. So if we kill the buffalo in us, it means we go beyond the concept of time, which is the ultimate goal of Wisdom – the going beyond limitations, the Liberation. It will be interesting to note that the word MAHALAYA, which adds up to seventeen, stands for the subtle body which consists of seventeen elements, namely the five Pranas, Manas, Buddhi, and the Ten Indriyas, the control of which leads us to get over the eighteenth, the Casual Body, which is the Vasanamaya Kosa or Avidya or Ignorance, the victory over which is symbolised by the killing of the Buffalo Demon in the end. Then, are we not entitled to celebrate VIJAYA, the Victory - the Victory of the Higher Self over the lower self? This celebration is within, not without. It is the exuberance of the human soul. And it is again very significant, it is VIJAYA DASAMI. Dasami is the tenth day, in this instance from the New Moon to the Full Moon – from total darkness to the total light progressively. It symbolises our victory over the sense organs (Dasami for Ten) in our progress towards light, the five organs of perception and the five organs of action, of which we are the slaves today. Intellectuality is not the goal, but illumination. And once we achieve victory over these ten organs, do we not become STITHA PRAJNAS or JEEVAN MUKTAS? This seems to be the philosophy behind the Mahalaya, the Mahishasura Mardana, and Vijaya Dasami. Once we realise this, external revelry will stop because we have gone beyond the ten sense organs and their field of play. We will begin to revel internally within ourselves. And that is the real "VIJAYA". Again,

234

the cumulative value of the three letters DA-SA-MI comes to eighteen reminding us of the Vijaya or the Victory which we should win over ourselves, and which is the summun bonum of human birth and existence.

And it is **DURGA**, whom we worship during these ten days. The meaning of the Sanskrit word "Durga" is that which is difficult to be reached, – namely the State of Liberation after the annihilation of ignorance and all undivine qualities symbolised by the combined form of Mahisha and Asura. The letters DA and GA in DURGA stand for 8 and 3 respectively, inviting us to go beyond the eight Siddhis and the three States, at the same time warning us with the internal meaning of the word that it is a diffcult state to be reached. At the same time we are consoled by the Lord that there is nothing impossible to be attained if we develop and maintain the requisite **ABHYASA** and **VAIRAGYA**. And the series of Pujas ultimately ends with the worship of Kali – "Bhadra Kali" to be precise. Uma, Karthyayani, Gouri, Bhadrakali, Hymavati, Iswari, Sivaa Bhavani, Rudrani, Sarvani, Sarvamangala, Aparna, Mrudani, Chandika, Ambika, Parvati, etc, are all the names of the different aspects of the Creatrix or the Primordial Sakti, each name having an importance and significance of its own in connection with some episode or other. The epithet "Bhadra Kaali" – has a special connotation here. According to the "Katapayadi" formula, there is a numerical value for every letter in Sanskrit, and it is by this formula that the stanzas in our ancient Astronomical treatises are deciphered into their proper numerical values for astronomical calculations of time and distance. (We are unable even to comprehend the greatness of those authors.) The word "Bhadra" means "safe and secure". "Kali" is the female counterpart of Kala, the concept of Time. The numerical value of the word "Bhadra" is 24, and it stands for the twenty-four Tatwas (Prakriti and its evolutes) under the Sankhyan Philosophy, namely Mahat, Prakriti, Ahamkara, Manas, the five Tanmantras, the five Mahabhutas, the five Jnanendriyas, and the five Karemdriyas – all of which function under the concept of Time, as against the twenty-fifth Tatwa – Purusha, which is beyond Time, and so, eternal. So, in the worship of "Bhadra-Kali", we progressively go beyond the above-said twenty-four Tatwas in time, and reach Purusha – the twenty-fifth beyond time. It is the worship of the one within time and the Timeless. And the goal is "Bhadra" – spiritual safety and security – called "Shreyas" in philosophical terminology.

Before writing down the Mahabharata as dictated by Vyasa, Ganapati had to understand what he was going to write. In this we have a moral. Let us try to understand the significance of what we are doing and what we are going to do. That makes all the difference. That knowledge will change our attitude, and ultimatley lead us to beatitude.

— HARI OM —

R.S.NATHAN

DEEPAVALI OR NARAKA CHATURDASI AND ITS SIGNIFICANCE

Which else shall beautify a home
But the flame of a lovely lamp
Which else shall adorn the mind
But the Light of Wisdom deep.

Few proofs of the essential oneness and solidarity of this vast country are more convincing than the institution of her festivals. No doubt, Bharata Varsha has been, from the very beginnings of her recorded history, criss - crossed with a large number of kingdoms and sub-kingdoms, peopled with so many stocks and clans. Each of these had its own characteristic way of life, social outlook and practice and tended to pride itself on its own ways and belittle those of others. In a well-known episode of the Mahabharata, Karna, the stalwart of the Kuru's cause, pours ridicule and contempt upon the customs of the Madra people in a manner that indicates a very concrete and sharp divergence and a lively sense of rivalry among the different peoples of the land. Yet overriding and overshadowing all the local variations stood like a sentinel the one master tradition that has spread all over the country and not only welded it into a living whole, but has continued to this day to hold it together. That is the undefinable **DHARMA** – the spiritual, the religious and, in a larger sense, the cultural tradition of India. From Kamrup to Dwarka, from Kanyakumari to Kashmir, it is the same conception of man's quest, the same high roads along which course the strivings and

237

expressions of the life force and thought, individual and communal, that grip our attention.

India is a land of vast dimensions. Intersected with gigantic rivers and mountains, impenetrable forests and endless plains, this country was never served, till recently, with proper means of communication. And yet we find that the Dwija of Khatmandu recites the famous prayer to the Sungod, the Gayatri, in precisely the same intonation, the same accents, to the very syllable, in which another does on the banks of the Kaveri. And Gayatri is just one Mantra of the thousands that have been handed handed down from mouth to mouth and preserved throughout in their pristine form. We do not know if there are many parallels as this unique phenomenon dating from a dateless past. We cite this as just illustrative of the sameness of tradition which is more spectacularly brought to the eye of our cycle of festivals.

A PICTURESQUE WEB

An Indian festival like Deepavali (Deevali) is a picturesque web into the making of which so many strands have gone – religious, social and cultural – a raiment that adorns the entire fabric of society, cherished and preserved by all alike, men and women, old and young, in all the quarters of the land, north and south, east and west. There maybe variations in details, differences in the social values attached thereto, observable in the celebrations in the different parts of the country. Thus, for instance, in Maharashtra Deepavali is not merely a religious festival, but an occassion for family reunions, the meeting of brothers and sisters, and also the commencement of the fresh crop year. But in the south of Maharashtra in the Western Ghats, the occasion is looked upon more as the parting of the seasons and coming in of the sunny weather. In Bengal it is still different. But these details are really inconsequential. The event which this occasion is understood all over to celebrate is one and one alone. Divali, or more correctly Deepavali meaning the Row of Lights, is the joyous celebration of the death of the Titan of Hell, Narakasura, at the hands of Lord Krishna : The Lord has eliminated at long last, the Beelzebub, the champion of darkness; the contamination that afflicted the Earth has been washed away, and myraid lights are put on to signalise His victory, which was indeed won for us, His dear children.

The origin of this celebration is, of course, to be traced to our mythology. But a myth, be it noted, is no yarn. It was Ruskin who described the myth as a story with a meaning attached to it other than what is apparent; and a characteristic feature of it, he went on to add, is something extraordinary about its circumstances. And if we proceed here to narrate the story of Narakasura, it is with a view to drawing the attention of the reader to the deeper significane of the festival, which is usually lost sight of in the socialities that have crowded round it.

THE STORY OF NARAKASURA

The earliest mention of this story is to be found in the Mahabharata — Sabhaparva in its southern recension. But is also found with slight variations, in the Bhagavata. Briefly told, this is the episode :-

Bhauma, son of the Earth, also known as Narakasura, was the king of Pragjyotishapura. By virtue of his prowess and the boon secured by merit of tapas, he became all-powerful and an intolerable menance to the gods, sages and all men of piety. He conquered and plundered not only the earth but heaven as well. He carried away the daughter of Twashta, the divine architect, and also the fair daughters of the gods, gandharvas and others, numbering about a little more

239

than sixteen thousand, and imprisoned all in his mountain retreat. As a crowning piece of effrontery, he robbed Aditi, the mother of the gods, of her ornamental ear-rings. This was too much for the gods to bear, and, headed by Indra, they supplicated Sri Krishna at Dwarka to kill Narakasura, as no one else was equal to the task. Sri Krishna readily consented and proceeded to the capital of Narakasura. Alone, unaided, he fought the hosts, and eliminated his five commanders.

The course of his advance, as described in the narrative, is interesting. First he had to rip open the six thousand sharppointed fencings (pasha), then surmount a rocky and mountainous region, and then wade through the red waters of a river (Lohitaganga); after crossing another river, he reached Pragjyotishapura. He met and killed the demons in their thousands and then plunged into the very bowels of the earth, the Patalaloka, the nether regions, and confornted the Titan. There ensued a fierce encounter. Sri Krishna dallied with him, as it were, and Naraka aimed his powerful Shakti towards Sri Krishna. But the latter was unhurt, and he stood as if he had been only "hit by a garland". And before Naraka could use the next weapon, his head was cut asunder in the twinkling of the eye by the famous disc "Chakra" of the Lord. Bhumi, the Earth rose and handed over the ear-rings of Aditi to the Lord and said :-

He (naraka) was created by You
He is ended by You as well;
May You sport in your glory!

Sri Krishna thereafter rescued the imprisoned damsels, who were pining for Him, the Liberator long-heralded by Sage Narada, and, at their earnest prayers, took them as His wives. The ear-rings were returned to Aditi and all was well once more.

240

CELEBRATION

This in brief is the legend. And it is this deliverance of the Earth and her people from the clutches of the Dark Asura of Hell that is celebrated with such joy and enthusiasm by a grateful people. Early in the morning, before sunrise, they get up from their beds, anoint themselves with oil for a holy bath to wash out the contamination caused by the very existence of Naraka. Bathed, they celebrate the day with sweets, presents and mutual visits. In Maharashtra, there is a system of the sister in the house worshipping with Arati her brother or brothers. The brother stands for Sri Krishna who did the meritorious deed. Before stepping into the special square, lined with various designs in corn-powder, to receive the worship, the brother tastes a particular bitter fruit (Karith, in Marathi) which Sri Krishna is said to have tasted before setting out for the kill. As the evening approaches, all the houses are lit up, rows after rows of lamps and lights are lit, the "Deep-avali"; there is no darkness anywhere, it is slain. All is Light and only Light.

Such a beautiful myth as this cannot be dissected and analysed without doing violence to its rounded perfection. We would rather leave the reader to feel the poetic imagery of the conception underlying this Saga of Lights, by himslef, in the privacy of his soul. We would only draw attention to a few striking features of this narration.

SIGNIFICANCE

Prag-Jyotisha-pura, the City of Lights in the East, East being where the light first breaks in, is the scene of the battle. The contestants are Sri Krishna, the Avatar of the Supreme God Vishnu, and Bhauma — born of Bhumi, i.e. the son of the Earth, also known as Narakasura, the Titan of Hell. This Titan has made life

241

impossible on earth. He even strays into the region of the celestials, robs the ornaments of Aditi, the Great Creatix of the gods and conceals them in his mountain retreat. Who else can this Titan be but the Dark Force of Ignorance – that is born of the Earth – that afflicts the life of the Earth and her people, the Ignorance that imprisons Light and Knowledge? The correspondence between Bhauma's imprisonment of these Kanyas and the concealment of the Vedic cows by Vala or the Panis, is too patent to be missed. Also glaring is the similarity in the means of their deliverance. The Mighty God Himself has to come, smash away every obstacle, thick and hard, and kill the arch-enemy with a decisive blow. There it is Indra that does it; here it is Sri Krishna. Once this is done, the daughters are liberated and are wedded to the Lord towards whom they rightly aspire. The theme is the same – a decisive conquest of the challenging Darkness and Ignorance by the Liberating Power, which results in the release and the flooding of the concealed Light.

There are other legends current in different parts of the country in connection with Deepavali. But the most ancient and sanctified by hoary tradition is the Krishna Narakasura episode, with which we associate this festival, in common with great men that have gone before us. The path is cleared and man's journey towards his destiny has been rendered safe by the Leading Power. This is the message flashed out by the little leaping flames which all of us, Indians, delight in lighting up once a year to remind ourselves, as it were, that the period of sloth, tamas, is past, the days of progress and endeavour have come.

M.P.PANDIT
(Grace of the Great and other Essays)

242

THE HOLI – ITS ORIGIN
AND SIGNIFICANCE

When the soul of man danced
In a burst of spring-flower colours...

The most famous and interesting of the village festivals is the Holi, which is held in the early spring, at the full-moon of Phalgun. One account of its origin describes it as founded in honour of a female demon or Rakshasi called Dundhas : meaning, "She who would destroy many".

Another account connects the observance with the well-known legend of Hiranyakashipu, the 'golden-dressed', and his son Prahlada. Hiranyakashipu was, it is said, a Daitya who obtained from Siva, the sovereignty of the three worlds for a million years and persecuted his pious son Prahlada because he was such a devoted worshipper of Vishnu. Finally the angry God in his man-lion or Narasimha incarnation, slew the sinner.

Harnaka, as the father is called in the modern version of the story, was an ascetic, who claimed that the devotion of the world was to be paid to him alone. His son, Prahlada, became a staunch devotee of Vishnu and performed various miracles such as saving a cat and her kittens out of the blazing kiln of a potter. His father was enraged at what he considered the apostasy of his son and, with the assistance of his sister Holi or Holika, commenced to torture Prahlada. Many attempts on his life failed, and finally Vishnu Himself entered a pillar of heated iron, which had been prepared for the destruction of the child Prahlada, and tore Hirnaka to pieces. Then Holi tried to burn herself, and the child Prahlada together, but the fire left him unscathed while she was consumed by the fire. The fire is now supposed to be burnt in commemoration of this tragedy.

This legend has been localised at a place called Deokali, near Irichh in the District of Jhansi, where Hiranyakashipu is said to have had his palace. Just below it is a deep pool, into which Prahlada was said to have been flung by the orders of his father, and the mark of the foot of the martyr is still shown on a neighbouring rock.

Another legend identifies Holi with the witch, Pootana, who attempted to destroy the infant Krishna under the orders of Kamsa by offering the child her poisoned nipples to suck.

Lastly a tale at Haradwar brings us probably nearer the real origin of the rite. Holika or Holi was, they say, the sister of Sambat or Sanvat, the Hindu years. Once, at the beginning of all things, Sambat died, and Holi or Holika, in her excessive love for her brother, insisted on being burnt on his pyre, and by her devotion he was restored to life. The Holi fire is now burnt every year to commemorate this tragedy.

Lighting of Holi Fire

The next day the Holi fire is lit. By immemorial custom, the boys are allowed to appropriate fuel of any kind for the fire, the woodwork of deserted houses, fences and the like, and the owner never dares to complain. We have the same custom in England too. The chorus of the Oxfordshire song sung at the feast of the Gun-powder plot runs:

A stick and a stake
For King James' sake
If you wont give me one,
I'll take two.
The better for me
The worse for you.

This is chanted by the boys while collecting sticks for the bonfire, and it is considered quite lawful to appropriate any old piece of wood they can lay hands on after the recitation of these lines.

Throwing of Powder

In the Indian observance of the Holi, next follows a series of performances characterised by rude horseplay and ribald singing. On the next day comes the throwing of the powder. Handfuls of red powder, mixed with glistening talc, are thrown about unto the balconies above and down on the people below and seen, through this atmosphere of coloured cloud, the frantic gestures of the throng, their white clothes and faces all stained with red and yellow patches, and the great timbrels and branches of peacock's feathers, artificial flowers and tinsel stars stuck in their rims borne above the players's heads, and now and then tossed up in the air, combine to form a curious and picturesque spectacle.

Then follows another mock fight between men and women, conducted with perfect good humour on both sides and, when it is all over, many of the spectators run into the arena and roll over and over in the dust, or streak themselves with it on the forehead, taking it as the dust hallowed by the holy feet of Krishna and the Gopis.

Holi in Marwar

Colonel Todd gives an interesting account of the festival as performed at Marwar. He describes the

people as lighting large fires into which various sub-
stances as well as the common powder are thrown, and
around which groups of children dance and scream
in these streets like so many infernals; until about three
hours after sunrise of the new moon of the month of
Chait, these orgies are continued with increased vigour;
then the natives bathe, change their garments, worship
and return to the ranks of sober citizens, and princes
and chiefs receive gifts from their domestics.

Ashes of the Holi Fire

The belief in the efficacy of the Holi fire in prevent-
ing the blight of crops, and in the ashes as a remedy for
diseases, has already been noticed. So too, in England,
the Yule Log was put aside and was supposed to guard
the house from evil spirits.

Origin and Significance

The Holi, then, in its most primitive form, is possi-
bly an aboriginal usage which has been imported into
Brahminism. This is specially shown by the functions of
the Kherapat or the Village Priest, who lights the fire.
He is sometimes a Brahmin, but often a man drawn from
the lower races too. As we have seen, his duties among
the Dravidian races are performed by the Baiga, who is
always drawn from the non-Aryan races. It seems proba-
ble that the legends connecting the rite with Prahlad and
Krishna are a subsequent invention, and that the fire is
really intended to represent the burning of the old year
and the birth of the new, which they pray may be more
propitious to the families, cattle, and crops of the worshippers. The observance seems also to include certain
ceremonies intended to scare away the evil spirits which
are supposed to bring famine and the diseases. The compulsory entry of the local priests into the fire can hardly
be anything but a survival of human sacrifice, intended

to secure the same results, and the dancing, singing, waving of flags, screaming and the mock-fight and the throwing of red powder, a colour supposed, as we have seen, to be obnoxious to the evil spirits, are probably based on the same train of ideas.

Of the mock fight at the Holi, it may be merely a fertility charm. Of these mock fights, we have numerous instances in the customs of Northern India. Thus, in Kumaun, in former days at the Bagwah festival, the males of several villages used to divide into two bodies and sling stones at each other across a stream. The results were so serious that it had to be suppressed after the British occupation of the country. The people in some places attribute the increase of cholera and other plagues to its discontinuance. In the plains, the custom survives in what is known as the Barra, when the men of two villages have a sort of a Tug-of-War with a rope across the boundary of the villages. Plenty and prosperity are supposed to follow the side that becomes victorious.

WILLIAM CROOKE
(From the Popular Religion and
Folklore of Northern India – Vol. II)

247

JANMASHTAMI

This is a sacred day dedicated to Lord Krishna. For centuries together, the story of Krishna has been repeated on this day in our country. Krishna was born on this day in Mathura and we are inspired by the story year after year. Later, Krishna married several wives and perhaps divorced some. Thus we have brought Him down to our own level and think that we are not as bad as Krishna. This was the ideal for a very long time. Perhaps this is the superficial meaning of the story and it has become a slogan for the cheap missionaries to be blasphemous of Hindusim.

The significance of this story is very great. Hinduism accepts no history to be worth remembering. All history which Hinduism accepts is only His Story. This His story is clouded in mystery, for it is but My-story. Actually there is no mystery in His-story. Everything is so very scientific and logical. The seeming mystery has been explained to be always My-story. Because He is Me and I am He. "The Son and the Father are one," says the Bible. Thus from His-story it happens to be, an enquiry, a revelation of my story. It gives a straight answer to the question "Who am I?"

When Vyasa wrote the Puranas, he was not writing any story of Krishna. We do not want any story in the Puranas. Vyasa wrote not for the sake of mere writing. He was a great student of Knowledge, a master of the Vedas. He was a realised Soul. He compiled the Vedas into four parts and then wrote the Brahma Sutras. These were not useful to the ordinary folk. They could not comprehend the power behind the body, mind and intellect,

248

which gave these the glow-of-life. So he wrote a figurative narration in the form of the Puranas. Thus from birth to death, the narration of Krishna was not a story.

There is a Higher Power pulsating in us. It is the Light of Intelligence. It illumines the thought and feelings in us. 'I am happy' 'I am aware of ideas'. The Light illuminating all these faculties is one and the same in all. It is represented as Sri Krishna. Krishna is Infinite Wisdom. He came forth for the first time in the world in the thick jungles of the Himalayas. He was born in the prison. That prison is the bosom of the Rishis, who were contemplating on the mysterious problem of Life. We know that scientific Truths are discovered in the quiet caves of the rare Intellectuals. The Rishis were contemplating on the great Goal of Life, the Purpose in life. Man is not born to die away as the donkey or the pig. Man has a better purpose in life. The Rishis in the quiet silence of the Himalayas rediscovered the Truth.

Krishna is Truth, He was born in the quiet heart-caves of the Rishis. Those Rishis gradually transmitted their knowledge to their disciples. Thus Krishna was removed from the prison to Yasoda's house – the disciple's. There is no pain in this unique delivery. The Guru gives out the child without the agony of labour pains. While we are sleeping in fatigue and exhaustion, wearied in production and destruction, we know not, that there is born a baby, called Knowledge – Krishna – in our bosom. Engaged perpetually in procuring, keeping and spending, we are fatigueo, and in the deep sleep of midnight, the child is born, the senses are the gatekeepers who slept off when Krishna was born in the prison.

As long as we are engaged in these outer activities, the scriptures do not open their secrets to us. When we get fed up with these and go to sleep to forget them, in meditation, this child is born. When we have fully enjoyed life in all aspects and find no peace out of them

– in that quiet sleep, the maturity of understanding, the Light dawns. The Scriptures are taught to such a heart.

Today a young man is not satisfied with mere theories. He wants a rational reply. The Bible cannot be questioned. To question it becomes blasphemy. The West cannot understand the logic and so the West is unhappy. Until the war came, they were satisfied with their material advancements and the general hoarding, maintained and expanded by bombs and superbombs. Now Materialism has broken down. There is plenty of wealth but there is no peace. Achievement is there but no delight in those joys. Wars have come and gone, but peace has not come. The war-mongers are more happy than the peace-lovers.

Western thought is ransacked by all these contradictions. A French philosopher expressed his realisation that behind all these struggles, there is an Infinite Reality which he could not comprehend. He has summed it up that there is a great Power behind all these conflicts, something Beyond. The Intellect cannot understand and bring it to scientific apprehension. The Intellect cannot reach there, it is like a dark screen. We cannot penetrate it. Trying to probe Beyond it is like a tiny mosquito attempting to crash into a rocky fort by repeated headlong attacks. So there is a screen between man and the Infinite, and man thus thinks he is insignificant.

But, in spite of misery and sorrow, pangs and struggles, if he fights, toils hard, he will push himself forward. He can reach Him. In and through life he can enjoy His smile. The West could not penetrate this darkness because the body, mind and intellect cannot penetrate the darkness. That darkness is this night of Krishna's birth. When everybody is sleeping in the prison of his Ego, when the sense organs are all asleep, the mysterious

250

Light shines forth during meditation, and in that darkness the blue boy of Brindavan is born.

He was first born in the hearts of the Rishis. They brought him to Yasoda, in you and me. The Scriptures are that little baby. The Light of Krishna, then, comes to us. Yasoda looks after that child, the Blue Boy. She thinks it is her own child because he is supposed to have been born to her while she was asleep. Material prosperity terminates into spiritual progress. The pursuit of material life and sensuous attachments is transformed.

We have to look after that Baby. It is not an easy job, with a mischievous baby. From minute to minute he steals from the house and also from the neighbouring houses. When Yasoda wants to punish him, his very looks make her forget her own intentions. Everything she forgets. The Gopis may complain again and again, but nothing can be done. A thousand worries, a thousand shames the mother bears for his acts, but she cannot punish Him. Try any number of times, we too cannot control Him. We too are deceived by His looks.

We have left the picture house on this holiday for the sake of Spiritual Knowledge. Once, if in His Light we are working, there is joy, and happiness increases. This is the second stage. We become firmly established with Krishna. We look after Him in all aspects – with body, mind and intellect. He illumines and helps us. We need not help Him.

When the third stage comes, we study the Sastras. We are convinced. Then the city of Dwaraka is constructed. After Sravana and Manana, we rise above the heart and try to meditate. Thus the Blue Boy of Dwaraka is the Lord of Consciousness in the Heart. He is building a house in my heart. The Lord in the pooja room is in my heart. The Light of Consciousness in me is He. What I perceive is due to this Light. That is the Dwaraka

251

Krishna. Krishna born in the jail, is the birth of Knowledge in the heart of the Rishis. They explained it to their disciples. The Leelas of Krishna are the Spiritual activities in us, the Realisation of the Self.

Fulfilment is here and now – to serve humanity, to generate a revival movement. The virtues of the Hindu culture are brought out in the story of the Mahabharata war. Krishna guided the war, whether it was good or bad. He did not take up any weapon. Appearance (Avatar) is only the Life of Construction in true Cultural values, and disappearance (Tirodhanam) is the gradual diminution to the Life of Knowledge. After rediscovery we become the hope of the age. The nation can be led to a greater momentum, the culture of the Rishis.

Hinduism is accused of too much introvertedness. But really it is only Realisation. There is no religion that preaches complete extrovertedness. Christians kneel down with eyes open and pray to the Lord Yonder. The Hindus close their eyes and meditate upon the Lord within. They are supposed to forget the world and its worries.

It is only a wrong reading of the picture from an uncomfortable distance. If the picture is looked at correctly we understand that the Rishis see the Scriptures in the temple of their hearts. They do not close their eyes. The foreigner's view is hasty, shortsighted and perverted. The Rishis do not close their eyes fully. It remains only half-closed. Their steady mind looks out, it is called Shambavee Mudra. They are fully conscious of their within and without. They know that the light they see outside is the reflection of the Light of Consciousness shining from inside. The Infinite and finite are one and the same for them. Peace and harmony reign in them. Their eyes are never fully closed. They are not fully introvert to the detriment of the outer world and its progress.

When Krishna was born in the secret prison, He was delivered to Yasoda. When He had grown up sufficiently, He went to Dwaraka. There He established order. Then He went to Hastinapura. In the battle of Kurukshetra He gave out His wisdom to bless the nation. When you have developed a good faculty, you do not enjoy it yourself but give it back, improved, to the society. Thus, Krishna also gave out to the society the Knowledge of the Geeta.

The history of the cultural beauty of a society is in waves of Darkness and Brightness. These waves of cultural history can be traced from creation. If the symbolic Krishna has failed, it means the cultural beauty is lost. This power is in everyone of us. It is for us to make it bright. To invoke Him is only to claim Him. "He alone gains Him, who chooses Him."

Today is a wonderful day. The Lord is coming, so people fast. Devaki is in pains, therefore you do not eat food. Fasting is Upasana i.e., to live near the Lord (Upa-asanam). Attunement to the Lord through meditation is fasting. While contemplating, it is an agony to eat. For intellectual work, eating food and indulgence in the world outside is detrimental, for Krishna's birth is Enlightenment. Food means satisfaction for the senses. Starve the senses. Uplift them to contemplation. The thick darkness has come. Be brave, light will dawn. There must be no fear. The Sun has dawned in our bosom. Thus we turn inward in meditation. In that silence of the heart, in spite of thunders, we must remain sufficiently long. Then only, in that long earned tranquillity will we experience, the Birth of Krishna, The Light.

SWAMI CHINMAYANANDA

GURU POORNIMA

Receive the fire,
And convert it into Light

KRISHNA DWAIPAYANA BADARAYANA VYASA was born of the sage Parasara, the grandson of the great Vasishta, and the charming fishergirl, Satyavati. He was named Krishna because of his complexion, and because he was born on an island in the river Yamuna, he was also called Dwaipayana. (Because he did his tapasya at Badrinath, he came to be known as Badarayana also.) The Pournima signifies illumination, and Vyasa Pournima exemplifies spiritual illumination.

According to the scholars, he was born about the time the Vedic age came to an end, that is to say, between B.C. 1,200 and 950. He took to the life of an ascetic at a very early age. He was a man of great insight and a master of words. He collected all the Vedic hymns extant at that time and gave them a standard form and accent. Because of this great work, he came to be called Veda Vyasa (the person who divided and codified the Vedas) and he has been revered for the last three thousand years as no one else has been.

Vyasa's masterpiece has been, however, the Mahabharata, in which he has left for us the entire wisdom he had gathered. This was the saga of the Bharatas, the most universal story of the human race, by writing which he "lit the lamp of knowledge". It has been well-said that along with the Ramayana, it represents the collective Unconscious of India.

254

Jawaharlal Nehru regarded it as one of the out-standing books of the world. "It is a colossal work" he says in his ' Discovery of India ', "an encyclopaedia of tradition and legend, and political and social institutions of ancient India... It is a rich storehouse in which we can discover all manners of precious things."

It is full of a varied, abundant, and bubbling life, something far removed from that other aspect of Indian thought which emphasised asceticism and negation. The teaching of the Mahabharata is summed up in the phrase : "Thou shalt not do to others what is disagree-able to thyself."

There is an emphasis on social welfare, and this is note-worthy, for the tendency of the Indian mind is sup-posed to be in favour of individual perfection rather than social welfare. It says : "Whatever is not conducive to social welfare, or what ye are likely to be ashamed of, never do."

Again, truth, self-control, asceticism, generosity, non-violence, constancy in virtue, – these are the means of success, not caste or family. Virtue is better than immortality and life. True joy entails suffering. There is a dig at the seeker after wealth : "The silkworm dies of its wealth."

In depicting the character of Bhishma, a great war-rior and a man of learning revered by all, Vyasa has placed before us a great problem of mankind. Bhishma was well versed in the Vedas and in the science of right-eous conduct, Dharma Sastra, but we occasionally find in his conduct something contrary to righteousness and even a certain confusion of mind.

Finally, the Mahabharata contains a great Gospel of Life – The Bhagavad Geeta, another memorable episode in that vast drama. William Von Humbolt regards it as "the most beautiful, perhaps the only fine philosophical song in any known tongue". It is a gospel of life exhorting us to strive constantly for the control of the senses, sincere but unselfish performance of our duties, cultivation of equanimity of mind with the elimination of passions like lust, anger and greed, silent meditation, and finally surrender to God's grace leading to supreme peace.

No wonder he is considered the Guru of all time, and the day dedicated to him is called Vyasa Poornima or more popularly Guru Poornima!

K. THIAGARAJAN

MAKARA SANKRANTI

This is a very important religious observance and festival. About 70 years ago it occurred on the 12th or 13th January according to the several Indian almanacs then current, but now it falls, owing to the precession of the equinoxes, on the 13th or the 14th of January in the month of Pausa. "Sankranti" means 'the (apparent) passage of the sun from one rasi (sign of the zodiac) to the next following' and hence the rasi in which the sun enters is designated as the Sankranti of that name. When the sun leaves the rasi called Dhanus and enters the Makara rasi that is called Makara Sankranti. The rasis are twelve and the Sankranti names with their western equivalents are given... as Aries, Taurus, Gemini, Cancer, Leo, Virgo, Libra, Scorpio, Sagittarius, Capricornus, Aquarius and Pisces.

The Observance

The person should offer to a self-restrained Brahmana householder three vessels containing edibles together with a cow intending them to be for Yama, Rudra, and Dharma and repeat four verses one of which is as follows : "As I do not make any difference between Siva, Vishnu, the Sun and Brahma, may Sankara (Siva) who pervades the universe be always a bestower of welfare on me". The person should make, if he has the means, further gifts of ornaments, a bedstead and golden jars (two) to the Brahmana. Then he should take his meal without oil and should others according to his ability. Women also should perform this vrata.

257

Great merit was attached to a bath in the Ganges on a Sankranti, on an eclipse and on new and full moons, as such a man reached the world of Brahma. A bath with ordinary water (not heated) was obligatory (nitya) on every sankranti, since the Devi-purana declares : "The man who would not take a bath on the holy day of sankranti would be for seven lives diseased and poor; whatever offerings are made to gods and pit-rus by men on Sankranti are returned to them by the Sun again in the several future lives".

The Time

It may be stated that in ancient texts the entrance of the Sun alone in a rasi is not regarded as a holy time, but the entrance of all planets in nakshatra or rasi is deemed to be a holy time. Hemadri and the Kalanirnaya quote three verses specifing the holy times (punya-kala) of the passage of the sun. The punya-kala is 16 ghatikas before and after the moment of the Sankranti; for the moon it is 1 ghati and 13 palas on both sides, for Mars 4 ghatikas and 1 pala, for Mercury 3 ghatikas and 14 palas, for Jupiter 4 ghatikas and 37 palas, for Venus 4 ghatikas and 1 pala, for Saturn 82 ghatikas and 7 palas. (60 palas make a Ghatika, and 2½ ghatikas make one hour).

Though the planets also have Sankrantis, later writ-ers hold that the word 'Sankranti' by itself means only Ravi-sankranti, as stated by the Smriti Kaustubha.

The twelve Sankrantis in the year are grouped into four classes : viz. there are two Ayana Sankrantis (that is Makarasankranti from which Uttarayana starts and Kar-katasankranti from which Dakshinayana starts), two Vis-huva Sankrantis (that is, Mehsa and Tula Sankrantis when the day and night are equal in length), the four Sankrantis called Shadasitimukha (i.e., Mithuna, Kanya, Dhanus and Mina) and Vishnupaid or Vishnupadi (that is Vrishaba, Simha, Vrschika and Kumbha).

Identification with Durga

Sankranti gradually came to be deified and the Devipurana identified it with Durga herself. The Devipurana says : "Devi is all-pervading on account of the division into very small and large parts in the form of year, ayana, season, month, fortnight, day and the like. Devi bestows rewards in accordance with the·divisions into meritorious and sinful actions. Even one act done at that time (of Sankranti) yields results multiplied crores of times. From dharma (righteous acts) increase spring of life, kingdom, progeny, happiness and the like, from adharma (unrighteous conduct) soaring diseases, sorrows and the like; whatever is donated and whatever japa is performed near (i.e., at the time of) Vishuva (Mesha and Tula) Sankrantis and at the ayana (Makara and Karkata sankrantis) becomes inexhaustible; the same holds good about Vishnupada and Shadasitimukha".

The exact moment of time when the Sun leaves one rasi and enters the following rasi is impossible of being marked by the eyes of flesh (ordinary human eyes). Therefore, thirty ghatikas (twelve hours) before and after the moment of Sankranti are said to be the time.

In order to convey how infinitesimally small is the time of the Sun's entrance into a rasi after leaving another, the Devipurana has the following : "The thirtieth part of the time taken by the throb of the eye of a man sitting happily at ease is called a 'truti'; one hundredth part of a 'truti' is the (duration of) time of the Sun's passage from one rasi into another." As it is not possible to perform during such an infinitesimally small point of time the rites prescribed for performance at Sankranti, one has to accept periods of time near this moment as the proper time.

259

A Time to Offer

The great merit collected by gifts on Sankrantis is set forth by the Rajamartanda in two verses. "The reward (of gifts) on an Ayana Sankranti is a crore times (as much as of the same gift on an ordinary day) and on Vishnupadi a hundred thousand times; it is declared to be 86,000 times on Shadasiti. Gifts on the eclipse of the moon is a hundred-fold (in merit) and a thousandfold on the solar eclipse, one hundred thousand times on Vishua days and of endless duration on the full moon days of Ashadha, Kartika, Magha and Vaisakha." The Bhavishya highly praises a bath in the Ganges and Ayana and Vishua Sankrantis : "He who bathes in the waters of the Ganges on Ayana and Vishuva secures the fruit of bathing in the Ganges for half a year."

Social Festival

In modern times, Makarasankranti is more a social festival than a religious one. No fast is observed and hardly anyone performs sraddha, though many people bathe in the sea or in tirthas like the Ganges at Prayaga and elsewhere. Sesame is very much in evidence, particularly, in the Deccan, and people greet each other by giving articles made from simple sesame and jaggery to artistic sugared preparations of sesame, coloured with saffron, and go about saying, 'Take this sesame and jaggery and speak sweet words' (in Marathi).

According to the modern astronomical calculations, the winter solstice occurs on 21st December and on that day commences the Sun's apparent march towards the north. But in India people who follow the almanacs based on the ancient methods and data think that the Sun's march towards the north takes place on the 14th of January. They are thus about twenty-three days behind the correct Makarasankranti, owing to the precession of the equinoxes.

**COURTESY : HISTORY OF
DHARMA SASTRA VOL. PART 1**

ONAM AND ITS SIGNIFICANCE

The Onam festival in Kerala is a unique feature. The entire social set-up there is based on this festival. The social fabric in Kerala is so knitted that no human activity is segregated from the divine.

Divinity pervades everywhere and in every being. The several facets of human life are but an expression of the divinity that is all pervading. Man, being the crown and jewel of creation, has to recognise this and live up to it. The aesthetic sense, the cultural beauty, the intellectual ability, nay, his dress, food and walks of life should be attuned in such a way that he should remember the divine in him, the divinity tha tis all-pervading and their essential unity. Sacrifice is the secret source of achieving this unity but it does not mean any total giving up or morbid denial of life. It only means the sacrifice of the congested ego-centric existence at the altar of the Lord of all beings. Life is a splendid opportunity given to us by God, so that we may ourselves rise to His own stature. So, the path to Godhood is not by a negation of life, but by its acceptance as a gift. The entire life is to be fully lived and viewed as an integral whole.

We always miss the above truth, because ordinarily we live only a three dimensional life, that is, the life of the waking, dreaming and deep sleep experiences. But all of us are capable of living a life of divine consciousness, called the fourth plane of consciousness. The experience on this plane of existence is transego. This is the depth in our personality from which all noble virtues spring forth automatically. If an individual can reach this stage of development, we can say that the flower of his life has fully blossomed and has started wafting its fragrance. This is the underlying theory in the charming festival of Onam.

Mythologically, Onam is associated with the incarnation of Maha Vishnu as "Vamana". In the evolutionary order of the incarnations of the Lord, we find that Vamana is the first incarnation with a human body. By now, the animalistic features are discarded and man is born, along with it. Here we have to note that Vamana was not born outside, but in the mind of the Rakshasa, Mahabali Chakravarthi, who, though a Rakshasa till then, sticks to truthfulness and charity. He rises, prepared to sacrifice his everything. To the Brahmin boy, in the form of Vamana, he not only gave all the three worlds he possessed but also allowed the boy to place his foot on his own head. Thereby Mahabali made the greatest sacrifice — the absolute sacrifice of his own ego. The three worlds stand for the three planes of consciousness, the waking dreaming and deep-sleep states. Vamana with the touch of His feet scaled or transcended not only these three planes of consciousness, but also dethroned King Bali or the ego-centric existence. But He did not kill the rakshasa. He subjugated him and allowed him to live in such domains where he is fit. This is the story of the man-man becoming victorious over the Rashasa-man on reaching the fourth plane of consciousness, which is beyond all pluralistic idea. Once a man reaches a divine state of consciousness he becomes one with and experiences the divinity in himself and the divinity all-pervading and comes to recognise and experience their essential oneness.

"Onam" is celebrated to symbolise this flight to the "Peak" in life. Let us examine what they do during this festival. Onam is usually celebrated for ten days. These fall during the August-September months of the English calendar. And this is the spring season in Kerala. The blue sky is clear after the heavy rains. Paddy and all fruits are available in abundance. The work in the fields has not yet started. The gardens and fences, the bushes and the forests are all green with the touch of new life, and they blush with the new flowers that make tham droop their heads. The rivers are full with clear water and the back waters are all calm and navigable. In this backdrop, we find young children collecting flowers early in the morning to decorate their courtyards everyday for ten days prior to the main day, which is known as "Thiru-Onam" (the auspicious or the divine Onam). Each day, the dimensions of the flower decorations expand in concentric circles until the last day, when it grows to its largest size. The children in the neighbouring houses compete with one another in the size and beauty of this decoration. This is to indicate the blossoming of the flower of life in man. The aesthetic, artistic and rational developments in man at the physical and psychic planes are acheived, or flower forth, petal by petal, as these flower decorations are replaced by the installation of a temporarily built deity. This "Lord of the Onam" – as it is called – is usually made of clay or mud, in almost a shapeless shape, with a square bottom, four faces and a pointed top. The four faces stand for the four-phased life of a full-grown man. The ascent from the square bottom to the pointed top indicates the ascent of the animal-man to the one infinite point Godhood through a four-dimensional life.

The Malayalees throughout Kerala make this festival an opportunity for reuniting their family ties. Relatives at distant places visit their "homes". The family members get new clothes and presents from the heads of the families. The children and adults too, play a lot of indoor and outdoor games. This is also the season for

263

boat races in Kerala, a special feature in those parts. Rich food is prepared and lavishly served to all, especially to the poor and the working classes. The farmers bring presents to their landlords, and in turn get presents for themselves in the form of clothes, cash and food.

All these external hilarity and customs produce the salient effect of bringing a sense of oneness among the people. The younger generation gets an opportunity to improve their finer sentiments and appreciate the beauty of creation. Creativeness of the various talents in the grown-ups also find a new gush. The bright side of life is invoked everywhere. Thus man is made to recognise the essential unity in all the diverse ways of life. Hence the local bards and the womenfolk in Kerala go about in this season, from house to house, singing and dancing the glory of the Lord.

BR. GOVINDAN KUTTY

VINAYAKA CHATURTHI

VIGHNESWARA, one of the popular deities worshipped by all Hindu sects in India, is represented by a figure with the head of an elephant and a human body. He is the God of Knowledge and is invoked at the commencement of any function. It is believed that, in the fulfilment of human desires, his assistance is absolutely necessary. He is the God who can protect his devotees from any vighnam (obstacle) and hence the name Vighneswara. He is more popularly known as Ganesh or Ganapathy, as he was made the chief of the ganas by his parents, Siva and Parvati.

Mythological stories reveal that, one day when Parvati wanted to take her bath, Siva was away on his mount Nandikeswara. So the goddess made a protective figure and infused life into it. She asked the boy to stand at the gate and mount guard with strict instructions not to allow anyone inside. When Shiva returned, he was refused entry. The boy had neither seen Siva before, nor had the God seen the boy. In anger, Siva cut off the head of the boy and came in. Parvati was upset. She could not tolerate this act of Siva, and also did not want her creation mutilated. So she asked Siva to bring the boy back to life. Siva sent his ganas in search of any living thing, and the first creature they met was an elephant. Its head was cut off and attached to the human trunk of the boy. The boy came back to life, and the name Ganapathy was given to him.

Some legends say that Vighneswara himself wrote down the Mahabbarata, to the dictation of the Saint and

Seer, Veda Vyasa. It is also said that Vighneswara lost one of his tusks in a scuffle with Siva's disciple, Parasurama.

Vighneshwara is considered most intelligent. When Sage Narada brought a fruit for Siva, both the sons, Vighneswara and Karthikeya, wanted it. A challenge was thrown before them : Whoever went around the globe and returned first, will have the fruit. Karthikeya started on his mount, the peacock, went round the globe and returned, which took quite sometime, while Vighneswara went around his parents thrice and claimed the fruit, saying that, by going round Siva and Parvati, who represent the entire universe, he had satisfied the condition of the contest. When Karthikeya returned, he saw Vighneswara munching at the fruit. He got angry, shaved off his hair, and went into isolation at the Palani Hills. But Vighneswara loved him and helped him at the time of his marriage with the maiden, Valli.

Hindus, in the South particularly, are quite familiar with all these anecdotes relating to Vighneswara, and the more they read about him, the more they get attached to him. Ganesh Puja is celebrated with great devotion and enthusiasm by all the members of the family, and in particular by children. In Tamil Nadu, wet clay image of the God is brought in the morning. These come in various sizez, shapes and colours. It forms the livelihood of a class of people who make these idols for Vinayaka Chaturthi as well as Navaratri. In the South, Ganesh images in various positions, sitting, standing, with our without consorts, going in chariots, etc. form part of many processions.

Ganesh worship has become very popular now-a-days, and the temples dedicated to the deity are brilliantly lit, drawing enormous crowds. Every temple will have an altar for Vighneswara, and, on Ganesh Puja day, the due rites will be meticulously performed. There will be numerous music performances by leading artistes, and Bhajans for several days. Besides the temples dedicated to Vighneswara, one can see the images of the deity under banyan trees, on the roadsides and on the bunds of tanks, of rivers, as Vighneswara is believed to be a highly protective influence.

The idols of Vighneswara are seen both in stone and bronze. Sometimes the God is represented with five faces, when he goes by the name Panchamukha Vinayaka. Vighneswara with the paws of a tiger and a female form is known as Sakshi Vinayakar. Uchhishta Ganapathy and Vallabhi Ganapathy are two versions of Vighneswara in the company of women. Narthana Ganapathy depicts the deity in a dancing pose. There are even figures representing Vighneswara with musical instruments.

(Ganesh Puja was prevalent in Maharashtra since ancient days, but it was Shri Bal Gangadhara Tilak who revived it to great dimensions in modern times. Today Ganesh Puja is celebrated in Maharashtra just as Navaratri in Bengal or Dusserah in Mysore.

Let us all therefore on this happy and auspicious day of Vinayaka Chaturthi, remember with gratitude the ideal placed before us by the concept of Vighneswara and rejoice in the pleasures bestowed upon us by God for His own delectation.

K.THIAGARAJAN

267

VIJAYA DASAMI

Man's real nature is Absolute Bliss and Knowledge. He tries to reach this state with the help of his mind and intellect. But the mind constantly gravitates to the sense objects for sensual pleasures and the intellect goes on seeking knowledge from the external world. By such extroverted pursuits man gets involved more and more in the world of objects and accumulates desires which veil the divinity in him.

Man is thus in a helpless condition consumed by numerous desires. The ancient masters knew that he has to turn his attention inwards to gain the state of Absolute Bliss and Knowledge, which he foolishly seeks in the external world. With this view in mind, they introduced various rituals and festivals throughout the year, to remind man of his supreme goal and ideal. One such festival is Dusserah.

The Dusserah festival is celebrated throughout the country for ten days. During this festival, everyone spends his time in worship, devotion, and study of the sastras, and every house assumes the sanctity of a temple. The ten days are divided into three stages of three days each, for worship, and the culmination of the festival on the tenth day is called Vijaya Dasami.

In the first three days, Goddess Kali, also called Durga, is invoked. In the next three days Goddess Lakshmi is worshipped, and the following three days are dedicated to Goddess Saraswati. On Vijaya Dasami day, a huge bonfire of the devil is made, and this marks the culmination of the festival. Such festivals are not only reminders for man to seek God, but they also contain in them the very path and technique by which man can reach Him. The great day of Dusserah indicates, as the word suggests, Dasa-Papa-Hara, or the end or liquidation of the ten sins. The ten sins are attributed to the ten sense organs through which the mind contacts and gains knowledge of the phenomenal world, and also reacts to the stimuli received from the world of objects. Therefore the idea is that on this sacred day the ten sins are ended which signifies the end of the mind and therefore the end of the world of plurality when one becomes rooted in the transcendental experience.

One can gain the experience of the Reality by following the right invocations in the required sequence. The invocation of Goddess Durga is done first, with a particular purpose. Durga is described in Puranic literature as "The Terrible Power" that vanquished and killed the demons who terrorised devoted religious seekers. Similarly, in the bosom of man there are destructive monsters of desire, passion, lust, greed, jealousy, and so on, which have to be annihilated before he can successfully seek spiritual unfoldment. Hence Mother Durga is invoked. By worshipping Her for three days man merely invokes his own power which lies dormant within, to discover and destroy the negative forces lurking in his bosom.

Destroying one's evil tendencies is only a negative approach to spirituality. So the next stage is to practise the positive aspect of the Sadana. This is done by Shree Lakshmi Puja for the next three days. Lakshmi is the Goddess of Aiswarya. Aiswarya is not to be understood in the narrow sense of material wealth and possessions alone but as including the divine wealth of love, kindness, devotion, patience, endurance, charity, ahimsa and the like. Again, these are not to be gained from without, but are to be engendered from within by the invocation of the Goddess within ourselves. By the end of these three days, these divine qualities should replace the devilish tendencies which had usurped and enveloped our bosom.

With the development of the divine, traits, the seeker is fully qualified and becomes an Adhikari for philosophical study, contemplation and meditation. The invocation of Saraswati, the Goddess of Knowledge, is therefore the last and the final stage in the spiritual evolution of man. Just as she brings out the music and melody from her well-tuned lute, one can manifest the divinity and harmony with a well-integrated mind, by the study of the Sastras, constant reflection and meditation. After the three stages are gone through, on the last Vijaya Dasami Day the devil is burnt down indicating the transcendence of the ego, when man attains the great victory – Vijaya – over his sense-life and revels in the ecstatic experience of the Transcendental Reality.

SWAMI CHINMAYANANDA

SYMBOLISM
IN
HINDUISM

PART IV
SACRED ARTICLES
VAHANAS OR VEHICLES
AND
ABSTRACT FORMS

THE RUDRAKSHA

Ardent devotees of Lord Siva, especially those of the Saiva Siddhanta School, wear a string of beads known as the "Rudrakshamala", which they use for counting when repeating their Mantra. The number of beads in the string varies according to the way it is worn. Even today, one can see Sadhus wearing these beads in their ear-lobes, round their wrists, on the crown of the head, tight round the neck, or falling like a garland on the chest. Three beads are worn on each ear, twelve round each wrist, thirty-six over the crown of the head, thrity-two or twenty-seven tight round the neck, and a hundred and eight when worn as a garland. It is this last form of "Mala" which is generally used for Japa the repetition of a mantra, although the Padma Purana declares that the use of a mala of twenty-seven beads gives a special potency to the mantra chanted.

These beads are the seeds of the Rudraksha tree which grows in the Himalayas. Both the Skanda Purana and the Padma Purana speak highly of the efficacy of wearing them. Two Sanskrit Sastras, the "Upadesa Kandam" and the "Suta Samhita" give extensive accounts of Saints who are said to have attained liberation through them.

The seeds are generally seen to be of four colours. The most highly prized are the white, the reddish, the golden, and lastly the dark. The first and the third varieties are rare, and the other two are common; so their traditional order of superiority is not on the basis of rarity. It may be on the a basis of assimilation of the four 'Varnas', white

273

being suggestive of the Brahmin, red of the Kshatriya, gold of the Vaisya and the dark of the Shudra.

The seed has a soft core through which a hole is pierced for threading it. A number of lines run over the surface from end to end of this core, dividing the surface up into a number of crescent shaped sections. Beads with five sections are the most common, but there may be any number from one to fourteen.

According to the "Yoga Sara", spiritual powers corresponding to the gods, abide in the beads according to the number of sections or 'faces', and this therefore determines the type of mantra for which they are meant or suited. A bead with one face is said t be sacred to Lord Siva, with two Siva and His Sakti, i.e., Parvati; three to Agni the god of Fire, four to Brahma the creator, five to Kaalari, i.e. Siva as the destroyer of Kaala or Yama, the god of Death; six to Skanda or Subranmanya the god with six heads, i.e. Shanmukha; seven to Aadisesha, eight to Ganapati or Ganesh; nine to Bhairava that is Siva in His ferocious aspect; ten to Vishnu; eleven to the Ekadasa Rudra i.e. the eleven Rudras; twelve to Surya the Sun; thirteen to Kaamadeva the god of Love; and fourteen to Nilakanta i.e. Siva conceived as the blue-throated Lord. A Sadhak is expected to choose his beads to suit his mantra. The most favoured Rudrakshamala among devotees is that with six faces i.e. the mala of Subramanya who is the second son of Siva and Parvati, the god of War.

The name Rudraksha is a compound of the two Sanskrit words 'Rudra' meaning Siva; and 'Aksha' meaning eyes; so Rudraksha is the eye of Siva. This is the mythological third eye implying spiritual insight or realisation.

There is a mythological story, symbolical like all other such stories, describing the origin of the

Rudraksha. Three Asuras or Demon brothers, Tarakaksha, Kamalaksha and Vidyunmali, performed such austerities that they were able to extort boons from Siva, (there are a number of such stories showing that intelligently planned and inflexibly performed austerities produce powers, even so to speak despite the gods, that is to say, without purity or enlightenment) and thereby made themselves invincible and acquired three flying citadels of gold, silver and iron repsectively, in which they roamed the earth and conquered not only this world but also the world of gods. That is to say, by their occult powers, they were able to dominate not only this world but the subtle worlds also. But even such powers evaporate before the face of Truth. The Devas prayed to Lord Siva in their distress. He appeared before the asuras with a terrible look and yet at the same time with an bengin smile, as Truth is terrible to him who has rebelled against it and yet at the same time is compassionate. The citadels were burnt up and the asuras destroyed. At the same moment a tear drop fell from the eyes of the Lord, and falling to the earth, became a seed from which sprouted a tree bearing Rudraksha seeds in its turn for the welfare of the world. The seed that had its origin in the Lord's eye thus became 'Rudraksha'.

Rudraksha beads are generally seen in three sizes :

1. Big ones generaly of the size of the Amalaka furit (Emblica Myrobalans)

2. Medium ones of the size of the fruit of Jujuba, and

3. Small ones

It is stated that the smaller the size of the bead, the greater is its efficacy. The single phased and double-phased Rudrakshas called 'Brahmarupa' and 'Gowri-Shankar' respectively are considered to be the most efficacious irrespective of their sizes.

The 'Rudraksha jabalopanishad' mentions that "In the crust of the Rudraksha dwells Brahma; in its hollow rests Vishnu; and in its mouth is located Siva; while in the Bindu abide all the celestials."

The Rudraksha bead that has a natural opening to allow the string to pass through (not made artifically) is considered to be most sacred and efficacious (Swayameva krutam dwaram Rudrakshesyadhikottamam) and it should also be free from worms and deformities.

It is said that besides the Himalayas, Rudraksha is seen to be growing in Gowdadesa (North Bengal); the region around Mathura and Ayodhya; some part of Ceylon; Malayachala (Southern portion of the Ghats running from the south of Mysore froming the eastern boundary of Travancore); the Sahyan ranges (Western Ghats as far as the junction with the Nilgiris). and Varanasi.

Medical science is beginning to accept that wearing of a genuine Rudraksha has a salutary controlling effect on Blood Pressure, Jaundice, Cancer, etc. The orthodox section has recoginised and accepted it from very early times.

PROF. N.R. KRISHNAMOORTHY

THE GREATNESS OF THE SACRED ASHES – VIBHUTI

It is difficult for the mind engrossed in forms to conceive of a formless state. The aim of all scriptures is to turn the mind inwards towards realising such a state. Sri Ramana Maharshi said that somehow a beginning has to be made towards the path of Truth and effort made to bring about such a turning point. Scriptures, ritual worship, revelations of sages and their teachings, have this aim for their objectives. They are thus not goals but signposts to direct the mind towards the Ultimate in stages, according to the aptitude of the seeker. Gradually the mind becomes attenuated. For the gross mind, gross forms are necessary for worship. When it becomes a subtler "rupa-arupa" (with and without form) worship takes its place. Hence the importance of the Linga worship whose "rupa-arupa" is symbolical of the Oneness of Spirit and Matter, the Self immanent in all manifestations.

Similarly Vibhuti, the Sacred Ashes, is one of the most sacred means of rupa-arupa worship. It represents Lord Siva and denotes primarily the destruction (of samsara and Karma), which is the greatest good or wealth, hence its literal meaning 'Aiswarya' or 'Bhuti' (wealth). Lord Siva's boon to his devotees is always Vairagya or dispassion, and destruction of all limitations, the destruction of non-existent illusion. Everyone can apply Vibhuti irrespective of caste, creed or religion. It has the profound symbolism of reminding one of the transience of all created things ultimately turning to ashes, an incessant process of catabolism ending in earth and ashes, the last stage of burning.

Vibhuti indicates Kala — time. It does not stop there, but reminds us to make efforts to reach Kaalatheetha (the One beyond time namely Lord Siva), turning our minds in the right direction to the Unchangeable amidst changes. Fire inherent in all objects becomes visible only in objects consumed by fire. It is formlessness manifested amidst forms.

In 'Arunachala Mahatmyam' by Eswaraswamy, he says that, as fire makes the cowdung cake take the form of its flame and then remains as sacred ash, so does the Lord give His form to one who attains Him in the fire of meditation and merging in Him remains as Infinite Wisdom.

Saint Gnanasambandha composed a song in praise of the sacred ash 'Tirineeruppathigam' in which he says that the sacred ash is the true form of Lord Siva. The same truth is expressed by the great sage Tayumanavar. When a disciple of this sage asked him how to attain salvation, he was told to be always thinking of death. This would make him onepointed, which would help him to attain the goal. The wearing of Vibhuti induces the thought of the end of the body as ash, and hence the ephemeral condition of everything in the world except the Lord.

The following passages from the talks of His Holiness Sri Samkaracharya of Kanchi Kamakoti Peetham, are relevant to the subject :

Vibhuti (the sacred ash) is held as most sacred and one would necessarily have it smeared over the body. Vibhuti in Sanskrit means wealth, and no wonder it gives all kinds of wealth to one who wears it — I mean the spiritual wealth.

278

Vibhuti which is actually the ash of cow-dung, by itself a great disinfectant and cleanser, can remove the most obnoxious odour conceivable, say even that of such a sharp smelling substance as kerosene.

The very colour of Vibhuti, white, signifies so much. It points out to nothing less than the Paramatman the Supreme Self. As the Geeta says : "Just as fire reduces firewood to ashes, Gnana destroys all Karma." The sacred ash symbolises the Gnana which remains after all karma is burnt out. Anything put into a fire may turn black for a while but eventually it has to turn white. So whiteness is the ultimate state. Iswara is the greatest Vibhuti we smear over our body. Hence the Vibhuti we smear over our body will ultimately take us to Him — of course, if done with the right understanding and attitude.

The smearing of the sacred ashes reminds us of a great principle. Whether one is a prince or a pauper, one has to end up in a handful of ashes. All life is Maya, but is beginningless.

In the Geeta verse quoted, the meaning driven home is not that nothing remains after karma is burnt out, but that what survives is the Supreme Self when everything is put into the fire of Jnana. So the wearing of the Vibhuti emphasises the Reality of the Self and the unreality of the world and its objects.

The example of Sri Bhagavan (Sri Ramana Maharshi) whose daily routine included applying Vibhuti after his bath every morning, has a special significance for his devotees and sadhaks, since he did not particularly advocate orthodoxy or its opposite.

Sri Bhagavan also used to take and wear Vibhuti and Kumkum brought to him on a plate after Arati at the Mother's shrine on important occasions or in connection with special rituals in the Ashram. One vividly recalls Sri Bhagavan's appearance on such occasions and his characteristic posture showing attentiveness adding dignity to the solemnity of the scene. He used to tilt his head backwards and with a steady and even pressure of the fingers rub the Vibhuti on the forehead till a uniform and fairly thick coating was obtained. The tilting of the head was to avoid the Vibhuti falling to the ground which was considered improper.

The hospital room in the Ashram, in which the third operation for the sarcoma on Sri Bhagavan's arm took place, was not equipped with the articles of Sri Bhagavan's daily use. The attendants forgot all about Vibhuti, probably assuming that he may not need it at such a time. But Sri Bhagavan asked one of his attendants whether he did not have Vibhuti with him (Sadhus generally carry a tiny bag of it in the folds of their dress). The attendant did have his Vibhuti and Sri Bhagavan applied it as usual.

SEIN

(Courtesy : The Mountain Path)

SYMBOLISM IN THE OFFERING OF THE COCONUT

There are many rituals among the Hindus, which suggest the mode of transcending the personality layers and realising the Self within. One such ritual is the offering of coconuts in a temple. The coconut represents the Karma Phala or the fruits of one's past actions, which are in the form of one's Vasanas. Offering of a fruit in a temple or to a Guru symbolises the surrendering of such Vasanas.

A coconut has a nice smooth skin covering a mass of twisted and knitted coir within. Beneath the coir is a hard shell, and in the inner portion of the shell is the white kernel containing the milk. Before a coconut is offered to the Lord, the priest removes the skin along with the coir, leaving behind a small tuft of coir at the head of the coconut. The shell is then broken and the tuft is removed to expose the three eyes of the coconut. The milk inside is allowed to flow out at the feet of the Lord.

This ritual has a deep significance. The outer skin represents the gross body which has an external show of beauty, but carries in its bosom an abominable cluster of desires and attachments which comprise the subtle body. Man has to renounce all his desires to the exception of one which is to realise the Truth. The retention of the tuft indicates this idea. When one approaches a Guru with this pointed desire and a spirit of surrender, the Guru breaks the hard shell of the intellect and exposes the pure Satwic Vasanas (the white kernel in the case of the coconut) to the Lord. The last lingering desire to realise the Truth is also transcended which is demonstrated by the plucking of the tuft away and exposing the three "eyes" on the shell. The third eye refers to the "Eye of Wisdom" known as the "Jnana Chakshu" which gives the intuitive vision of the Self. The milk flowing out at the feet of the Lord represents the merging of the individual's self with the Infinite Self.

: KUWAIT YAGNA SOUVENIR – 1972

THE SANKHA OR THE CONCH IN HINDU THOUGHT

The Sankha or the Conch occupies an important place in Hindu thought. It is said to symbolise the Pranava or the mystic symbol OM. The sound that emanates from it is 'Omkar'. Lord Vishnu holds it in one of his hands symbolising Nada Brahma or God in the form of Sound. The Brahma Vaivarta Purana has this to say of the Sankha :

> "Sankha sabdo bhaved yatra
> Tatra Lakshmischa susthira
> Sa snatha : sarvateertheshu
> Ya : snatha : Sankhavarini
> Sankhe Hareradhishtanam
> Yata : Sankho tato Har :
> Tatraiva satatam Lakshmi
> Dooribhootaamamgalam"

Where the sound of the Conch is heard, there stays Lakshmi (wealth and prosperity) forever. He who bathes in the water from the Conch, bathes in all the holy waters. The Conch is the abode of Lord Hari. Where the Conch is, there Hari resides. There stays Lakshmi driving away all inauspiciousness."

Sankha Sadma Purana says :

> "Kapilaksheeramadaya
> Sankhe snatwa Janardanam
> Yajana-ayutasya sahasrasya
> Snapayitwa labhedphalam
> Kshiptwa Gangodakam Sankhe

283

Ya : snapayati Madhavam
Namo Narayanetyuktwa
Muchyate yonisankatath
Darsanenapi Sankhasya
Kimu tasyarchanenacha
Vilayam yanti papani
Hima Suryodaye yada.''

One who bathes Lord Janardana with the milk of a black cow, from a Conch, enjoys the fruit of performing a million Yagnas. One who bathes Madhava with Ganga water, from a Conch, uttering "OM Namo Narayanaaya" will escape all further births. While the mere sight of a Conch dispels all the sins as the Sun dispels the fog, why talk of its worship?

The origin of the Conch is described in the Brahma Vaivarta Purana as follows :

Lord Siva took from Hari the Trident, which shone resplendently like a thousand mid-day Suns, and flung it playfully against the Asuras. The Asuras with all their chariots were burnt to ashes as a result, and consigned into the sea in the end. Those ashes formed themselves into Conches of different varieties which became invested with holiness for the worship of the Gods.

DAKSHINAVARTA.

Among the Conches the Dakshinavarta or the right turned Conch is said to be rare, most auspicious and of the highest value. Its highest market-value is thus accounted for by its rarity and its great virtues described in the Varaha and Skanda Puranas.

In the former it is said that one who bathes in the water from such a Conch is freed from all sins.

Incidentally, the water from a Sankha should never be sipped but respectfully received in the palm of the right hand and sprinkled on one's head with devotion.

About this Dakshinavarta Sankha the Skanda Purana says :

"Dakshinavarta-sankhasya toyena yo-archayet Hareem Sapta Janmakrutam papam tadkshanaadeva nasyati".

Bathing Lord Hari with water from a Dakshinavarta Sankha will instantly remove one's sins accumulated through the past seven lives.

The right-turned Sankha is also considered a ratna or jewel.

On the sea-shores of Saurashtra and other places, it is said, Sankhas are found. Of these the best ones are those that are shiny, soft, white as the moon, with pointed ends and rather heavy. Of these some have the cavity turned to the right. They are the Dakshinavartas. Most of them have the cavity turned to the left. They are called Vamavartas. About the Dakshinavarta Sankhas it is said :

"Dakshinavarta Sankhastu Kuryaadaayu yaso dhanam".

i.e. "Dakshinavarta Sankhas will bestow on the possessor long life, fame and wealth". The above effects are in proportion to its largeness, sheen and whiteness. Should there be some blemishes even in such a Conch, when mounted on gold the defects and the harm will be overcome.

Conches were used as bugles in war, and in ancient India each warrior had his special famous conch. For instance Lord Krishna's Conch was known by the name "Panchajanya", that of Arjuna as "Devadutta", that of Bhima as " Poundra Khadga"; "Ananta Vijaya" of Yudhishtira; "Sughosha" of Nakula and "Mani-pushpaka" of Sahadeva.

The god, Kubera, is said to possess a mystical treasure or Nidhi by name "Sankha". That accounts for his inexhaustible wealth.

According to Samudrika Sastra, lines resembling a Conch on one's palm or sole makes one exalted and rich like a king. The Science of Omens too considers the Sankhanaada or the sound of the Conch as very auspicious.

The therapeutical properties of the Conch are said to lie in the cure of the effects of the disturbance of Pitha and Vatha, and endowing beauty and strength.

V.A.K. AIYAR

THE PURNA KUMBHA

The representation of the Purna Kumbha at Sanchi, Brihat, Mathura, Begram, Amaravati, Nagarjunakonda, Anuradhapura, Borodudur and several other places, and on ancient Indian coins and seals in the form of a decorated pot placed on a pedestal from which the leaves, buds and flowers of a lotus come out, poses the problem as to how this art form originated.

Unfortunately the sculptures and architectural pieces of a period anterior to those of Bharhut and Sanchi, are few and far between in India, Ceylon and Java. We get no representation of Purna Kumbha on Mauryan terracotta panels nor do we get many representations of this form on the Indus Valley seals. There is only one seal at Chanhudaro where the Purna Kumbha motif is seen.

In the Indus Valley civilisation and later, in the Mauryan period, however, we get earthern pots bearing lotus designs on them. We can therefore presume that they might have been used as Purna Kumbha by filling them with water and putting flowers and leaves on them.

Harbinger of good fortune.

Today, in India, the Purna Kumbha is decorated with the design of Swastika, etc. and filled with water. The leaves of five trees, the Aswatha, the Vata, the Amra, the Pansa and the Bakula, (Ficus Religiosa, Ficus Indica, Mangiferra Indica, Artocarpus Integrifolia and Mimusope Elanga) are put in its mouth and a bowl of rice with a coconut at the top is placed over it.

It is supposed to be a harbinger of good fortune and success in life. We get references to people placing Purna Kumbha at the doors of their houses, in Skanda Purana. We also have a reference to the worship of Purna Kumbha in the Matsya Purana.

God Varuna

Much akin to this is the Purna Kumbha used today for worshipping Varuna in our marriages and other functions. At Rameshwaram, even today, a decorated Kumbha full of water is placed during the temple-ritual to represent Varuna.

The association of Varuna, the god of the seas, with the Purna Kumbha seems to be based on the conception that the seas brought wealth or that people trading by the seas amassed riches.

We get a reference to Purna Kalasa in the Rig-Veda where the pot is full of water and appears to be connected with Indra, the god of rain, who brought in his turn agricultural prosperity.

"Apurna asva kalasah svaha sekteva kosam sisice pibadhavai Pradakshinidabhi somas Indram" — Overflowing is the vase of the Yajamana, glory to him. As a bounteous power I have filled the cup for you all to drink."

In another hymn we have a reference to a Kalasa made of gold. The worship of the Kalasa finds mention in yet another hymn :

"Etani bhadra Kalasa Kryama Kuru Sravana dadato maghani."

Another word for Kalasa we get in the Rig-Veda is Kumbha, which evidently denotes an earthern pot and used to be employed for carrying water.

"Satam Kumbha asinctam Surayah."

The Lotus Motif

However, we do not get any reference regarding the association of Kalasa or Kumbha with the Lotus in this Samhita.

In the Atharvaveda we find people wishing to have the Kumbha full of honey and the Kalasa full of curds. A reference to the Purna Kumbha in the Atharvaveda is where womenfolk are asked to bring such pots to the Yagnasala for the success of the sacrifice. At another place we get in the Atharva Veda :-

"Purna Kumbhodhi Kala ahitastam vai pasyame bahudha nu santah". "The Purna Kumbha is the firm substratum of time, we behold it manifesting in various forms." Here we have the endless stream of time compared to the liquid of the vase which is the source of its fulness.

In Vajasaneyi Samhita also we come across the word Kumbha but not Purna Kumbha.

Thus we see that a pot full of water had some special significance and was usually considered the bestower of good fortune.

In other Religions

The word "Ghatha Katah" is used in Chullavagga for the water pot, and "Purna Ghata" often occurs in Pali. We get a reference to "Purna Ghata Parimandita ghars" in Dhammapada Atthakatha, which points to the belief current even in those days regarding the auspicious character of this symbol.

This word "Ghata" to denote a pot appears in Sanskrit literature at a later date : for Painini explains 'Ghata' to mean 'intensely occupied or busy'. It is only in Manu Smriti and the Yagnavalkya Smriti that we find the word 'ghata' used for the water pot. The word

"Kumbha" is however older. In Manimekhalai also we get a reference to the pot full of water. "Do therefore decorate the city; the great royal roads and the halls of faultless learning; put in ther appropriate places jars full of water, seed-vessels with budding sprouts, and statues holding lamps."

The Lotus and Lakshmi

The connection of Lakshmi with the Lotus is too well-known to need any elaboration, but the Lotus also represents the "tree of life" springing from the navel of Vishnu as mentioned in the Lalitavistara. It is therefore not surprising to find Varuna or Budha being worshipped with a Purna Kumbha with lotus flowers coming out of it.

From these references we conclude that the philosophy of the full-blooming, over-flowing contents of life comparable to the plants and foliage luxuriating from the mouth of a jar filled with life-giving fluid (Jivana) is present in our Vedic literature and has continued to exert its influence on the Indian mind afterwards.

An Indigenous Idea

Thus we can be sure that this idea was indigenous and ancient as we get the first representation of a Purna Kumbha with lotus flowers in one of the seals of the Indus Valley mentioned earlier.

How did the idea of a Purna Kumbha, which was adopted as a popular art motif, originate?

Its shape from a simple earthen pot with leaves and flowers — a poor man's image of the goddess of fortune, Lakshmi-developed, as time passed, into an elaborately decorative symbol which was considered auspicious and the bestower of luck and prosperity.

290

As such, it was later employed to decorate the border of the panels, the door jambs, the crown of the pillars, the capitals of the temples, the 'Sikhara' of the Stupas and the like.

– Hari Om –

DR. RAI GOVINDA CHANDRA

THE SALAGRAMA

Note : (Generally people pronounce this word as 'Saligrama', but the correct Sanskrit word is "Salagrama". The word 'Salagraman' is one of the names of Vishnu. The origin of this word is traced to a remote village called "Salagrami" near the source of the river Gandaki in Nepal. There Vishnu is known as "Salagraman" and it is a piligrim centre too. The stones used there to prepare the image of Vishnu came to be called "Salagrama". There, in the Gandaki river, "Salagramas" are natural formations of stones, which are worshipped as different types of Salagramas. – Refer to Mahabharata, Vana Parva, Chapter 84, Stanzas 123 to 125.

(Er)

"Aajanmakruta paapaanaam
Praayaschittam ya Icchati
Salagramasilavahi
Paapahaari namostute :"

"Obeisance unto you, O water, sanctified by the washing of Salagrama ! You grant deliverance unto him who seeks you, from all sins accumulated from birth."

Amongst the valued possessions and hallowed objects of worship in a devout Hindu's home, are the Salagramas, those pebble-like objects, smooth to the touch, spheroid in shape, and black, red, or mixed in colour, and kept closed in the Puja box.

That they are, for the most part, a hereditary possession of the family, handed down from generation to generation, is sufficient testimony to the veneration bestowed upon them by our ancients. Not to be purchased

292

or sold, it is a prized gift or dana, and it is given as a valued gift in some places to the bridegrooms along with the bride.

The salagramasila is considered the embodiment of Vishnu. Its mantra has Shri Bhagvan for Rishi or Drashta, and Narayana as Devata or the object of worship.

The Salagrama is a peculair kind of stone which is normally found in the river Gandaki in Nepal.

> *"Gandakyamcha uttare teere*
> *Girirajasya dakshine*
> *Dasayojana vistheernaam*
> *Mahakshetra Vasundharaa*
> *Salagramo Mahadevo*
> *Devi Dwaravati bhaved*
> *Ubhayossangamo yatra*
> *Muktisttattra na samsaya."*

"To the north of the river, Gandaki (also called Narayani), and south of the Himalayas, there is the holy region of Salagrama, which is ten yojanas extent, where Dwaravati merges into Salagrama. Undoubtedly such a place is capable of vouchsafing Moksha."

Actually, about 140 miles from Khatmandu, is situated Muktimati or Muktikshetra, also called "Salagrama-kshetra".

Salagramas are distinct from the oval 'lingas' in that the former have some sort of a natural cavity drilled into them. Besides, there will be several natural markings like Sankha, Chakra, etc. on them.

Legend has it that once Brahma was exasperated at the rate of increase of the sinners among his creation. Then drops of sweat rolled down his cheeks (Ganda), ultimately collecting themselves into the form of a female child calling herself 'Gandaki'. She took it into

293

her head to do a severe penance which became so over-
whelming that the Devas started trembling before her.
As usual they offered her the bait of a boon in return for
her stopping her penance, but they met a Tartar in her, for
she wanted to mother all the Devas.

Not having the power to grant such a boon, the
Devas pleaded their inability, at which Gandaki became
furious and cursed all the Devas to be born as worms
on the earth below. The Devas in their turn placed a
countercurse on her head that she should become 'Jada'
or inert matter.

Naturally, Brahma was concerned with this unex-
pected development. Unable to find a way out, he con-
sulted Indra and Rudra. With them also he drew a blank.
Finally, all the three turned to Vishnu, who said : "Inas-
much as the curses have been already pronounced, they
cannot be revoked, and both the parties affected must
suffer them. The problem is how to make them work to
their mutual and ultimatley universal benefit."

After consideration, Vishnu said : "I shall take up my
abode in the Chakra Teertha near Salagramakshetra. You,
Devas, shall migrate to this hallowed region as 'Vajrakitas'
eating into the pebbles. Gandaki shall in the form of a river
fill the universe enveloping the shilas hallowed by me."

Thus it would seem Salagrama stones are but divine
manifestations of Lord Vishnu cum the Devas. There are
othher legends too.

There are also found on Salagrama slabs certain
stripes, looking like the conch, the discus, etc., which are
usually seen on the outside as well as the inside. Based
upon these distinct marks, the Salagramas are classified
as different manifestations of Lord Vishnu. Here are
some of them :-

"Naanavarnamayam chaiva
Naana bhogena veshtitam
Tatha Varaprasadena
Lakshmikantham vadamyaham"

One that is multi-coloured and surrounded on all
sides by snake-like hoods is called "Lakshmikantha". It
is said that this is a veritable treasure as it is capable
of giving what all one wants.

"Narayanodbhavo deva
Chakramadhye cha karmana
Tatha varaprasadena
Lakshmikantham vadamyaham"

That which carries the symbol of a discus inside, is
also called Lakshmikantha, with identical results.

"Krishne silatale yatra
Sookshmam chakram sudryusyate
Soubhagyam santateem dhatte
Sarvasoukhyam dadaticha"

That Salagrama, which being black in colour carries
a fine replica of the discus in it, is capable of besotwing
on the owner, great happiness, wealth, health and children.

"Sreedhara : sukare vame
Haridvarnastu drusyate
Vasudevasyachinhani
Drushtwa papai : pramuchyate"

That which contains emblems of Sri Krishna, like
green colour on the left side, will drive away all sins at
the very sight of it.

That which contains the symbol of the tortoise or
the foot of the cow, is called Varaha . Yellow colour
denotes the Devas; the red ones are fearful as they are
said to represent the Narasimha form; but they are said to

be capable of giving Moksha. One with the symbol of a conch is said to be Vamana. Damodara will be a large one, at the centre of which there will be the marking of a discus. Also there will be yellow rays and a large cavity.

The shape of an umbrella will make one a monarch; a circular one will give plenty of wealth. One that has the shape of a flat nose will bring grief, and that which has a pointed edge will lead to war.

If the forehead of a Salagrama has the look of a serpent's hood, or has the golden shine, or a discus of golden hue, it is 'Vamadeva' and is good.

If the Salagrama has a resemblance of Lakshmi Nrisimha, back on the left and down on the right, or the figure has an elongated lip, it will bring utter penury; if it has reddish lips, disaster; if holding the Chakra, will cause ill health; if actually cleaving, then positive death.

It is clear from the above that icons too are permitted to be carved out of Salagrama stones, as indeed are the idols of Badrinath Temple and other famous temples. Adi Samkara is reputed to have established a Salagrama Nrisimha at Badari. Famous deities are made to wear garlands made of Salagrama beads.

Now, no blemish is attached to the Salagrama even if it is broken or defaced, burnt in fire, or otherwise disfigured. It does no harm.

The worship of Salagrama does not call for elaborate Puja; not even mantras, sacred water etc. are necessary. Its very presence assures happiness.

Normally it is worshipped with the Purushasookta mantra. It is said that its presence at Sraddha ceremonies is most pleasing to the souls of the ancestors.

> "Brahmahatyadikam paapam
> Mano vak-kaya sambhavam

Seeghram nasyati tatsarvam
Salagramasilarchanaat"

All sins including even Brahmahatya (killing of a Brahmin) and those accruing out of the activities of our mind, words and body, all die instantaneously with the worship of the Salagrama.

One should sprinkle the water sanctified by the bathing of a Salagrama on one's head and wear the Tulsi used in its worship on the head, and partake of the food offered to Vishnu (in the shape of the Salagrama). One who does so will live for several aeons in Vaikuntha. The sipping of the sanctified water purges one of all the sins accrued in crores of births. Therefore, one should not spill the sanctified water on the earth, which will multiply one's sins eightfold.

In the Padma Purana, Lord Samkara explains the significance of Salagrama to his son Skanda wherein he quotes Vishnu as having affirmed :

"Nivasaami sadaa Sambho
Salagramodbhavosmani".

"O Siva ! I always abide in the Salagrama stone".

What more proof is needed than the declaration of Lord Siva Himself ?

"Mallinga kotibhidrushtii :
Yad phalam poojiti : sthuthai :
Salagrama silayaamtu
Ekasyamiva tad bhaved"

"The Punya obtained by seeing and worshipping crores of my Lingas is equivalent to that obtained by worshipping a single Salagrama"

. **NISHKINCHIN**

OUR GODS AND THEIR VEHICLES

The Hindu Scriptures abound with an innumerable number of gods and goddesses doing several functions and helping their devotees in several ways. Almost all of them have *Vahanas* of their own, which they make use while moving about. Who are these gods, and how did the Rishis come to know of these *Vahanas* ? Why are particular *Vahanas* allocated to particular gods ? A study of this aspect of Hinduism makes an interesting reading.

A devotee full of sweet love for the Lord, needs the concept of the Lord in a personal form, whom he can serve with love. He derives joy out of such service. When he is in difficulties, the devotee requires the prop of the personal god, so that he can touch the feet of the Lord and pour out his sorrows. The great Rishis, knowing the need of the human heart, provided sufficient variety of forms of gods, that would give succour to the devotee when invoked with intense love. In order to keep the devotee's mind fixed upon the Lord, various stories and incidents connected with each form of gods have also been narrated. The *Vahanas* attributed to the various gods are part of this process of bringing to the finite mind the glories of the Infinite Lord. A devotee invoking a god gets the vision of the god as described by the Scriptures, through the intensity of his feeling. The god is real to him. But it does not stop here. This intense love ultimately turns the attention of the devotee to the presence of the Supreme Lord in his own bosom. He finds his identity with the Supreme and attains Salvation. Thus the Rishis undertook the double-task of providing with an outer prop to the loving mind, and an inner guidance to the evolved intellect, of the Sadhak when they conceived the forms of gods and their *Vahanas*.

Each god represents a particular potency which can be attained by a Sadhak by controlling a negative tendency and by cultivating a positive tendency. The *Vahanas* of a god indicates a wrong quality which has been controlled by riding over it; or a helpful quality that carries the potency to be cultivated.

Again, the expressions of the Supreme Reality are found in the world in various capacities, sustaining the world show by bringing forth varied experiences to the individuals through the changing phenomena in the world. All these expressions are called gods or goddesses and the *Vahanas* that are attributed to these gods and goddesses are suggestive of the nature of the power that is expressed through them in order to discharge the function.

A close examination of the well-known gods and goddesses and their *Vahanas* will give us an idea of the amount of wisdom that is hidden in the seemingly simple and silly descriptions.

THE TRIMURTHIS

Brahma, Vishnu and Maheshwara, are the Trinity in charge of the creation, sustenance and destruction of the world. Hamsa Garuda and Vrishabha are their respective Vahanas. Hamsa is a bird that is stated to have the capacity to separate milk from water and drink only the milk from a mixture of milk and water. This is indicative of a discriminative intelligence, which faculty is an essential requisite for the creation of anything. Hence Brahma is said to be carried by Hamsa. Maintenance of the world requires the continuous demand of the people who dwell in it. An individual in the world really sustains the continuity of the world. His three aspects, as Knower through the intellect, as Enjoyer through his mind, and as Doer through his body, demand the continuation of the world. The knowledge and enjoyment are interdependent and vary simultaneously, while the actions of a man affect his knowledge and enjoyment too. Thus Garuda, having the two wings of mind and intellect balanced by the tail of the body, is the carrier of Vishnu. Thirdly, the destruction of the world or the individual takes place when the vasanas which necessitated the creation have been shed and there is no need for continuing the manifestation in that particular pattern any more. Vrishbha is called so because of this shedding. (Varshanaat Vrishabha .... Nirukta 9-22). Hence Siva is stated to be carried by a Vrishabha.

Besides their functions aforesaid, the Trimurthis have their own families, most of the family members having Vahanas of their own. In their family background the gods give us another message.

BRAHMA'S FAMILY

Brahma's spouse is Saraswati, the goddess of learning. Sanaka, Sanandana, Sanatana and Sanatkumara are his our mind-born sons, who are great Jnanis, while Narada is another son, who is a great devotee and goes about propogating Bhakti in all the three worlds. Saraswati also has Hamsa for her Vahana while none of the sons is endowed with any Vahana. Creative power, knowledge, inner realisation, and outer glorification of the Lord are all based upon one quality, namely, that of the discriminative faculty. The experience within and the expression in the outer world are the outcome of the wisdom and the creative urge. Hence the sons have no Vahanas of their own.

'Hamsa' is an abbreviation of the twin terms "Aha Sah" : (I am He). The creation is a manifestation of the

Lord moving in time-space continuum. Everything in creation moves incessantly declaring "I am He". The sun, the moon and the stars move in their respective orbits proclaiming "I am He". The wind blows, the water flows, and the earth rotates and revolves, constantly declaring "I am He". The trees wave their branches, the bird fly and the fish swim declaring "I am He". The breath of the sun comes out and goes in declaring "I am He". Thus the whole creation is proclaiming the great truth that, all that is seen and heard is "He". This is Brahma on Hamsa. He who understands this becomes enlightened and released from the bonds of matter.

VISHNU'S FAMILY

Vishnu has two spouses, Sridevi and Bhudevi. One son is Brahma, the Creator, and the other son is Manmatha or Cupid. Vishnu and his two spouses are carried by Garuda. Brahma has Hamsa, while the other son Manmatha has Suka or the Parrot for his *Vahana* Bhudevi is static and motionless, while Sridevi or Lakshmi is restless and fickle. Vishnu is thus the Lord of all that is moving and unmoving in the world. All the three are carried by the individual who is endowed with the three equipments of body, mind and intellect. These equipments are for ever hooked on to the world and thus the world is sustained. To them are born the offsprings, the creative genius on Hamsa, the discriminative faculty, and the deluder, Manmatha, who rides on Suka. The Parrot is a bird which repeats everything that it hears without knowing its meaning. Where the discrimination is lacking, the result of living in the world is only delusion. The man falls into the snares of the world and gets tied down.

When a man makes use of the discriminative faculty and lives properly developing the two wings of devotion and knowledge, and also cultivates the tail of Karma Yoga that propels him forward, he rises like an eagle in his meditation and becomes a *Vahana* of the Lord—meaning one through whom the Lord reaches the hearts of other people. He even supports the total world by his glorious experience.

In some texts there is a mention that Lakshmi Devi has her own *Vahana* namely *Uluka* or the owl. The message is clear. The owl is a bird that is blind during the day, and it cannot see what is obvious to others. So too is a man who has love for material wealth alone, but has no devotion to the Lord. Leaving the Lord, if a man adores the goddess of wealth alone, he is lost. He wastes away his life and opportunities in vain pursuits. The other spouse of *Vishnu,* namely Bhudevi,being static, has no need for a *Vahana.*

SIVA'S FAMILY

Siva also has two spouses, Parvati and Ganga. Seated on the head is Ganga, and sharing half the body is Parvati. They automatically use the *Vrishabha* as their *Vahana* too. Independently Ganga rides on *Makara* or the crocodile . Parvati rides on *Simha* or the lion . Their sons Vinayaka and Kumara,with the *Mooshika* and the *Mayura* as their respective *Vahanas.*

As the god of destruction (constructive destruction at that), Siva requires two things, Matter that perishes, and movement that creates time. In 'time' alone everything gets destroyed. Parvati represents the matter that undergoes continuous destruction and Ganga represents the movement. "Gam...Gam..." going is her nature. In movement, time is perceived, and the changes are seen. Thus Lord Siva, along with his two spouses who are the aspects representing matter and movement, rides on the Vrishabha. Every creation is intended for the "load-shedding" of a set of *Vasanas.* When the scheduled *Vasanas* are shed, the destruction takes place.

In the combination of Matter and Spirit, the individual is born with his higher personality of discriminative intelligence, and his lower personality, namely the man perceiving and enjoying the world around him. These two selves are depicted as Vinayaka on the mouse, and Kumara on the peacock. Vinayaka's elephant sized head, with the trunk both sensitive and powerful, indicates the superior intelligence that can keep the destructive ego, the mouse, under control. Before the discriminative intelligence, the ego looks ridiculously small, because the raptures of a fine cultured intellect cannot be compared to the silly joys of an egoistic man. Hence the huge Vinayaka on the tiny *Mooshika*.

The six-headed Kumara is the psychic personality of the five senses and the mind seeking the joys of the objective world and riding over the most beautiful but vain body called the peacock. Every man is in fact a Kumara riding over the peacock of the physical body. But the ordinary man becomes a real Kumara, a god fit to be worshipped, only if he does what Kumara's peacock does. The *Mayura* always keeps a writhing snake under its feet. The snake of ego is to be kept under complete control if a man wishes to transcend the sorrows of the world.

Siva's destruction comes every now and then whenever a man's life-span is over. But it is not the final end, because we are born again and again to exhaust our *vasanas*. How to attain the final salvation? The *Vrishabha* indicates how. Nirukta (9-22) gives another derivative meaning for Vrishbha : "Atibrihati reta iti", i.e., roots out of the seed. When a Sadhak serves the Lord faithfully just as an ordinary bull serves his master day in and day out, without demanding or seeking anything for himself, then this very attitude sheds the seed of vasanas and he will no more be born again. The Vrishabha attitude is the carrier of the most auspicious of all, the release from the bondage of life.

Ganga Devi in her independent role is *Vahini.* As explained above, she is movement personified. Gam...Gam...Gam...l that is, going. By the movement 'time' is made. *Makara'* means the maker of time. Ma + Ka = time + maker.

Parvati Devi rides the *Simha* or the lion Parvati has two aspects. Turned away from Siva, she is known as *Avidya Maya.* Turned towards Siva she is known as *Vidya Maya.* Turned away from the Spirit she rides over the *Simha* curelty personified All harshness and cruelty emanate from the forgetfulness of Spirit. When the same matter-vestures are used to reach the Lord, Parvati is Vidya Maya leading the Sadhak nearer to the Lord. Then she is riding on Simha, which is derived by the reversal of 'himsa'. (Himse va syat vipareetascha-Nirukta 3-18) Cruelty reversed is kindness. A Sadhak dedicated to the Lord can never be unkind to others.

As Rajarajeswari, the Mother of the three worlds, Creatrix of all, she rides over all the animals in her various forms and aspects. 'Lalitha Sahasranama' makes mention of all her aspects and the *Vahanas* too. In fact as Mother Nature, she rides over all forms and is carried by all of them.

ASHTA-DIKPALAS OR LOKPALAS

The eight quarters are protected by eight deities cumulatively known as *'Dikpalas',* the protectors of the quarters or *'Lokapalas',* the protectors of the world. They are invariably mentioned in the following order :-
East – Indra on *Airavata*S the elephant, and *Ucchaisravas* the horse.
South-East – Agni ōn *Mesha* or the he-goat
South – Yama on *Mahisha* or the he-buffaloe
South-West – *Nirurti* on Aswa or the horse
West – Varuna on *Makara* or the crocodile
North-West – Vayu on *Mruga* or the deer

North — Kubera on *Nara* or man
North-East — Isana on *Vrishabha*

The world is no doubt maintained and guided by the Supreme through its various expressions, but the direction in which the world moves and its duration are determined by the cumulative tendencies and attitudes of the denizens of the world. These tendencies are responsible for the creation of the world, and its running. These tendencies and propensities are termed as the protectors of 'Dik' or the directons and also of 'Loka' or the perceivable worlds. They are always mentioned in a particular order since they are in a series, one leading to the other, and finally culminating in the projection and continuation of the world. The names of the gods as well as their *vahanas*, play a significant part in indicating the stages of development.

1) INDRA ON AIRAVATA AND UCHHAISRAVAS

Indra is the perceiving ego (Idam Darsanaat Indra : Nirukta 10-8) and Iravata is *Gaja* an elephant. Airavata means pertaining to Ira or matter. Gaja is from 'Gaj', to get confused. Indra on *Airavata* is the ego that gets confused by its fascination for matter.

Uchhaisravas is an Aswa or horse. The word Uchhaisravas means 'high knowledge'. 'Aswa' means the 'great eater' (Mahasano bhavat — Nirukta 2-27) Indra on *Uchhaisravas* thus means the ego which is the seeker of high knowledge.

Thus the beginning point of the direction of the individual or the total Cosmos is in two directions, getting confused with material enjoyments or seeking higher evolution. This begins with the ego.

2) AGNI ON MESHA

'Agni' means 'leading' (Nitat-Nirukta 7-14) *Mesha* is so called from 'winking' (Mishate — Nirukta 3-16) Wink-

305

ing is a sign of thinking.

The second stage is the leading in thought of what the ego has provided as basis. The thought moves towards the material side of the evolutionary aspect.

3) YAMA ON MAHISHA

Yama means control. It can be self-control, as well as a limitation which puts limits over one's capacity. *Mahisha* means greatness, and also indicates the dullness of the buffalo.

Thus the third stage indicates what follows. When an ego is moving in the direction of higher knowledge, self-control becomes the natural characteristic feature of such a personality, and this self-control is carried by loftiness and greatness. When the ego is heading towards the materialistic enjoyments, the animal of ignorance puts limitations and controls over the personality.

4) NIRURTI ON ASWA

Nirurti means both enjoyment and calamity (Niramanaat – Richata : Nirukta 2-7). *Aswa* here indicates runner (Asnuveet Aswa – Nirukta 1-12).

The fourth direction is towards enjoyment or fall, both speedily in the path of evolution or devolution earlier taken.

5) VARUNA ON MAKARA

Varuna means both the choicest things, and the veiling. (Varuna : Vrunoti : Ni. 10-3) Makara is the hand of time or the hand of measure, namely the limitations of the world.

The world that we get or understand will be in accordance with the direction that is given earlier. A man on the path of evolution gets the choicest things in the limited world while the man in the path of devolution

306

gets veiled by the limitations of the world.

6) VAYU ON MRUGA

Vayu means arrival. (Eteh : Ni : 10-1) *Mruga* means that which goes in death or the perishable world. Finally the man appears in the world of changes.

7) KUBERA ON NARA

Kubera is in charge of all the wealth of the gods. He is reputed to have three teeth and eight legs. The gods are the sense-faculties, and their wealth is the objective world of matter. This matter is eight-fold Prakruti, which always moves and hence is described as having eight legs representing the eight directions. The world of matter gets ready for the man who arrives as described above. The world is perceived by the man by the Triputi – the seer, the seen and the seeing. These three are the three teeth of Kubera, who is carried by the Nara. The individual sustains the world with his preceptions.

8) ISANA ON VRISHABHA

When , each individual thus makes or mars this life by the direction taken by him, the one direction in which the Lord Isana guides the world, is towards the pouring out of the accumulated *vasanas.* 'Vrishabha' is the pouring out (Varshanaat : Ni : 9-22). The Lord comes riding over the *Vrishabha* to exhaust the accumulated vasanas of the Jeevas.

The stopping of all the directions is the final culmination of all Sadhana. To indicate this, in the ritualistic Pooja, before the actual Pooja starts, Ashta-Dik-Bandhana is done. Then the mind of the individual is arrested from taking any direction. He discovers his own true nature.

307

THE NAVAGRAHAS

The Navagrahas are the nine gods worshipped together in the temples. They are :-

1) Surya on the one-wheeled chariot drawn by seven horses,
2) Chandra on a white chariot drawn by ten horses,
3) Kuja on *Mesha* or the he-goat,
4) Budha on *Simha* or the lion.
5) Guru on *Hamsa,*
6) Sukra on *Mandooka* or the frog,
7) Sani on *Kaka* or the crow,
8) Rahu on *Simha* or the Lion, and
9) Kethu on *Grudhra.*

The nine Grahas represent the sun, the moon and the five planets : Kuja (Mars); Budha (Mercury); Guru (Jupiter); Sukra (Venus); Sani (Saturn); which are nearest to the earth in the order of their distances from the Sun, and finally Rahu and Kethu, which are the ascending and the descending nodes of the moon as it enters and ecliptic and leaves it. These nine are said to have the greatest influence on the physical and psychic conditions of the living beings on the earth. Thus they have a very important place in Astrology. The future of a being is decided by the position of these nine in the Zodiac at the time of his birth. Whenever an individual or society is passing through difficult times, "Navagraha Santi" is performed in the temples according to pre-scribed rites.

Astrology is not a mere superstition of gazing at the stars and making fantastic predictions, but is based upon the firm tenets of the doctrine of Karma and rebirth, of Hinduism. Every individual is born to go through his Prarabdha and exhaust his urgent vasanas by performing certain actions. Thus he chooses a par-ticular time and place to be born, when and where he can live a life suited for the purpose. The time of his birth at that particular conjunction of the planets indicates his fate if a correct assessment can be made by the astrologers. Since it is the individual's mental mood that decides his world and the position of the planets, the Sastras prescribe the Poojas and Santis to change his mental mood and thereby his world. The same rule applies even to the country. The world is arranged by the psychology of a nation and can be re-ordered and shaped by changing the psychology into a better one.

As in all else, the Navagraha deities do not stop by this mere indication. They have a deeper message to convey. The position in which the deities have to be installed in the temples gives an inkling as to what they are actually meant to represent to man. The idols are to be installed with the Sun in the centre. The other eight deities stand surrounding him in such a way that no deity faces another. The Sun in the centre also faces none of them. The eight Grahas surrounding the Sun represent the eight-fold lower nature of the Lord, and the Sun represents the higher nature of the Lord which becomes the Jeeva. The world play is the play of the two natures of the Lord attracting, catching and pulling one another. Since the nine catch one another, they are called the Navagrahas, the nine Catchers. All the restlessness of man is due to the mutual attraction of these two. When a man knows how to keep the two natures within him separate from one another, he stands at peace with himself and with the world around.

How to separate these two? A new understanding of the position is to be gained. 'Nava Graha' literally means a "New Grasp". An investigation into the names of the deities and their *vahanas* gives us the new understanding about life and its mysteries.

1) SURYA ON A RATHA DRAWN BY SEVEN ASWAAS

Surya means 'promoter' (Sveeryate – Ni. 12-14) 'Ratha' means 'movement'. (Ranhate iti Ratha : Ni. 9-11) *Sapta Aswa* stands for the seven types of appetites (Aswa Mahaasano bhavati – Ni. 2-27). The superior nature of the Lord entering into the individual *vasanas* promotes the seven types of appetites – of the five senses, the mind and the intellect.

2) CHANDRA ON A RATHA DRAWN BY DASA ASWA

Chandra means the allurer. (Chandate : Ni. 11-5) Dasa stands for the sense objects, (drishtaartha : Ni. 3-10) Aswa means 'ephemeral' (Na + Swa = No tomorrow). To the Jeeva who is hungering for the lure of the sense objects offered by the world.

3) KUJA ON MESHA

Kuja means stealing, from Kuj : to steal. *Mesha* is winking, that is thinking. (Mishate : Ni. 3-16) A continuous brooding on or thinking about the attractive objects steals the individual away.

4) BUDHA ON SIMHA

Budha means recognition. A knowledge of how the wisdom is being stolen away comes to man on self-mastery. *Simha* means 'mastering'. (Sahanaat Simha : Ni. 3-18). A man of self-control alone can recognise how he is becoming a slave to the sense-objects by his unintelligent brooding over them.

5) GURU ON HAMSA

Guru means the remover of darkness. *Hamsa* is that mythical bird that is capable of separating milk from a mixture of milk and water, accepting only the milk and rejecting the water in it. Thus the actual removal of the ignorant attraction is not by recognition alone but by proper discrimination.

6) SUKRA ON MANDOOKA

Sukra means bright illumination. It comes on satisfaction. *Mandooka* means those who dwell in satisfaction, (Manda Esham Oka iti : Ni. 9-15) on perfect contentment and applying themselves to the contemplation of the higher Reality, when the illumination dawns.

7) SANI ON KAKA

Sani means slowness and laziness. *Kaka* means that which is to be driven out. (Apakalayitavyo bhavati : Ni. 3-18). In the matter of Sadhana, there should be no relaxation or laziness — such tendencies should be firmly eliminated.

8) RAHU ON SIMHA

Rahu is the combinatioin of two roots Raa and Hu, meaning to surrender and offer in sacrifice respectively. Simha is Himsa turned back, that is non-injury cultivated. Non-injury is the carrier of the spirit of surrender and sacrifice to the Lord.

9) KETHU ON GRIDHRA

Kethu means *Prajna* (Ni. 3-9) or Pure Consciousness. *Gridhra* is from the root *Grigh* which means to endeavour to gain. An effort to gain Consciousness is the carrier of the Knowledge, which cannot be gained without proper effort.

A new understanding of the true position thus gives peace to the individual because he perceives clearly that he can get what all he wishes to gain, by proper application, in the right direction. Nothing outside can any more trouble him.

The Hindu Scriptures make use of all imaginable symbols and forms to convey to man the true goal of life, the ultimate human destiny, what is to be done and what is to be avoided in order to gain or attain it. In the esoteric mission of the Scriptures, the *Vahanas* of the various deities play quite a significant part.

— HARI OM —

SWAMINI SARADAPRIYANANDAA

THE BULL – NANDI

*(The Vrushabha or Nandi
in the Siva Temple)*

The Bull is conceived in our Puranas as the vehicle of Lord Siva. Puranas are not meaningless and absurd stories, as many people are prone to take them to be. In fact, there is no absurd or meaningless talk at all anywhere in any of our Scriptures. All stories in our Puranas as well as in the Epics, are nothing but material loaded with mystic symbolism. So, instead of discarding them as meaningless narrations, one does well if one is able to understand and appreciate their true significance by deciphering the mystic symbolism implied and inherent therein.

Siva is the One, eternally pure and auspicious. In Him there can never be any contamination of the imperfections of Rajas and Tamas. Non-apprehension of Reality is Tamas, and misapprehension of Reality constitutes Rajas. From one standpoint, the Bull is the symbol for both, Tamas (non-apprehension of Reality) and Rajas (misapprehension of Reality), which project themselves as the two horns of the Bull. Thus the Bull is the symbol for the extrovert man. Siva, the Self, is riding this Bull; and in this Siva is neither Tamas nor Rajas; He is Brahman, He is Siva. 'Sa Brahma Sa Siva.....' as declared by the Kaivalya Sruti. This is the reason why Siva is said to be riding the Bull. This Bull is the one we see outside the sanctum sanctorum of the Siva temple, the Bull that is the Vahana, the conveyance of Lords Siva.

313

The word 'Vrushabha' has two meanings : one the ordinary meaning and the other the inner concealed meaning. The ordinary meaning is the Bull : which is known to everybody as the vehicle of Lord Siva. The inner meaning is 'Sreshta' (the best) because 'Vrsham Bhasayati iti Vrushabha' – one who illumines right actions, their results and all dhramas. So the Bull can be taken as the symbol of a perfect man, the realised soul, the 'Jivanmukta,. The Bull we see inside the temple of Lord Siva stands for this.

This Bull is also called 'Nandi' in the Siva temple. 'Nandati iti Nandi' – one who is full and happy is called Nandi. The perfect man, the realised soul, alone can enjoy fullness and complete happiness. So, Nandi is again proved to be the symbol of the perfect man, 'the Aryan', who has completely purified the inner equipment of the mind and intellect and sought identity with the Self that he is.

The realised soul, the Jivanmuktah, always revels day in and day out, and in every moment, in the vision of the Self, his own essential nature, the Supreme Reality. Hence, in the Siva temple, we find that the Bull 'Nandi' is placed right in front of the deity, Lord Siva, in a contemplative posture. The 'popular bull', which stands for the ego-centric entity, is dead and gone, and the real Bull, the enlightened Buddhi that is overwhelmed by its content, 'Awareness', freed from the matter-envelopments, revels in the vision of the Self, Lord Siva, in the highly inspired mood of deep contemplation.

When we go to the Siva temple, we first offer our salutations to the Nandi, the Bull in front of the deity. Placing the two fingers, the index finger and the thumb of the right hand on the two horns of the Bull, we have the vision of the silhouettee of Lord Siva through the circle thus formed. There is an underlying symbolism in

314

this. 'Nandi', as aforesaid, is the symbol of the 'Sreshta Purusha', the realised soul, who is Brahman - Brahmavid Brahmaiva Bhavati' – (Mundaka Sruti). So we first offer our prostrations to Nandi as soon as we enter the temple of Lord Siva. This is 'reverence', which is a form of love at the mental level, and 'respect' at the intellectual level, which is the first and primary sign of progress in the path of perfection. Then we try to identify ourselves with this perfect soul, and endeavour to enjoy the vision of the Self, Lord Siva, in the same way as the Bull does, by transcending the matter envelopments, the five kosas. The index finger represents the Jiva, and the thumb represents the Self. At present they are far removed from each other, each faciang a different direction, so we do not have the vision of the reality, the Self within. When we place the thumb and the index finger on the two horns of the Bull, the index finger Jiva, the ego-centric entity, gets resolved in the contact with the thumb Reality, in the circle of 'fullness' that is formed through the two horns of the Bull, which stand for the Viveka and the Vairagya, enjoyed by the man of perfection symbolised by the Bull. Then we are rooted in the vision of the Self, which is the 'Darsan' of Lord Siva. Here incidentally, the value of 'Sat Sanga', the company of the evolved souls, is also highlighted. When we come in contact with the realised souls or men of perfection represented by the Bull here, we are exposed to the beneficial influence of their virtues of Viveka and Vairagya, and we imbibe these two virtues through the mind and intellect represented by the two fingers in the symbolism, with the help of which we will be able to lift ourselves from the clutches of matter vestures, the five kosas, so as to enjoy the vision of the Lord, the Self that we really are. "Uddharet atmanaatmanam". The 'Jeevanmukta' is always in Samadhi, irrespective of whether he is seen sitting in meditation or not, and whether he is preaching or not; so also the Bull here is always in Samadhi and his eyes are not closed to indi-

315

cate that he is not in 'Jada Samadhi', stone-like meditation making all preaching impossible. Through the preaching of such Jeevanmuktas, we have the opportunity of our having 'Sravana', 'Manana' and 'Nidhidhyasana', namely Listening, Disquisitional reflection and Contemplation respectively, through which we gain perfect Viveka and Vairagya, and we are permanently, naturally and effortlessly rooted in the vision of our own essential nature, the Self. Once this vision of the Self is gained, there is no question of going back from it — 'Yad gatwa na nivartante tad dhama paraman Mam' — as Bhagvan Sri Krishna Himself says in Sreemad Bhagvad Geeta. This is also indicated by the fact that the Bull inside the Siva temple is always seated in a contemplative mood (Samadhi) before Lord Siva, not moving away from Him at any time even for a split second.

— HARI OM —

BR. KANDASRI (KRS PRASAD)

ULUKA — THE OWL

"O! Clever Uluka! Penetrator of darkness!! Lead us safely through the dark alleys of greed and sin, so that we may not be blinded by the dazzling splendour of Goddess Lakshmi whom you carry."

Uluka is a lesser known vehicle of Lakshmi, the Goddess of Wealth and Prosperity, and the consort of Lord Vishnu. Also called Pechaka, the owl is worshipped in Bengal during the Lakshmi Puja.

In Hindu, Greek and Roman mythology, the owl symbolises wisdom and intelligence because of its ability to presage events. But it has also come to be looked upon as a bird of ill omen, a symbol of darkness, disgrace, inauspiciousness and misfortune.

Lakshmi, the Goddess of Wealth, has all the three attributes 'Maya' is composed of. In her enlightened aspect of Satwaguna, she is manifest as charity and benevolence, and accompanies Vishnu on his Garuda. When connected with the quality of activity of Rajoguna, she is carried by the elephant Gaja. It is when she is connected with the dark quality of Tamoguna, which stands for the dark side of wealth and its pernicious influence, such as intrigues, dishonesty and avarice, that she is conceived as riding on Uluka, the owl, who is blind in the light, dazzling her subjects with her splendour.

The contradictory, magical and mysterious qualities of Uluka make it an appropriate 'Vahana' (Vehicle) for Lakshmi. When Uluka carries Lakshmi, people are blinded by wealth. They forget the good aspect of riches, such as proper use and charity, of what they are sup-

317

posed to hold as in trust: They become greedy and destroy themselves with their own wealth. On the other hand the Uluka is a recognised symbol of wisdom, and without wisdom wealth cannot serve its lofty and useful purpose.

The Sanskrit word 'Vahana' – that is Vehicle – is used for the animals, birds and men, who serve as the carriers of the gods in Hindu mythology. They are offered due worship along with their presiding deities by people who follow the Hindu way of life. Their idols and pictures are placed in the shrines and their living counterparts are provided a sanctified existence.

Accepted as a part of our cultural heritage from very ancient times, the concept of Vahanas has helped to create a sympathetic understanding of the animal world. Their selfless service, devotion to duty, mute patience and all the ideals they stand for, have inspired the 'humane' man through the ages. These have also been, to a very large extent, the inspiration behind the evolution of our philosophical thought.

AJNATANAMA

Courtesy – Mafatlal Industries Ltd.

SARVAM KHALVIDAM BRAHMA
THE PRANAVA OM

Of all the *Mantras* the most powerful and the significant one is the single-syllabled incantation called the *Pranava*. This is the 'OM'.

The available literature upon the significances of these Vedic *Mantras* is almost voluminous. Nowhere in this world can we meet with a more sacred symbol that has got such a vast amount of significance.

From vedic times until the present day the word 'OM' has been taken as a symbol and as an aid to meditation by spiritual aspirants. It is accepted both as one with Brahman and as the medium, the Logos, connecting man and God. The entire history of the syllable is in the revelations of the Vedas and in the declarations of the Upanishads, and this history, in the hands of the later philosophers, developed into what came to be known as the *Sphota-vada* or the philosophy of the word. The perceptible universe is the form, behind which stands the eternal inexpressible; the *Sphota,* the essential mateiral basis for all ideas or names, is the power through which God creates the universe. *Iswara* – the Brahman conditioned by Maya-first manifests Himself as the *Sphota,* the inexpressible word, out of which He evolves as the concrete, sensible world.

There is a verse in the Vedas : *"Prajapati vai idam agre aseet"* (In the beginning was Prajapati, the Brahman); *"Tasya vag dvitiya aseet"* (With whom was the Word); *"Vag vai Parambrahma"* (And the Word was verily the Supreme Brahman). The idea belongs to Hinduism

319

and in the fourth Gospel of the New Testament we read it repeated; "In the beginning was the Word and the Word was with God and the Word was God." This *Sphota* has its symbol in the word 'OM'. Thus, in the *Maitrayana Upanishad*, after it has been said that there is one Brahman without words, and a second, a Word Brahman, we are told that the word is the syllable 'OM'. The sound of 'OM' is also called *Pranava'*, meaning that it is something that pervades life, or runs through *prana* or breath.

The very central theme of *Mandukya Upanishad'* is the syllable 'OM', through which the mystery of Brahman is gathered to a point. The text of this Upanishad first treats 'OM' in terms of the Upanishadic doctrine of the three states of waking, dream and sleep, but then passes on to the 'fourth' *(Turiya)*, thus transporting us beyond the typical Upanishadic sphere into that of the later "Classic-Advaita-Vedanta". Speaking of 'OM', *Taittiriya Upanishad* says : 'Thou art the sheath of Brahman'. That is 'OM' is the container for the Supreme and therefore, invoking 'OM' is invoking the Supreme.

In every piece of music there are three aspects, *viz.* (1) the meaning of the song; (2) the laws of music and (3) the sound of the song. Similarly, in 'OM' there are three aspects. The first is the mere sound, the mere *mantra* as pronounced by the mouth; the second is the meaning of the syllable, which is to be realised through feeling; and the third is the application of 'OM' to your character, singing it in your acts and so through your life.

"OM" represents the Self, which is the Supreme Non-dual Reality. The Self is known in four states, namely, the waking-state, the dream-state, the deep-sleep-state and the fourth state, called the *"Turiya"*. All these states are represented in the three sounds of 'OM' (i.e. A, U and M), and the silence that follows and surrounds the syllable.

The sound 'A' represents the waking-state; the sound 'U' represents the dream-state and the sound 'M' represents the deep-sleep state. The waking state is superimposed on the 'A' sound because it is the first of the three states of consciousness and so is 'A', the very first of the letters of the alphabet in all languages. The dream is but a view within the mind of the impressions that reflected on the surface of the mental-lake during the waking state. Besides, the dream-state occurs between the waking and the deep-sleep state and comes second among the three states of consciousness. And so, 'U' being next to 'A' in the order of sounds, and also between 'A' and 'M', it is treated as representing the dream state. On the 'M' sound of 'OM' is superimposed the deep-sleep state. The comparison between the last sound of 'OM' and sleep lies in that it is the closing sound of the syllable, just as deep-sleep is the final stage of the mind in rest. A short pregnant silence is inevitable between two successive OM-s. On this silence is superimposed the idea of the "fourth-state" known as *"Turiya"*. This is the state of Perfect Bliss when the individual Self recognises its identity with the Supreme.

In OM, the sounds A, U, and M are called *Mantras* or forms; there is also in AUM the common principle called the *Amatra*-OM that which signifies the Thing-in-itself, running through and pervading the threefold phenomena of Waking, Dream and Deep-sleep. The law of memory is that the rememberer and the experiencer must be one and the same individual, or else memory is impossible. So, as we can remember all our experiences in all the three different planes, there must necessarily be a single common factor which was a witness of all the happenings on all the three planes. There must be some Entity within ourselves Who is present in the waking world, Who moves and illumines the dream, Who is a distant observer in the deep-sleep world, and

321

yet Who is not conditioned by any of these three realms. This Entity conceived as the fourth state *(Turiya)* is the Real, the Changeless, the Intelligent Principle.

The syllable 'OM' symbolises both the spheres : *(a)* the phenomenal, visible sphere of the *'Jagat'*, wherein the Manifestations of time and space appear and perish, and *(b)* the transcendent, timeless sphere of the Imperishable Being, which is beyond, yet one with it. Thus, 'A', the 'Waking-state'; 'U', the 'Dream-state'; 'M', the 'Deep-sleep' and the Silence, *"Turiya"* all these four together comprise the totality of this manifestation of *Atman-Brahman* as a syllable. Just as the sound 'M' manifests itself, grows, becomes transformed in its vocal quality and finally subsides into the silence that follows, so too the four 'states', or components, of Being. They are transformations of the one experience, and, taken together, constitute the totality of its modes, whether regarded from the microcosmic or from the macrocosmic point of view.

The A and U are as essential to the sound as M, or the Silence against which the sound appears. Moreover it would be a mistake to say that AUM did not exist while Silence reigned; for it would be still potentially present even in the Silence. The actual manifestation of the syllable, on the other hand, is fleeting and evanescent; whereas the Silence abides. The Silence, indeed, is present elsewhere during a vocal pronunciation of AUM, that is to say (by analogy), transcendentally, during the creation, manifestation, and dissolution of a universe, and is indeed the first manifestation of Divine Wisdom. Thus OM is truly symbolic of God.

'OM' thus represents the entire manifested world and the unmanifest, and also that which lies beyond both the manifest and the unmanifest – the Brahman, which

322

is the changeless substratum for the changing objects of the world of expriences.

To every *mantra* 'OM', the *Pranava*, is added on. And without 'OM' no sacred-chant has its power. Just as living body has no vitality when the life-giving breath is not flowing through its veins, so too a *mantra* has no life in it without the addition of the *Pranava*.

Vedantic students generally practise the repetition of and meditation on the symbol provided by the *Pranava*; this is called *Pranava Upasana*.

It may be asked why this particular word 'OM' should be chosen as the word representative of the "thought" out of which the universe has become manifested. The answer may be given in Swami Vivekananda's own words.

"This OM is the only possible symbol which covers the whole ground and there is none other like it. The *Sphota* is the material of all words, yet it is not any definite word in its fully formed state. That is to say, if all the particularities which distinguish one word from another be removed, then what remains will be the *Sphota*. Therefore, this *Sphota* is called the *Nada-Brahman*, the Sound Brahman. Now, every word-symbol intended to express the inexpressible *Sphota* will so particularise it that it will no longer be the *Sphota*. That which particularises it the least and at the same time most approximately expresses its nature, will be the truest symbol thereof; and this is the OM, and the OM only; because, these three letters A, U, M, pronounced in combination as OM, can alone be the generalised symbol of all possible sounds. The letter 'A' is the least differentiate of all sounds. Again, all articulate sounds are produced in the space within the mouth — beginning with the root of the tongue and ending at the lips; the throat-sound is 'A' and 'M' is the last

323

lip-sound; and 'U' exactly represents the rolling forward of the impulse which begins at the root of the tongue, continuing till it ends in the lips'.

If properly pronounced, this OM will represent in itself the whole phenomenon of sound production, and no other word can do this, and this, therefore, is the fittest symbol of the *Sphota*, which is the real meaning of the OM. And as the symbol can never be separated from the thing signified, the *'OM'* and the *Sphota*, are one. And as the *Sphota*, being the finer side of the manifested universe, is nearer to God.

SWAMI CHINMAYANANDA

OM IS THE ONE - OM IS THE MANY

— Swami Chinmayananda —

ओमिती ब्रह्म । ओमितीदँ सर्वं ।।

OM iti Brahma, Omitedam Sarvam

The sacred sound OM is Brahman. All this is the syllable OM.

The mystic syllable OM is the choicest point' of concentration prescribed for the benefit of the student of Vedanta,who is constitutionally more intellectual than emotional. In their early attempts at developing a highly concentrated mind and intellect, such students too need the help of a symbol or an idea which has infinite possibilities to entertain them with its inexhaustible contents. The genius in the Vedic Masters gave us OM as an ideal-idol to worship in the inner temple.

Life is a constant flow of experiences, and these experiences, when observed, are found to fall in three layers, as the experiences of the waking-state, of the dream-state, and of the deep-sleep-state. The life of everyone of us is certainly influenced by our experiences on all these three different planes of consciousness, and they all have totally a positive influence in moulding our character and personality. This would read slightly strange to the modern young man, because Western philosophy has been so far striving to discover the fundamental in life by an analysis and close study of merely the life available for us in our waking-state. It is indeed difficult, if not almost impossible, to come to a right evaluation of life and its meaning by observing only a third of its field.

When the Rishis more and more closely observed these three fields of experiences they discovered that an individual indentifying with his physical body comes to live his waking-state of outer gross objects as the 'waker'.

The same entity, totally in oblivion of his body and the outer world, when he exclusively gets identified with his mind and intellect, comes to revel in an inner world of dream, and experiences subtle objects of imagination, as a 'dreamer'.

When, again, the very same entity becomes forgetful of His body and its outer world, the mind and intellect and their feelings and thoughts, and comes to expreience a world of nothingness, no doubt peaceful and joyful, but conscious of nothing but 'nothingness', he becomes the 'deep sleeper'.

The 'dreamer' experiences are totally different and sometimes even contrary to the 'waker's life' and the experience of the 'deep sleeper' is common to all and seems to have no relationship with the waking and dream conditions of experiences. Yet, it is the experience of all of us that we can remember, on our waking, all about our experiences during our last 'waking-state', yesternight's 'early dreams' and also the 'peaceful sleep' that we had afterwards. From these observations the Rishis conceived their bold and adventurous theory.

The 'Law of Memory', is that one cannot oneself remember the experience of another. If one can remember anything at all, they are all actual experiences of the individual himself. That is to say, the law of memory enunciates that the rememberer and the experiencer must be one and the same individual or else, memory is impossible. I can never remember any of your past experiences; nor can you remember any of my experiences.

326

Applying this 'Law of Memory' as a test, we find that the 'waker' and the 'dreamer' and the 'deep-sleeper' are strangers among themselves, each living in his own world, and has seemingly no passport to travel beyond its frontiers. Since we can remember all our experiences in all the three different planes, there must necessarily be a single Common Factor which was a witness of all the happenings in all the three planes.

To make it clear, let us suppose that we have one idle afternoon, and a friend in our drawing room starts revealing a slice of his biography in which he explains his despairing days in Madras, his disastrous failures in Madurai, and his glorious successes in Delhi. Now we all know that Madras is not Madurai, nor is Madurai one with Delhi. But our friend is describing his experiences in all the three places from his own memory. Again, the despairs of Madras are different from the disasters in Madurai and both these sets of experiences are separate from the glorious successes in Delhi. But our friend is explaining all of them from his own memory. Under such circumstances we instinctively understand that he, our friend, lived his despairing days in Madras, and himself went to Madurai where he spent his days of failures, and then he himself left the Madurai-Madras zone for Delhi to reap his glorious successes.

Similarly, there must be some Entity within ourselves who is present in the 'waking-world', who moves to illumine the 'dreams', who is a distant observer in the 'deep-sleep-world', and yet, all the same, is not conditioned by any of these three realms. The Entity is, as it were, conceived as the 'fourth', who is the Real, the Changeless, the Intelligent Principle.

The Sages of the Vedas, after indicating this much to the students of Vedanta, want them to experience the Pure Subject who, in the waking-world becomes the 'waker', in the dream becomes the 'dreamer' and in the sleep becomes the 'sleeper'.

The sound OM is constituted of three syllables, A, U and M; and while chanting continuously the sound OM in the mind, the Upasaka is advised to superimpose upon these three sounds the three different planes of consciousness we have been describing so far, viz., the 'waking', 'dream' and 'deep-sleep'. The process of superimposition is the same as the principle underlying all idol worship. We have already discussed this technique by which the Mighty is seen or imagined in the meagre; Siva-Tattwa in the Siva-linga; the Divine Mother of Knowledge in the River Ganga; Sri Narayana in the Saligram; Christ on the Cross!

The practitioner at his meditation thus trains himself consciously to superimpose the waker in him on the sound A; and then, as the sound A merges with the sound U, he gains a mental dexterity to forget totally his identity with the waking state experiences and to come to live in meditation consciously the entire identity with the 'dreamer' in him; so too, when he comes to the sound M, he is able to black out the entire state of plurality and arrive at a state of semi-conscious experience of all negation. Thereafter his spiritual growth is assured in proportion to the intensity of his pursuit, purity of his life and his intelligent sense of detachment.

Even this practice of keeping oneself fully conscious and making the sounds A, U, and M each marching into the other and getting telescoped into themselves, is in itself a severe training for the mind at concentration. The conscious superimpositions unfolded, and again folded up as explained above, is an equally all-absorbing occupation for the entire intellectual capacity in us so that the true practitioner, if he be sincere and regular, gains in a very short time an infinite amount of integration both in his mind and in his intellectual equipments.

Thereafter, the sensitivised instruments of the within become subtle in him so as to dare seek the Pure Awareness which, in the grosser three planes, illumines the objects and sustains the mirage personalities of the 'waker', the 'dreamer' and the 'deep-sleeper'. The silence between two successive OMs is the point of concentration which the Yogi attempts to merge with, and experience thereby the infinite contents of one split second completely divorced from the past, and entirely free from the mental slavery to the future. To live thus dynamically free from within and from without, one second of a human life, is all that is needed to peep over the veils of ignorance and realise for ourselves eternally thereafter the True Nature of the Self, the Godhood.

As we explained above, since OM represents a symbol for the waking, the dream and the deep-sleep states of consciousness, and since our entire life is the sum total of different experiences on all these three planes, OM, the symbol, represents 'All This'. As OM is the symbol of the Infinite Reality that is behind the seeming multiplicity and painful plurality, it becomes self-evident that the Rishis were not illogical or deliberately mystical when they declared that OM is *all this universe*.

Mud is the reality. All pots of all colours, all shapes, all sizes, irrespective of their contents or condition, are nothing but mud. Gold is the reality behind all ornaments; be they thin or thick, be they intricate or simple, be they for the neck or for the legs, they are all nothing but gold. The ocean is the reality, for all the waves, be they mountainous or small, frothy or clear, are nothing but the very ocean itself. It is in this sense, OM, the idol of Reality, has been explained in the Mantra here as a symbol that represents 'the entire universe' — experienced outside as objects and within as thoughts and ideas.

SWAMI CHINMAYANANDA

THE SIGNIFICANCE OF
THE MYSTIC SYMBOL "OM"

The greatest achievement of man in the field of philosophy is his comprehension of the idea of the Infinite, and his attempts to bring the Infinite down to some sort of understanding at the finite level, or to transcend his finite equipments and thus reach or evolve into the Infinite. All religions of the world agree on this basic principle, and they are but various attempts at expressing the Infinite in finite terms as is intelligible to the finite equipments with which we perceive and gain all our knowledge and experiences.

The basic expression is the thought, which manifests itself as the word. Hence the importance of the spoken word. The great seers of the past, who had evolved themselves to perfection or to near perfection, and had realised and identified themselves with the Infinite BRAHMAN as termed in the great and most ancient of all the living religions of today, SANATANA DHARMA, wrongly yet popularly known as Hinduism now, the Mother of Religions, – Jivanmuktas, who still functioned under their upadhis to live out their residual Karma (?) yearned to express their sublime experience so that aspirants of posterity could visualise and concentrate on this Infinite and thus make the progress to the summum bonum of human birth and existence – liberation. For this they had to coin a short, yet all comprehensive symbol in the shape of the spoken word and thus reduce the Infinite to the finite level of understanding in form and name-"Vikara and Namadheya". The result is this mystic symbol "OM". 'Sadhakaanaam hitarthaaya

330

Brahmani roopakalpate" — it is said for the convenience of the aspirant that Brahman the fromless, has been assigned a form, to facilitate concentration.

Now let us examine, subject to our limitations of knowledge and capacity, how far this mystic symbol 'OM' is all comprehensive, and what could have been the reasons for the great seers for selecting this symbol to represent the Infinite Brahman.

"Aksharam Brahma Paramam
Swabhavo-adhyatmamuchyate" — Geeta VIII-3

Brahman is Akshara — inexhaustible, that which cannot be spent, therefore Eternal. The spoken letter in Sanskrit is also called "akshara". Once the letter or word is spoken, the effect is eternal. So they must have decided to have an "akshara" to represent the "Akshara".

"OM Ityekaaksharam Brahma
Vyaharan mam anusmaran
Yahprayati tyajan deham
Sa yati paramam gatim" — Geeta VIII-3

Bhagvan Himself tells Arjuna that he who leaves this body chanting the one mystic Akshara "OM", reaches the "Paramam Gati" — the final Supreme goal of beatification.

Because the great men who know the Vedas accept this "akshara" as representing Brahman and as the Vedas themselves point to the Brahman, the akshara 'OM' can be said to be the quintessence of the Vedas

The "eternity" of the spoken word is emphasised in all the Upanishads, and the first component of the compound letter "OM" is the first vowel "Akara".

"Aksharanaam Akaarosmi" — Geeta X-33
"Kirtih Sri Vak cha Nareenaam" — Geeta X-34

Among the aksharas, I am "Akaara" and I am the spoken word "Vak".

This is exactly what is stated in the Christian Bible too : "In the beginning was the word. The word was with God and the word was God." This is accepted in principle in all the known religions of the world.

In the beginning, before creation (if there ever was such a time, as we believe Srushti is anaadi—here 'anaadi' should mean only 'unknown' to us), before the "SPAN-DAN" occurred, when Brahman was unmanifest or, to be more correct, the mind was not there to cognise and hence perception was not there, the whole of Brahmanda was enveloped in darkness and it was nothing but space unlimited, AVYAKTA. There was nothing but a booming continuous sound in the Brahmanda. Mythology has it that this continuous booming sound was being emitted by the Conch (Sankha) that is in one of the hands of HARI, which symbolises the eternal sound. Even today, if we retire to the top of a hill in the centre of a vast expanse of virgin forest with giant trees all around, where even the sun's rays meet with some kind of opposition to peep in, and sit in communion with Nature, this primal sound can well be heard or felt. Pilgrims to Sabarimalai who go in the traditional and orthodox way through the conventional route could have had this experience, if they were lucky enough. It can well be presumed that the sages who constantly communed with Nature under such sylvan atmosphere coined this monosyllable "OM" after this basic sound that enveloped the Brahmanda, from their own experience.

The sages have proved that Man is a miniature Cosmos, that everything that is contained in the Cosmos is contained in the human body, of course not anatomiclly. This is called the "Brahmaanda-Pindanda theory" – in English the theory of "Macro-cosm and Micro-cosm". The monosyllable 'OM' is the result of the harmonious combination of the three basic sounds which contain in themselves all the sounds which can be produced by the human system, and it can be seen that the entire vocal mechanism of the human being comes into full play when he pronounces the sound 'OM' according to the Vedic injunctions.

AKAARA Produced from the very depth of the human system, the place where Kundalini is posited, the throat taking the most prominent part in the expression of the sound

UKAARA The second stage where the sound starting at the throat, rolls outwards, as it were, to the tip of the tongue.

MAKAARA The sound concentrated at the extremity of the human vocal system, the lips.

Thus it can be seen that, in producing the sound 'OM', the entire Pindanda, the Microcosmic representation of the Macrocosmic Brahmanda, comes into full play, and therefore the monosyllable can correctly be said to represent the all-pervading, all-comprehensive Brahman.

The significance of the Mantra (this is also a Mantra coming within the definition "Mananaat thraayate iti Mantra", a redeeming instrument, by reflecting on which we are liberated) "OM" though ocurring in various Upanishads and in almost all Hindu scriptures throughout, is seen to have received special mention in Taittireeya, Chhandogya and Mandookya Upanishads, to mention only the more well-known ones. The eighth Anuvaka of the Siksha Valli of Taittireeya Upanishad is almost entirely devoted to the mystic symbol "OM".

OM ITI BRAHMA
OM ITI IDAM SARVAM
      OM ITI ETADANUKRITI, etc.
        OM ITI SAMAANI GAAYANTI, etc., etc.

"OM," according to this Upanishad, is the point of concentration for the aspirant who is more intellectual than emotional, for the man in the path of Gnana Yoga than in the path of Bhakti Yoga. 'OM' is the idol for the intellectual worship in the inner temple. While concentrating on the monosyllable 'OM', its three component parts A, U and M are to be respectively meditated upon with special reference to the Jagrat, Swapna and Sushupti states i.e. the waking, dreaming and deep-sleep states, superimposing the waker in him on the sound A, passing on to the next dreaming state in U, and then on to the deep-sleep state in M and, transcending all these, come to live in the fourth state of Super-consciousness called the Turiya state, by progressive negation of all things Anatman and by constant practice of pointed meditation. As the sum-total of our experience is the totality of experiences in the Jagrat, Swapna and Sushupti states, 'OM' represents the entire Jagat, the World of Cosmos, and hence pure Awareness. That is how the great Yogis have declared that 'OM' is all the Akhilanda. "OM ITI BRAHMA."

The opening stanza of Chhandogya Upanishad eulogises the importance and efficacy of this mystic symbol 'OM'.

"OM ITI ETAD AKSHARAM UDGEETAM UPAASEETA OM ITI HI UDGAAYATI TASYA UPAVYAKHYANAM"

In Mandukya Upanishad we find :-

"OM ITI ETAD AKSHARAM IDAM SARVAM," etc.
"BHUTAM BHAVAD BHAVISHYAD ITI SARVAM OMKARAMEVA", etc., etc.

.According to 'Narada Parivrajaka Upanishad', wherein the Pranava 'OM' is exhaustively dealt with, it is made up of sixteen matras as under :-

"AKAARA, UKAARA, MAKAARA, ARDHAMATRA, NADA, BINDU, KALA, KALAATEETA, SANTI, SANTYATEETA, UNMANI, MANONMANI, PURI, MADHYAMA, PASYANTI AND PARA"

Out of these, it is said that four matras have their 'Laya' in the other matras, thus making twelve basic matras. 'Dhyanabindu Upanishad', which exclaims "Om iti ekaksharam Brahma dhyeyam sarvam mumukshubhi" and goes on to explain the greatness and the all-comprehensive nature of the Pranava (OM), has named these matras and has also stipulated the effect of each one of them on the Siddhi level :-

1.	Ghoshini	Results in attaining to super-conscious state
2.	Vidyunmali	Raises to Yakshaloka – next stage in evolution
3.	Patangini	Enables the Sadhaka to fly in the air
4.	Vayuvegini	Enables to travel at the speed of the wind
5.	Namadheya	Gives entry into Pitruloka
6.	Eindri	Gives entry into Indraloka
7.	Vaishnavi	Gives entry into Vishnuloka
8.	Sankari	Gives entry into Sivaloka
9.	Mahti	To influence the beings of Maharloka
10.	Dhrithi	To influence the beings of Maharloka
11.	Mouni	Enables the Sadhaka to reach the world of Munis
12.	Brahmi	Attains to Brahmaloka

When the Pranava (OM) is identified with Jagat :-

A-Kara is Iswara

U-Kara is Moolaprakriti, and

M-Kara is Mayasakti

See "Tasmai Makaaraaya Namah Sivaya"!

So, the combination A+U+M=OM which stands for Brahma + Vishnu + Siva, or the entire eternal Cosmic principles of Creation, Preservation and Dissolution (of which the last is a constructive destruction) completing the cycle of evolution and involution.

The mystic interpretation is that the vibration caused by the component sounds of A, U and M, created the disturbance that lead to the creation, preservation and dissolution respectively.

Now, we go to the efficacy of OMKARA Japa. Having realised the significance of this mystic symbol OM, and how it represents the Supreme Infinite Brahman, the aspirant does Japa with concentration on the "Pranava", the shortness of which is really conducive to concentration.

"JA" kaaro Janma vichheda

"PA" kaara Papa Naasana

This explains the efficacy of the Japa of any Mantra, of course associated with 'Manana' i.e. reflection.

Incidentally, Mantra is the mystic formula, Yantra is the machine (in this case the human body-mind-intellect complex in its three aspects of Sthula, Sukshma and Karana Sareeras, in the three different states of consciousness of Jagrat, Swapna and Sushupti – i.e. waking, dream and deep-sleep) and Tantra is the technique of applying the formula on the machine to produce best results.

To go to the metaphysics of this mystic symbol 'OM', the primary manifestation of activity in the Cosmos was through the principle of sound, whether we take it metaphysically or mythologically; metaphysically when we 'look back' into "Soonyata or Avyakta", and mythologically through the Conch of Hari, Damaru of Siva, or the tongue of Brahma (not Brahman), each one of which has its symbolic significance in the logical cosmic scheme of things. Everything is made apparent due to certain vibrations which our modern Science has lately discovered and accepted. Even the basic seven colours are seen by the human eyes due to different vibrations coming within the range or capacity of human vision. Every sound, in fact every thought, offsets innumerable vibrations in the cosmic field. The intensity of vibrations produced by the chanting of 'OM' (that is, if properly chanted ! Students of Sound may recall the principle of sympathetic resonance) is said to affect or effect the entire microcosm and macrocosm. Mantra has its full efficacy only if chanted with the proper pronunciation and intonation and it is even said that different modes of chanting produce entirely different effects.

'Mantroheena Swarato Varnato vajro
Midhya prayukto na chamarddha maha
Sa vak vajro Uajro Yajamaanam hinasti
Yadha Indrasatru : Swarato aparaadhaat"

The real "Swara" (mode of chanting) can only be learnt directly from the Guru. Mantra Sastra says that the Pranava (OM) can be chanted in 170 different ways (Madame Blavatsky has quoted from some ancient Indian work that it can be chanted in some 250 different intonations) and that the Siddhi attained by each method is different. The great Physicist and Sound Expert of Philadelphia, the late Mr John Worrel Keely, demonstrated to the world that the harmonious sound emitted from a violin could raise a machine from the ground, but others could not do it, as the feat depended on a certain level of personal spiritual advancement and achievement. Mr O. C. Ganguli of Calcutta wrote in the "Aryan Path" (issue : January 1937) about the efficacy of Swaras on the emotional field. Out of the seven Swaras, Sa, Ri, Ga, Ma, Pa, Dha and Ni, the Aarohana of Sa and Ri produce wonderment and hatred, Dha raises fear or repulsion, Ga and Ni pathos, and Ma and Pa love and delight. The Sapta Swaras have thus been formulated to produce and maintain all the basic emotions, not only in the human system, but even in animal minds.

"Pasurvethi Sisurvethi Vethi Ganarasam Phani"

It is explained in the Agamas that :-

A-kara kills krodha, (meditating on Akara in all aspects explained)
U-kara kills dwesha and
M-kara kills fear

While the compound symbol 'OM" in its entirety kills the ego in man.

'Mantra' is the expression of mental power, Iccha Sakti, and has been defined as the language that describes the thought vibrations that originated in and from Nada Brahman, the original manifestation of Universal Mind in the form of Universal Sound, and 'OM' is the original sound that enveloped the entire Brahmanda before the beginning (?) of Creation.

Thus we see the significance of 'OM', though this is only a bird's eye view of a gigantic subject that envelops, penetrates and permeates the whole of Brahmanda. Whatever be the level of explanation offered, logical, scientific, metaphysical or mythological or intellectual acrobatics resorted to, in attributing mysticism or sacredness to the symbol, it has to be understood that it is the mind of man, which is an integral part of the Universal Mind, and his intensity of faith that gives the real value to anything in the world. Says Christain D. Larson : "The mind of man is conscious and subconscious, objective and subjective, external and internal. The conscious mind acts, the subconscious reacts, the conscious mind produces the impression while the subconsicious mind produces the expression, the conscious mind determines what is to be done, and the subconscious mind supplies the mental material and the necessary power...... The subconscious mind is the "Great Within" – the inner mental world from which all things proceed that appear in the being of man". Every man is not deluded to see the "ghost in the post", neither does the same man see it under all identical circumstances. Any symbol that helps man to concentrate his mind-intellect equipment on the Supreme Reality, and thus make his progress in the path of evolution, is sacred, and the sages and seers only say that OM (AUM) – this mystic symbol–has been tried and found most efficacious, and it has been coined by taking into consideration all the various aspects of the Supreme Reality (accepted that the Supreme Reality has neither aspects or parts but this is Vyavaharika as cognisable to our meagre and limited equipments) in all its plurality of manifestation as known to them, visualised experienced and lived by them.

– HARI AUM TAT SAT –

R.S. NATHAN

WHY SECRET SIGNIFICANCE?

As an individual grows, in his earliest infancy, he is able merely to "perceive" with his sense organs, and it is only much later that the child develops his emotional responses to the world of things and beings around him. He likes some things and dislikes many other things. He feels charmed by some and really frightened by others. He develops his own self-interest, as in protecting his toys from others, and even covets to have, and if necessary, fights to gain, what another child has in his hand!!

It is again much later that the child learns to think, has ideals; develops some values, again visions of greater possibilities.

In short, through the entire span of his first 15 or 16 years of life, a child declares a definite pattern of development and growth within him. And this is universally so in every race.

Based upon this universal system of progress, which is clearly self-evident in every adult response — (first I see her.... later I get emotionally involved in her.... and much later I intelligently decide upon making her my wife or not).... the Rishis also evolved schemes by which each student can be guided slowly from each of his lower state into a higher state, step by step, and helped him gain the Supreme State of Pure Being.

To serve those at the stage of mere "perception", there is the vast temple edifice with its clean and wide courtyards, to visit which the child is specially bathed, dressed and lovingly taken there by his elders.

The sheer beauty of the decorations, the lamps winking at him, the throng, the singing, the temple instruments, perhaps the roaming bulls, (or the elephants, during festivals) all these are impressive experiences in "perception" for the growing child.

Each night, at bed-time, his grandpa or grandma tells him "stories" of the Lord. The early childhood of the fidgety, fretful Blue-boy of Brindaban touches the chords in the growing baby's heart. He wants to hear these stories again and again. In time he develops an emotional attachment, "love" for the Lord. He starts seeing a greater significance in the Altar.... a larger awareness of its divine representation comes to flint through his heart.

The child grows on.... he now gets distracted with toys, games, studies, fields of sports and play. Apparently he seems to leave his habit of visiting temples — yet, on his way, whenever he passes a temple, a soft refreshing breeze of memory of his early childhood associations flashes through his bosom.

Now the child starts meeting with various little problems, each of which, to him, becomes a great insurmountable challenge! Examinations, homework, sports, competitions.... at each of these challenges he tries to draw more courage and confidence from the "grace" of the Lord.

With each experience of success, his "Love for the Saviour Lord" becomes more and more ardent and he needs now the Form to fix his mind upon, in order to 'play' with his inner divine Love-Lord. He holds on to the beloved Form-Divine, talks to Him, misuses Him, absuses Him, then regrets and even weeps to Him — according to His mood at the given point in time.

He grows, and progresses in his education to expand his utilitarian point of view. His scientific training whispers to him doubts regarding the validity of this belief in the Lord. He reviews his religious fervour with this newly discovered equipment in himself, his own growing powers of judgement (logical thinking, scientific enquiry, etc.) of the intellect.

Natrually he comes to conclude that all religion is a myth, and all ritualism a bluff. The entire basis of his earlier faith slides away from under him. He is happy about his ability to discover this "hollowness" of religion, but at the same time, he feels helpless, orphaned, baseless, and he has no sure foothold when the unavoidable but normal calamities and shocks of life hit him from all sides.

Even the apparently most courageous and heroic, in this state, rushes into a sad state of inner despair arising out of his ineffectual sense of anger at himself and at the Creator who built up this restless world to victimise him mercilessly!

Everyone goes through this period of dark despondency, a painful time, when one loses one's own faith in oneself and one's belief in the world outside. In this blind state of inner despair many turn corrupt, vicious, wicked, dissipating themselves with wine, immoralities, excesses, drugs, women and cruelities deliberately planned and heartlessly perpetrated upon others. They become truly 'mad'.

It is after this dark and dreary span of sheer suffering that some, in their helplessness, turn to enquire upon the deeper significances of religion, the meaningful essence of God, as enshrined in all the scriptures. They approach scholars, men of study, masters and Acharayas. They read more and more of the spiritual books and sincerely study the philosophy of Vedanta.

It is then the eloquent siginificance behind the temple-structures, the Sanctum, the Altar, the Idol etc. becomes clear to such an individual. He discovers that the Deities are

342

all different aspects of the same One Supreme Self, expressing in different form-symbols.

This secret of reconvincing oneself of the meaning behind the representations has been revealed in the previous pages. Sri. R.S. Nathan has intelligently collected these ideas from my talks, from some 300 odd different platforms. I congratulate him. He has done a glorious job of pure seva in thus compiling these ideas so faithfully.

SWAMI CHINMAYANANDA